THE
CHAIN OF
TRADITION
SERIES

Volume V: Ḥasidic Thought

Ḥasidic thought

BY LOUIS JACOBS

Behrman House, Inc.

PUBLISHERS NEW YORK

for my granddaughter, Ziva

Acknowledgments

Between manuscript and bound book, there is much need for talent, acuity, and devotion. Both Morrison David Bial and Mrs. Gerry Gould have shown this and both the author and the publisher wish to acknowledge such.

Published by Behrman House, Inc.
1261 Broadway, New York, N. Y. 10001

Library of Congress Catalog Card Number: 76–15825
International Standard Book Number: 0–87441–242–0

Manufactured in the United States of America

Introduction

THE ḤASIDIC MOVEMENT arose in Podolia and Volhynia in the first half of the eighteenth century. So rapid was the progress it made, in spite of—or because of—the fiercest opposition, that by the end of the century a large proportion of Polish and Russian Jewry had become Ḥasidic. Even today the movement numbers many thousands of adherents, and thanks to the popularizing efforts of Martin Buber and Louis I. Newman and the scholarly work of Professor Gershom Scholem and his school, it is well known in both general and academic circles. There are books enough on Ḥasidism. The excuse, if such is required, for adding another is that there has been little investigation of the actual texts of the Ḥasidic masters. So far as I am aware, noṇe of the texts presented here has ever before been translated into English.

Historical details about practically every aspect of Ḥasidic life are readily available. (Bibliographies and much useful historical information are to be found in the numerous articles on Ḥasidism and the Ḥasidic masters in the new *Encyclopedia Judaica,* on which I have relied, mainly, in the matter of dating.) Only those historical details essential to an understanding of the texts have been supplied here. The reader is advised to read through the brief introduction to each series of texts before studying the texts themselves. The chart at the end of the book places each of the masters considered in the Ḥasidic "chain of tradition."

The method adopted is that of the other four volumes in the Behrman House Chain of Tradition series, to which there are occasional cross-references. The text in English translation is printed in bolder type, with the explanatory notes inserted in the text in lighter type so that "he who runs may read." The titles to the various pieces in the table of contents are mine, not those of the original authors. They are intended to encourage the reader to choose, in the first instance, the topics with a special appeal for him, with, as the Ḥasidim would say, something belonging to the root of his soul. In any anthology the principle of selectivity is complicated. But I have tried to choose passages from the main books used by the Ḥasidim and those which convey something of both the flavor of Ḥasidic thought and the rich variety of Ḥasidic expression. For this reason only one or two examples have been given of movements which developed a life of their own and produced a literature of their own within Ḥasidism—the Ḥabad movement, for instance. Emphasis has been placed on texts from standard Ḥasidic books rather than on aphorisms and the like quoted in the name of Ḥasidic thinkers, with the exception of such tendencies in Ḥasidic thought as Ruzhyn, Kotzk, and Belz, which produced fascinating Ḥasidic leaders but no literature to speak of. Although a real attempt has been made to be fair to the Ḥasidic masters, it would have been inexcusable to omit from this anthology that which might be called the darker side of Ḥasidism—Moses Teitelbaum's attitude regarding women or Zadok Ha-Kohen's strong opposition to all general learning, for example. The Ḥasidim often speak of the special value of that light produced from out of the darkness, and, in any event, a round picture of what Ḥasidic thought is really like has been the aim of this book.

Most of the texts are difficult and require some study, but the effort is worthwhile if it results in a more direct appreciation of what it is that the Ḥasidic masters were trying to say and do, why they were so successful and yet met with such powerful opposition, and what there is in Ḥasidic life and thought of significance to contemporary Jewry.

CHAPTER 1

The Baal Shem Tov
1700-1760

How the Maggid was converted
What is the role of the zaddik?
What is real and what is an illusion?

The founder of the Ḥasidic movement is known as the Baal Shem Tov, *"Master of the Good Name," the "Good Name" being the sacred name of God. Israel ben Eliezer was one of a number of folkhealers who used for their cures, in addition to herbs and so forth, various divine names believed to have magical power. These men were called* Baaley Shem, *"Masters of the (Good) Name." (The suggestion that Israel ben Eliezer was known as the "good" Master of the Name as opposed to the other healers who were "bad," or at least "not good," is erroneous. The term* good *does not qualify* Master, *but the* Name.) *He is also known as* Ribash (Rabbi Israel Baal Shem) *and in writing in the abbreviated form the* Besht (Baal Shem Tov). *The great difficulty in attempting to reconstruct the life of the Baal Shem Tov is that the numerous legends concerning him cannot easily be disentangled from the historical facts. We do know, however, that he was born in Podolia (although the town of Okop, where the legends say he was born, does not exist) and that he eventually "revealed" himself, i.e., he became a master of the spiritual life, gathering around him a number of associates and disciples. It was among the members of this intimate circle that the ideas of the Baal Shem Tov were first promulgated, leading, after to his death, to the emergence of the Ḥasidic movement.*

The chief legendary biography of the Baal Shem Tov is the Shivḥey Ha-Besht *(Praises of the Baal Shem Tov), first published in Kopys fifty-four years after the death of the Baal Shem Tov. (This work has been translated into English by Dan Ben-Amos and Jerome R. Mintz, Indiana University Press, 1970, but while this English translation and the copious notes are useful, the book contains a number of serious errors and must be used with caution.) This legendary biography is the main source utilized by historians of Ḥasidism who try to get behind the legends to the historical facts, a task fraught with obstacles but not entirely hopeless. The main sources for the actual ideas of the Baal Shem Tov are the works of his disciple Rabbi Jacob Joseph of Pulnoyye. In these works—*Toledot Yaakov Yosef *(published both in Meziboz and Koretz in 1780),* Ben Porat Yosef *(Koretz, 1781), and* Zafenat Paneaḥ *(Koretz, 1782)—Rabbi Jacob Joseph quotes sayings he had heard personally from the lips of the Baal Shem Tov, though the words he uses in conveying these sayings are his own, no doubt with considerable elaborations. These sayings were published in a separate anthology under the title* Keter Shem Tov *(The Crown of the Good Name) in Zolkiew in 1784. The following selections are from more recent editions of* Keter Shem Tov *(Jerusalem, 1968),* Toledot Yaakov Yosef *(Warsaw, 1881), and* Ben Porat Yosef *(Israel, 1971—photocopy of 1884 Pietrikow edition). It must be appreciated that the Baal Shem Tov wrote no works himself, so that in these words his ideas come to us at one stage removed. Allowing for elaboration and interpretation (as well as for changes of meaning inevitable in the translation into Hebrew of the original Yiddish in which the sayings were almost certainly first uttered), there is nonetheless little reason for doubting the basic authenticity of these sayings.*

On the general problem we can do no better than to quote from Simon Dubnow's splendid history of Ḥasidism, Toledot Ha-Ḥasidut *(Tel Aviv, 1967). Dubnow (p. 41) writes: "The historical figure of the founder of Ḥasidism appears to us shrouded in darkness, the thick darkness of wonder tales by means of which legend crowned the head of the beloved folk hero. A thick curtain, woven out of the imagination of his contemporaries and later generations, conceals the true picture of the Besht, so that it sometimes seems as if there were no such person and it is all a myth, a fictitious name used for the cause of a religious movement that took the Jewish world by storm. Nevertheless, those familar with the literature of that period can never be guilty of the folly of denying that the Besht ever existed. Apart from his disciples and associates, many of his contemporaries who opposed his doctrine testify to his existence, although only a pale shadow emerges from their testimony. If we read with a critical eye even the legendary biography of the Besht we see revealed there the features of a living person influenced by his surroundings and influencing them in turn, as well as a reliable picture of the eighteenth-century Ukrainian environment." Professor Gershom Scholem has shown us how to get to the historical truth in his Hebrew essay "The Historical Baal Shem Tov" (offprint from* Molad, *Av-Elul, 1960). The three selections quoted here are from: (I)* Keter Shem Tov, *pp. 107–8; (II)* Toledot Yaakov Yosef, *pp. 415–16; (III)* Ben Porat Yosef, *p. 252.*

I HOW THE MAGGID WAS CONVERTED

I heard a certain Ḥasid tell what happened when Rabbi Dov Baer of blessed memory heard of the fame of the holy Rabbi the Baal Shem Tov; how all the people flock to him and how he achieves awesome and tremendous things by the power of his prayers. Now Rabbi Dov Baer of blessed memory was a most acute scholar, thoroughly familiar with the whole of the Talmud and all the Codes and he possessed ten measures of knowledge in the science of the Kabbalah. Astonished at the reports he had heard concerning the high rank of the Baal Shem Tov he decided that he would journey to meet him in order to put him to the test. Since Rabbi Dov Baer was very industrious in his studies, it came about, after two or three days of his journey, during which time he was unable to concentrate on his studies with the same application as in his own home, that he was sorry for having decided to go. When eventually he came to the Baal Shem Tov of blessed memory, he thought that he would hear some words of Torah from him, but instead the Baal Shem Tov told him a tale of how he had undertaken a journey of many days during which he had no bread to give to his uncircumcised coach driver and how a poor Gentile came along with a sack of loaves so that he was able to buy some bread wherewith to feed his coach driver. He told him other tales of this sort. When he came the next day the Baal Shem Tov told him of how on that journey he had no fodder to give to his horses and it happened, etc. Now all these tales related by the Baal Shem Tov contained great and marvelous wisdom if one could only

understand it, but since Rabbi Dov Baer of blessed memory failed to appreciate this he returned to his inn, saying to his servant: "I wish to return home right away, but since it is so dark we shall stay on here until the moon shines brightly and then we shall be on our way." At midnight, just as Rabbi Dov Baer was getting ready to depart, the Baal Shem Tov sent his servant to summon him and he heeded the summons. The Baal Shem Tov of blessed memory asked him: "Are you a scholar?" and he answered in the affirmative. "So have I heard, that you are a scholar," said the Baal Shem Tov. "And do you know the science of the Kabbalah?" "Yes, I do," replied Dov Baer. The Baal Shem Tov then instructed his servant to bring a copy of the book *Etz Ḥayyim* (The Tree of Life) and the Baal Shem Tov showed Rabbi Dov Baer a passage in this book. Rabbi Dov Baer said that he would look at the passage and after doing so he expounded it to the Baal Shem Tov of blessed memory. But the Baal Shem Tov said: "You have not the slightest degree of understanding of this passage." So he looked at it again. He then said to the Baal Shem Tov: "The correct interpretation of this passage is as I have stated it, but if your honor knows of another meaning let him tell it to me and I shall judge which is more correct." Upon which the Baal Shem Tov said: "Arise!" and he rose to his feet. Now this particular text contained many names of angels and no sooner did the Baal Shem Tov of blessed memory begin to recite the text than the whole house was filled with light, and fire burned around it, and they actually saw the angels mentioned in the text. He said to Rabbi Dov Baer of blessed memory: "It is true that the meaning of the text was as you stated it to be, but your study of the text had no soul in it." On the spot Rabbi Dov Baer ordered his servant to journey home while he himself remained in the home of the Baal Shem Tov from whom he learned great and deep topics of wisdom. The Ḥasid heard all this from Rabbi Dov Baer's own holy mouth, his memory be for a blessing.

This tale is obviously legendary but may well be based on the actual events behind Rabbi Dov Baer's conversion to Ḥasidism. (Rabbi Dov Baer is the Maggid of Meseritch, the great organizer and leader of Ḥasidism after the death of the Baal Shem Tov.) The book Etz Ḥayyim *is the famous kabbalistic work by Rabbi Ḥayyim Vital (1542–1620). It is worth noting how the narrative dwells on Rabbi Dov Baer's extreme reluctance to leave off his studies in order to learn from the Baal Shem Tov and how he is disappointed that all the Baal Shem Tov can do is to tell him boring tales about coachmen and horses. The point here is that the Baal Shem Tov believed—and this became an essential feature of Ḥasidism—that God is present in all things and in all events, so that behind what seems to be dull stories about mundane happenings there is, in the language of our story, "great and marvelous wisdom—" i.e., reflected in them is the account of those spiritual forces through which God operates, as it were, as He governs the universe. The Baal Shem Tov wishes Dov Baer to overcome his reservations but does not seek to hurry the process. It is not until Dov Baer is about to depart that he receives a summons to come to the Baal Shem Tov. It is also worth noting that Dov Baer, despite his reservations, heeds the summons, propelled by the Baal Shem Tov's charismatic personality. This notion that "there must be something in it" seems, indeed, to have been the reason why some scholars initially hostile to Ḥasidism nonetheless came under the sway of the Baal Shem Tov, some of them becoming themselves devoted followers. Finally, the Baal Shem Tov wins over Dov Baer not by demonstrating his superior knowledge of the text, but by reciting it "with soul." The idea here is that mere knowledge of the Kabbalah is no different from knowledge of any other science. It certainly involves effort and intellectual ability, but is in itself devoid of mystical fervor. A man can be a keen student of the Kabbalah and even be an expert in the science without ever having had a mystical experience, a direct apprehension of God. The aim of the Baal Shem Tov was to "see" the angels of God, not simply to know all their names or converse about them. The story claims not that the Baal Shem Tov was more learned than Dov Baer, but that scholarship is not enough and that mystical fervor and burning enthusiasm are the true aims of the religious life. The etceteras are in the original text. This is a common device in this kind of literature, generally expressing a reluctance to complete the sentence and so suggest that there are mysteries here, as if the writer or the teller of the tale is winking at his audience, hinting to them that there is more here than meets the eye.*

II WHAT IS THE ROLE OF THE ZADDIK?

I heard from my teacher [i.e., the Baal Shem Tov] an interpretation of the talmudic saying: "Yes, in connection with Moses, it (the fear of God) was a small thing." The difficulty here is obvious. Moses was

not speaking to himself but addressing the people of Israel. He explained it as follows. The Talmud states that the verse: "Thou shalt fear the Lord thy God" (Deuteronomy 10:20) includes scholars. The Maharsha explains this on the basis of the saying: "A boor cannot be sin-fearing" (Avot 2:5). Consequently, when a man is a scholar he attains to the fear of God. That is why the verse includes scholars. Now of Moses we find it written: "And they were afraid to come nigh him" (Exodus 34:30). Since this was so, the people had had some experience of the fear of scholars and hence could easily progress to the fear of God. This is the meaning of "Yes, in connection with Moses it was a small thing," that is to say, since they had already attained to the fear of scholars "in connection with Moses," of whom it is said, "And they were afraid to come nigh him," it was a small thing for them to progress to the fear of God since one follows from the other. And the words of a wise man's mouth are gracious.

The talmudic saying is in tractate Berakhot 33b. Moses said: "And now, Israel, what doth the Lord thy God require of thee but to fear the Lord" (Deuteronomy 10:12). The Talmud asks: "Is the fear of the Lord such a small thing?", i.e., Moses states it as if it were very easy of attainment. To this the answer is given: "Yes, in connection with Moses it was a small thing." The difficulty to which our text calls attention is that Moses was not speaking to himself but to the people so that even if the fear of the Lord was an easy matter for him it was anything but an easy matter for those he was addressing. The answer given by the Baal Shem Tov refers to a comment on a passage in tractate Pesaḥim 22b of the Talmud by Rabbi Samuel Edels (1555–1631), author of a famous commentary to the Talmud. (This author is known as Maharsha: *Morenu* Ha-Rav *Shemuel* Edels, *Our Teacher, Rabbi Samuel Edels. Edel was Rabbi Samuel's mother-in-law, who supported his college out of her own funds; hence Samuel adopted her name.) In this passage the verse "Thou shalt fear the Lord thy God" is said to include scholars, i.e., one must have respect for scholars and be in awe of them just as one is in awe of God. This is extremely puzzling. How can any human being be compared to God? Maharsha seeks to explain it by quoting from* Ethics of the Fathers *(Avot 2:5): "A boor cannot be sin-fearing," i.e., only a learned man can have a full appreciation of true religion. Since this is so, says Maharsha, the "fear" of scholars and respect for them leads to the fear of God and that is why the verse "And thou shalt fear the Lord" can be said to include scholars. Now from the verse—"And they were afraid to come nigh him,"—we see that the people were in awe of Moses (because of the mysterious shine on his face; see the verse in full). They had experienced the awe of a scholar (Moses), and once having had this kind of experience it was easy for them to fear God. Thus the Baal Shem Tov gives a novel turn to the talmudic passage. It means, he says, that to those in connection with Moses, i.e., those associated with him, the fear of God was a small (i.e., easy) thing. The Baal Shem Tov makes use of the comment of Maharsha and applies it to the original saying. Jacob Joseph concludes, as he frequently does in his works, by quoting the verse from Ecclesiastes: "The words of a wise man's mouth are gracious" (10:12). This is a common form in this literature for bestowing high praise on someone else's comment, as if to say, "Bravo"!*

There is much more to the saying of the Baal Shem Tov as expounded by Rabbi Jacob Joseph than meets the eye. The term used in this text for scholars is the usual one found in the Talmud, namely, talmidey ḥakhamim, *literally, "disciples of the wise." But in Ḥasidic thought the term generally refers not to great experts in talmudic learning or Jewish law, but to the spiritual masters of the new type who emerged as leaders of the movement. The talmudic sayings in praise of the "scholars" are all applied to the Ḥasidic saint—the* zaddik. *What our text is really saying, by a skillful adaptation of the earlier literature, is that it is very hard for the ordinary man to fear God, but it becomes easy for him if he associates with the zaddik. Moses becomes the prototype of the zaddik. Just as the people were led by their awe in the presence of Moses to the fear of God, so the masses can be led to the fear of God through their awe of the spiritual grandeur of the zaddik. This demonstrates, incidentally, that the doctrine of the central role of the zaddik in Ḥasidism is not, as some would have it, a later invention, but was present in the movement from its inception. The doctrine is quoted here in the name of the Baal Shem Tov himself. It was precisely this idea that man requires the zaddik as an intermediary to God that the opponents of Ḥasidism, the* Mitnaggedim, *found so offensive.*

I heard this parable from him. There was once a king whose practice it was to go among the poor in order to attend to their needs. One of these poor men always used to declare, "Whatever a man does, whether it be good or evil, he does only for himself." The king, furious

at such ingratitude, ordered that poor man to be presented with a chicken stuffed with poison, and when this was given to him the poor man made the same reply. The poor man took the chicken home on the outskirts of the city and placed it there in storage. It came to pass that the king's son, tired and weary from hunting game, came to the house of the poor man and begged to be given something to eat. He was given that chicken, but the doctors who were with the prince first examined the chicken and discovered it to be poisonous. When the matter was brought before the king the poor man offered as his excuse that the king himself was responsible. The king was then obliged to admit that the poor man was in the right. The moral of this tale is obvious. And the words of a wise man's mouth are gracious.

The moral of the tale is left without application and one can only guess at its meaning. The king is God who has created man with what the Rabbis call "the evil inclination," the propensity to sin. But when a man sins he finds some excuse by recognizing that the king who poisoned the chicken is himself ultimately responsible, i.e., after all, if God had not made man the way He did, man would not sin. Needless to say, if this is what the parable means, the Baal Shem Tov does not intend to imply that man can sin with impunity. What he appears to be saying is that he should never yield to despair and be so oppressed with feelings of guilt that he gives up trying to lead the good life. Implied, too, perhaps, is the Ḥasidic doctrine known as "elevating strange thoughts." This idea, found early on in Ḥasidism, but later played down considerably as dangerous to spiritual health, is that whenever one is afflicted by "strange thoughts," sinful thoughts, an attempt should be made to lift these thoughts to God. For instance, if a man senses in himself feelings of pride, he should say to himself that all pride has its source in God and so every sinful thought should lead him on to take pride in being God's servant and to acknowledge that God alone is to be praised. In this way the sinful thought itself becomes the vehicle for religious emotion of a higher order. The "poison" was placed there by the king for a purpose. But perhaps the real meaning of our text is again to call attention to the role of the zaddik. He is the "king's son" who is in danger by eating the poisoned chicken. The zaddik, the "king's son" who resides in the palace, is at times obliged to go to the outskirts of the city far away from his father. There is spiritual danger in the zaddik's association with ordinary and even sinful folk, but he must take the risk of being "poisoned." In the end the poor man comes to the king and is vindicated, and so, too, the zaddik's "descent" brings about ultimately the elevation of the masses.

III WHAT IS REAL AND WHAT IS ILLUSION?

I heard this parable from my teacher. A king had three friends who, it was rumored, did not really love the king. He ordered each of them to feed a dog from the king's kennels. One of these men, being wise, used the money he should have spent on the dog's food to buy a crown for the king. The second one provided the dog with just enough to keep it alive. The third did his best to provide the dog with substantial meals. The king ordered the dog to attack the third man, but not so with regard to the one who provided the crown, etc. And the words of a wise man's mouth are gracious.

"Feeding the dog" probably refers to man's attention to his physical needs. Ḥasidism does not believe in asceticism. In the parable the king ignores completely the man who only gives the dog enough to keep it alive. Ḥasidism naturally disapproves of unbridled addiction to physical pleasure, since this only aggravates the problem. The dog that is too well fed is urged by the king to attack the man who feeds it. But there is no mention at all in the parable of the man who fed the dog in moderation, as we might have expected. The wise friend of the king concentrates on paying homage to the king and ignores the dog. The true Ḥasid, it seems to be implied, always has God in mind and neither torments nor indulges his body, but looks upon all worldly things as so many means of glorifying his Creator.

And I have heard from my teacher that he once said that the philosopher argues: "Since no place is empty of Him, when you deny idolatry you deny something that is from Him." My teacher explained that a man has a diaphragm. This is the mystery of: "And the veil shall divide unto you" (Exodus 26:33). Through it man pushes away the waste, etc. It is to be compared to a king who wished his son to have delight, but since this cannot be when it is permanent the king created the illusion of ten walls, etc. And the son of the king imagined, etc., but afterward it became clear to him that there is nothing evil at all.

This cryptic passage becomes clearer when seen in the light of further elaborations found in the works of Rabbi Jacob Joseph. The saying,

"No place is empty of Him" is Kabbalistic. It is used by the Ḥasidim to describe the typical Ḥasidic doctrine (best defined as panentheistic *—"all is in God"; not* pantheistic*—"all is God") that all things are part of the Divine. This doctrine was severely attacked by the Mitnaggedim, the opponents of Ḥasidism, who pointed out the extreme dangers in the doctrine in that it would seem to follow from it that God is present in evil as well as in good and would so tend to obliterate the demarcation lines between good and evil. This is the problem raised in our text by "the philosopher." Idolatry, so strongly condemned by Judaism, must also be from God; therefore, to deny the reality of idols is to deny something that is from God. The radical Ḥasidic answer is that evil does not really exist at all, but only appears to exist. Therefore, when one denies idolatry one is not rejecting something real, but rather affirming that only God exists and that idols only have the appearance of reality.*

Man's task in life is to see only God beneath the appearance of things. This is the "mystery" expressed by the veil which divides the holy from the unholy. This "mystery" is reflected in man in his diaphragm which divides the upper part of the body from the lower. (To this day the Ḥasidim wear a special girdle [the gartel*] for prayer to divide the upper part from the lower.) Man is to be constantly engaged in rejecting the waste products, in rejecting evil as unreal and so completing the process of "division." But if evil is only an appearance, why did God create the illusion that evil is real? Is not the illusion itself something positively evil? To this the Baal Shem Tov replies with a parable. The king wishes his son to have the greatest possible delight in life, but this is only possible in the presence of the king in his palace. However, all delight that is unceasing and permanent eventually becomes no delight at all since the senses become dulled with familiarity. Some opposition, some spur, is required. In the overcoming of opposition the delight is even greater. Consequently, the king, by his magic, builds around him imaginary walls so that the king's son feels obliged to make efforts in order to penetrate these barriers to the delight of the king's presence. If the prince in his love for his father is sufficiently determined to press on regardless of the barriers, he discovers that, strangely enough, the walls dissolve into nothingness. God creates the appearance of evil, He endows this nonexisting thing with the power to capture men by the illusion that it does exist, so that man can enjoy the greater delight of coming into the presence of his Creator after the effort he has made to shatter the barriers. If man is firm in his faith, he* *discovers that all the barriers between him and his God dissolve completely, so that, in reality, only good exists and God is everywhere with "no place empty of Him." This is one of the most typical of the Ḥasidic attitudes, and it is clear from our text that whatever special emphases and elaborations it received later, the doctrine is original with the Baal Shem Tov, although he probably developed it out of earlier Kabbalistic ideas. There has been a good deal of discussion about the sources behind Ḥasidic doctrine. Generally speaking, the contribution of Ḥasidism was not so much in producing entirely new ideas as in placing fresh emphasis on older ideas.*

CHAPTER 2

Jacob Joseph Katz of Pulnoyye
d. c. 1784

For its own sake
What can one learn from the clown?
How can religious sincerity be achieved?

Jacob Joseph [the name "Katz" is an acronym of Kohen Tzedek, *"a holy priest," a descendant of Aaron], disciple of the Baal Shem Tov, is the great theoretician of Ḥasidism. His* Toledot Yaakov Yosef *(The Generations of Jacob Joseph) was the first Ḥasidic book to be published and the main target of the Mitnaggedim. The author is referred to by the Ḥasidim, after the title of his book, as "the* Toledot*" (actually, in the Ashkenazi pronunciation used by the Ḥasidim, "*the Toldos*"). The title is based on the verse, "These are the generations of Jacob. Joseph, being . . ." (Genesis 37:2), used here in the sense of the "thoughts ["generations"] of Jacob Joseph." The other three works by Jacob Joseph similarly adapt verses dealing with the biblical hero Joseph for their titles. There are* Ben Porat Yosef *(Joseph Is a Fruitful Bough, after Genesis 49:22), first published in Koretz in 1781;* Zafenat Paneaḥ *(the name given to Joseph, Genesis 41:45), first published in Koretz in 1782; and* Ketonet Passim *(Coat of Many Colors, after the coat made by his father for Joseph, Genesis 37:3), published in Lemberg in 1866. The* Toledot Yaakov Yosef *is in the form of a running commentary to the whole of the Pentateuch,* sidra *by* sidra. Ben Porat Yosef *is a commentary to Genesis,* Zafenat Paneaḥ *to Exodus, and* Ketonet Passim *to Leviticus and Numbers.*

There is evidence that Jacob Joseph also wrote a separate commentary to Deuteronomy, but this has not survived. These works set the style for most of the subsequent Ḥasidic books, which are generally in the form of a running commentary to the Pentateuch and, occasionally, to other parts of the Bible. There is a full-scale study in English of Jacob Joseph's life and works entitled The Zaddik *by Samuel S. Dresner (New York: Abelard Schuman, 1960; paperback edition, New York: Schocken, 1974).*

Jacob Joseph was a distinguished rabbi when he came under the influence of the Baal Shem Tov. As a result of his new allegiance, viewed with extreme suspicion by his flock, Jacob Joseph was obliged to relinquish his position as Rabbi of Shargorod. When Aryeh Leib, the preacher (Mokhiaḥ) *of Pulnoyye, another disciple of the Baal Shem Tov, died, Jacob Joseph succeeded him in that position. Jacob Joseph had a fiery disposition, and his attacks on the rabbinic leadership of his day for their lack of spirituality were occasionally very intemperate, another reason for arousing the ire of the Mitnaggedim.*

I FOR ITS OWN SAKE

Toledot Yaakov Yosef, Bereshit (Warsaw edition, 1881), p. 21

I once heard the following parable. Two men entered into a mutual pact. After a time one of them became exceedingly wealthy. The other remained poor, but unlike his wealthy friend he walked in the way of the Torah. When the two met again they recalled the pact they had made, and the rich man gave his poor friend a sum of money with which to support himself. When the money had been spent the poor man came once again to his rich friend with whom he had made the pact. The rich man wanted to give him some more money, but the poor man said, "Rather than give me more money it is better that you teach how you made your money so that I can do likewise and also become rich." The rich man replied, "You walk in the way of the Torah and worship God. Since not every man is worthy of having two tables, how can you expect to have wealth in this world as well as the bliss that is stored up for you in the world to come? Give up the way of the Torah and you may then become rich." When the poor man heard this he decided to relinquish the way of the Torah and devote himself to gaining riches, but he was unsuccessful.

Returning to his friend the latter said to him, "The reason you have been unsuccessful was because your motive in giving up the way of the Torah was in order to become rich. If you resolve to give up the way of the Torah, come what may, whether you become rich or remain poor, you will then perhaps be successful." The poor man made this resolve, but was still unsuccessful. When he came again to his friend the latter said, "The reason you have been unsuccessful was because your very resolve to give up the way of the Torah, come what may, was itself for the purpose of acquiring riches. Evidently, there is no remedy for you." The application of this parable is obvious. It refers to its opposite, namely, when a man does that which is good and upright, it must be without any thought of reward. As the Tanna says: "Be like servants who serve their master without thought of reward" (Avot 1:3). The reward will surely come afterward, but your motive must not be in order to receive it. The whole of the above-mentioned idea applies here. Understand it well. And the words of a wise man's mouth are gracious.

"Be like servants who serve their master without thought of reward" is in the portion of the Mishnah known as Ethics of the Fathers (Pirke Avot). A teacher whose views are recorded in the Mishnah is known as a Tanna. *The remark about "two tables" is based on a talmudic saying (Berakhot 5b), that few people can expect to have a well-laden table both in this world and in the hereafter. The rich man in the parable sees the only hope for his poor friend who wishes to become rich is in giving up the Torah way. If he does this, he will lose his share in spiritual bliss in the hereafter and can then perhaps become rich in this world. But the poor man's motive for giving up the Torah way is not a "pure" motive. He only gives up the Torah way in order to become rich and not for its own sake. If he could become rich and still follow the Torah way he would do so. And even when he tries to do it for its own sake, this is because he comes to appreciate that only the "pure" motive will succeed in winning for him the riches he desires, and therefore this "pure" motive is tainted. The point of the story is that the poor man does not really desire to give up the Torah way; hence, whatever he does in practice, he does not, in fact, give it up at all.*

The application of the parable is obvious. The devout Jew believes that God will surely reward him for following the way of the Torah, but the only way that deserves to be called true worship of God is for a man to follow the Torah way for its own sake, to do it out of his love for God and not for the gain he will receive from it. If he engages in worship with this pure motive his reward will be all the greater. Realizing this, he tries hard to engage in worship without any thought of reward, but he may do this very thing in anticipation of the even greater reward that will be his by so doing. There is no way out, no remedy, for such a man. All his deeds and thoughts are tainted by self-interest. Even when he gives up the anticipation of reward, he gives it up only in order to receive reward. His giving is really in hope of taking.

The Ḥasidic answer to the problem is that man should not think of reward at all, but worship God in love. God will surely reward man for doing good, but this should never be his motive. Although the Talmud does urge a man to do good even where the motive is not of the highest, the Ḥasidim generally tried to rise above all thoughts of reward and had nothing but scorn for the self-seeking worshipper who is really not a worshipper at all. This is the Ḥasidic emphasis on Torah lishmah, *"Torah for its own sake." Ḥasidic strictness in this matter frequently led the Ḥasidim to denigrate rabbinic scholars whom they suspected of studying the Torah and practicing the precepts only in order to win fame and respect. The Mitnaggedim, on the other hand, attacked the Ḥasidic idea for its extremism, arguing that it is surely better, as the Talmud says, to persist in doing good even when the motives are not of the highest; otherwise men will neglect the Torah out of fear that their motives may be impure. This whole theme occupies a very prominent place in Ḥasidic-Mitnaggedic polemics.*

II WHAT CAN ONE LEARN FROM THE CLOWN?

Toledot, Va-yetzay (Warsaw edition, 1881), p. 51

Comment on: "And he lighted upon the place, and tarried there all night, because the sun was set; and he took one of the stones of the place, and put it at his head, and lay down in that place" (Genesis 28:11).

One should learn a lesson from the clown who, for the penny he receives, is ready to lose all dignity in order to make people laugh. How, then, can we fail to rejoice in God's service? The wise man will draw a similar lesson from the example of the stony-hearted who use every kind of strategem in order to do evil. In the same way one

should use every strategem in order to do good. We must add an observation I heard from my teacher. He said that when a soul comes down from the World of Emanation into the World of Action and observes how powerful the *kelipah* **is there and how little respect is paid there to the honor of the King's glorious majesty, he arouses himself all the more to praise the glorious King of the universe for he is not like them, etc. And the words of a wise man's mouth are gracious. Therefore, the verse says: "And he took one of the stones of that place, and he put it at his head." That is to say, he derived a lesson from the men of that place, who had hearts of stone, so that, relative to him, they were called "the stones of that place." And he "put it at his head," that is to say, it was foremost in his mind so that he could be clearly aware of it, and he praised God all the more in that he was not like them. "And lay down"—***va-yishkav***—"in that place," for there he had become even more worthy of inheriting the 310 worlds by means of the 22 letters. That is to say, he engaged in the study of the Torah with even greater enthusiasm because he realized that he was gifted with a heart of flesh and was therefore superior to them (who only had a heart of stone).**

Ḥasidism believes that nothing on earth is without purpose, nothing from which the Ḥasid cannot learn a moral lesson. From every event he witnesses the Ḥasid should derive some idea for the better service of his Creator. When the Ḥasid sees all the effort a professional clown puts into his work in order to make people laugh, the Ḥasid resolves that he, too, will rejoice in the service of God and bring this joy into the lives of others, too. Similarly, when the Ḥasid sees how much thought evil men give to their nefarious schemes, he resolves to give as much thought to his plans for realizing the good. The Kabbalah speaks of Four Worlds. The highest of these is the World of Emanation, the lowest the World of Action, which includes this world. The kelipah *("shell" or "husk") is the kabbalistic name for the demonic forces in the universe, evil surrounding the good and being nourished by it as the bark surrounds the tree or the shell the kernel of the nut. The lofty soul is profoundly disturbed to see how little regard men have for God, but paradoxically this experience helps to serve the good since it rouses in that soul an even greater love of God. If stony-hearted people can go about their business with such skill and enthusiasm, the man of lofty soul argues, how much more must*

I go about my business, which is to serve God and mankind, with even greater skill and enthusiasm.

The pun in the last part of the text is based on the Hebrew for "and he lay down"—va-yishkav. *The* va *simply means "and." This is disregarded and we are left with* yishkav, *which is read as two words* —yish *and* kav. *Now* yish *is made up of the two letters* yod *and* shin, *the numerical value of which (since each Hebrew letter has a number value) is 10 and 300 = 310. A passage in the Mishnah (Uktzin 3:12) states that God will give every saint in Heaven 310 worlds. The letters of the Hebrew alphabet, and hence of the Torah written in this alphabet, are 22.* Kav *is formed of the letters* kaf *and* bet, *20 and 2. Hence Jacob Joseph's interpretation of* va-yishkav. *The patriarch Jacob, when he saw the men of that place and noticed how stony-hearted they were, learned his lesson and studied the Torah with even greater enthusiasm; thus he came much closer to the spiritual delights of the 310 worlds in store for him and he studied the Torah written in the 22 letters with even greater industry and joy. The Ḥasid must never despair because men neglect their spiritual nature. On the contrary, this very fact should lead him to an even greater awareness of his own responsibilities.*

III HOW CAN RELIGIOUS SINCERITY BE ACHIEVED?

Ben Porat Yosef, Ḥayye Sarah (Pietrikov), pp. 82–83

The Mishnah in the first chapter of Avot reads: "Antigonos of Socho says, 'Be not like servants who serve their master in order to receive a reward; but be like servants who serve their master not in order to receive a reward; and let the fear of Heaven be upon you' " (Avot 1:3). This statement seems to contradict the statement in tractate Pesaḥim (50b): "A man should always engage in the study of the Torah and in carrying out the precepts even if his motive is unworthy (*she-lo lishmah,* literally, 'not for its own sake'), for as a result of doing it out of unworthy motives he will eventually come to do it out of worthy motives (*lishmah,* literally, 'for its own sake')." How then could Antigonos have put it so negatively: "Be not like servants etc." so that, as a result, Zadok and Boethus became heretics, as it is said there? You might argue that the passage in tractate Pesaḥim does not intend to convey a rule for saints (*mishnat ḥasidim*) and therefore states that a man should do it even if his motives are unworthy, for he will eventually come to do it, etc. Avot, on the other hand, is a

rule for saints, hence the negative form. But this cannot possibly be correct since the passage in Pesaḥim states: "A man should *always* engage, etc.," implying, that no distinction is to be made between a saint and an ordinary man who follows the normal rule and that to both of these the rule applies that they should do it even where the motive is unworthy, etc. Another difficulty is: Why does the text repeat: "Be not like servants, etc., but be like servants, etc."? Would it not have been preferable simply to say: "Be like servants who serve not in order to receive reward"? Furthermore, what connection is there between this and the concluding observation: "and let the fear of Heaven be upon you"? And we must also try to understand the very obscure verse in Psalms (37:37): "Mark the quiet man, and behold the upright; for the end of that man is peace."

The reference to Zadok and Boethus is to the rabbinic comment (not found, in fact, in Avot, but Jacob Joseph probably refers to the commentators to Avot who quote this from the book Avot De-Rabbi Nathan) *that Zadok and Boethus were pupils of Antigonos who understood him to mean that there is no reward for the righteous, so they became heretics. Some of the medieval commentators do try to resolve the contradiction on the lines rejected by Jacob Joseph at first, but Jacob Joseph is dissatisfied with the solution for the reason he states. Again in this passage we have the Ḥasidic preoccupation with* lishmah.

It appears to me as follows. The Rambam writes in his *Eight Chapters* to Avot, and also in the second chapter of *Hilkhot Deot,* that it is the way of the sages to prefer the way of moderation in all matters of the Torah except for the man who has gone from the middle way to one of the extremes. His remedy is to go to the opposite extreme for a time until he reverts to the middle way. Consult these works. Now you will understand the verse in Psalms: "Mark the quiet man," i.e., follow the middle way, the way of Jacob who is called a "quiet man" (Genesis 25:27). But there are times when it is necessary to grasp one of the extremes. This is called "upright," going beyond the strict letter of the law. Hence the verse says: "and behold the upright," namely, the man who has gone to one of the extremes. "For the end of that man is peace," i.e., when one has gone to an extreme his "end," i.e., his cure, is to go to the other extreme for a time so that eventually

he may come to follow the middle way that is called "peace," the harmony by means of which contradictions are resolved and extremes correlated. And this is easy to understand.

The Rambam *is Maimonides (1135–1204), so called after the initial letters of his name:* Rabbi Moshe ben Maimon. *The* Eight Chapters *form his introduction to Avot, and* Hilkhot Deot *(The Rules of Ethics) is part of his great code, the* Mishneh Torah. *The ideal is moderation in all things, but if a man finds himself going to one extreme he should counterbalance it by going to the other extreme for a time until he achieves equilibrium. For instance, ideally a man should be neither a miser nor a spendthrift, but if he senses that he is in danger of becoming a miser he should counterbalance it by acting as a spendthrift for a time and vice versa. The rest of this passage in* Ketonet Passim *involves a highly technical kabbalistic discussion and is omitted because it is incapable of translation into English. But what Jacob Joseph says basically is that Avot is, indeed, a rule for saints—the Ḥasidim—but one cannot expect to reach the ideal all at once, nor is it desirable that one should do so. As Rambam says, certain attitudes of mind and heart can only be acquired by trial and error. By knowing the harm of the extreme of unworthiness, one can have a better appreciation of the extreme of goodness. Hence the passage in tractate Pesaḥim states that a man should at first study the Torah and practice the precepts with an ulterior motive and only then can he gradually attain to the pure motive as stated in Avot. He must first go to the extreme of the ulterior motive and then, when he sees how ridiculous it is, he will be won over all the more to the pure, disinterested motive. That is why Antigonos uses first the negative and then the positive. This is to say, by all means begin with the unworthy motive, this is the only way at first. But do not remain always in this inferior state, but see to it that you progress toward the pure motive. And that is why Antigonos concludes: "And let the fear of Heaven be upon you," i.e., be sufficiently God-fearing to proceed from the state of self-interest as soon as you can.*

As we have noted, this whole discussion of lishmah *is basic to the Ḥasidic outlook. But not all the Ḥasidic teachers had precisely the same approach to the problem, and even among the writings of individual teachers it is possible to find different approaches, as we do, in fact, find in the writings of Jacob Joseph on this subject. In our text Jacob Joseph is realistic. He yields to none in affirming the central role of* lishmah, *of worship for its own sake out of the love of*

God, but appreciates that it takes hard and long training to attain to such a state. Moreover, unless the rise to pure motivation is gradual it tends to be self-defeating. Only after the struggle to overcome selfish motivation can the desire to worship in purity be firmly established. On the way in which the opponents of Ḥasidism reacted to the Ḥasidic ideal see the fine study Torah Lishmah *by N. Lamm (Jerusalem: Mossad Harav Kook, 1972).*

CHAPTER 3

Phineḥas Shapiro of Koretz 1726-1791

Illuminations
Should Jews wear non-Jewish garb?
Should prayer be silent?
How can pride be overcome?

Phineḥas Shapiro is known to the Ḥasidim as Reb Pinḥas Koretzer. He lived for a time in the town of Koretz (and hence his name), but there came into conflict with Solomon of Lutzk, disciple of the Maggid of Meseritch. Phineḥas settled later in the town of Ostrog and finally in Shepetovka, where he died. Although a prominent figure in Ḥasidism, Phineḥas pursued a line of his own. Not only did he differ in many matters from the school of the Maggid of Meseritch, but even in relation to the Baal Shem Tov he is best described as an associate rather than a true disciple. For all that, he was greatly influenced by the ideas of the Baal Shem Tov. His main disciple was Raphael of Bershad (d. c. 1816). Phineḥas did not write any books, but his teachings, in the form of gnomic sayings, like those of the Baal Shem Tov, are found in a number of Ḥasidic works. The work Midrash Pineḥas *(Jerusalem, 1971) is a collection of the sayings of Phineḥas and of Raphael of Bershad. It is evidently written by a disciple of Phineḥas who recorded the sayings as he heard them from his master, translating and occasionally quoting the original Yiddish. The Hebrew style of the work is extremely poor, being no more than a paraphrase of the Yiddish, but it is this which lends the work an air of authenticity.*

I ILLUMINATIONS

Midrash Pineḥas, p. 6, no. 9

The categories of *direct light* **and** *reflected light* **are present in all things. They are present in a loan, i.e., the loan is in the category of** *direct light* **and its repayment in the category of** *reflected light.* **But there is no category of** *reflected light* **in water.** *Mayyim* **("water") reads the same when read backward as when read forward. For water represents absolute simplicity. When the letters of** *mayyim* **are integrated they form the same word, e.g., the letter** *mem* **is formed of the letters** *mem, mem* **(so both are the same); the letter** *yod* **is formed of the letters** *yod, vav, dalet,* **the last two of which have the total numerical value of 10, which is the same as that of** *yod;* **and the same applies to the final** *mem* **of the word. That is why the Talmud states that people do not normally borrow water. [I once heard him <the Baal Shem Tov> say that it is dangerous to use the term** *borrowing of water.***] But fire does not have this property. When the word** *esh* **("fire") is read backward it reads** *sa* **("lift up"), for it is the nature of fire to rise upward. And the integrated letters of** *esh* **are not like those of** *mayyim.* **I also once heard him say that whatever a father gives to his children is in the category of** *direct light,* **which is mercy, whereas whatever children give to their father is in the category of** *reflected light,* **which is judgment. That is why people say, one father can support ten children but ten children cannot support one father.**

Direct light *and* reflected light *are kabbalistic terms. God's great mercies are described in terms of light. In His desire to have creatures whom He can benefit, God brought the world into being. But no creature can exist in the full splendor of the divine light. Consequently, the light has to be controlled and mediated gradually to finite creatures. This is done by beaming the light, as it were, so that after proceeding from God it first returns to Him before descending to the finite world. This process of beaming takes place, as it were, in the divine realm and from there comes down to earth. The* direct light *represents God's mercy, while* reflected light *(the control of the flow of mercy) represents God's judgment. Phineḥas observes that all things on earth have these two categories of* direct light and reflected light, except for water, which only has one. It is typical of the Ḥasidic approach to see mirrored in even the most mundane things the cosmic processes (see the story of the Baal Shem Tov and the coachman and horses in Chapter 1). Thus the twin processes are seen at work whenever there is a loan. The loan itself, as a pure, disinterested act of goodness, is direct light. The repayment of the loan is reflected light in that it reflects the original good intention. The borrower, when he repays his debt, is not acting out of pure mercy but out of justice. He owes the lender the money he has borrowed.

The kabbalists also make great play with letters and numbers, which to them are not mere symbols. The letters of the Hebrew alphabet are the form assumed on earth by the spiritual powers from on high. Take, for example, the Hebrew word for "light," or, formed from the letters alef, vav, resh. These represent various spiritual forces in the divine creative process, and when they are combined in this particular way they produce light. Thus when God said at the beginning of creation, "Let there be light," He combined the source of these letters on high and so produced light. It follows that a careful examination of Hebrew words shows the characteristics of things and events. By the "integration" of a word is meant the spelling out of each of its letters in full so that each forms a new word, e.g., or is alef, vav, resh; alef is alef, lamed, pey; vav is vav, vav; and resh is resh, yod, shin. The Hebrew word for "water" is mayyim: mem, yod, mem. These three letters still form the word mayyim even if spelled backward. Furthermore, by "integration" we get: mem = mem, mem; yod = yod, vav, dalet (the numerical value of yod is 10, that of vav 6, and that of dalet 4); mem = mem, mem again. Thus when either is read backward or "integrated," the word mayyim remains unchanged. For Phineḥas this represents the special character of water. Water never flows upward. It possesses none of the complexities of other things. It is pure and simple, the symbol of God's uncontrolled mercies; it is all direct light. Fire, on the other hand, does rise upward, back to God, as it were. That is why water represents mercy and fire judgment. The Talmud observes that people give water to one another, but do not normally lend it. This is quite natural, states Phineḥas, since water represents the capacity to give without thought of repayment.

The remark of the editor in brackets introduces a semimagical note. To use a term like borrowing of water is "dangerous" because the power of judgment is then introduced into the realm where all should be mercy. Finally, the love of parents for their children is said *to be completely selfless and self-sacrificing. It is pure giving—*direct light. *Children, on the other hand, owe a debt of gratitude to their parents for bringing them into the world and for looking after them. There is an element of duty and obligation, and this is consequently* reflected light. *Phineḥas endeavors to explain in this way why it seems to be true that parents are more devoted to their children than children are to their parents. (Freud also had something to say about this.) He concludes by quoting a well-known Yiddish saying. This is a further example of Ḥasidic fondness for reading mystical ideas into the sayings of ordinary folk.*

II SHOULD JEWS WEAR NON-JEWISH GARB?

Midrash Pineḥas, p. 13, no. 29

He remarked in connection with Gentile garments which Jews have nowadays taken to wearing such as the *pelts* **("fur coat") and so forth. These, he said, do not provide warmth, but only protect the wearer from the cold. For a garment represents the** *surrounding light,* **and with regard to the people of Israel the** *surrounding light* **enters to become combined with the** *inner light,* **but the Gentiles do not have the** *surrounding light.* **He once said, "Hear this clever observation: A simpleton cannot get dressed quickly, but first puts on one garment then waits a while and then, etc. For the** *surrounding light* **derives from wisdom, and the simpleton lacks the capacity of attracting wisdom speedily. A child also takes a long time to get dressed." I also heard him say, "When a man is sick he cannot bear to have the** *surrounding light* **all about him and he throws off his clothes. I once came to visit a sick man and found him lying in bed fully clothed and I declared that he would certainly recover."**

A further kabbalistic idea is that there are two aspects to the divine light by which all things are sustained: (1) surrounding light, *the light which transcends the universe, sustaining it from without, as it were; and (2)* inner light, *the divine light as immanent in the universe. God is both transcendent and immanent. Thus the two types of divine illumination are said to become combined and united. The view that Gentiles do not have* surrounding light *is curious and is based on the kabbalistic notion of the Jewish soul as inherently superior. (It would be probably reading too much into this passage to say that Phineḥas means that Gentiles stress the immanence of God to the virtual exclusion of His transcendence.) Phineḥas believes that Gentile-style garments, even when worn by Jews, have no power to warm inwardly, only to keep out the cold. (Perhaps Phineḥas is saying that Jews have guilt feelings about wearing Gentile-style garments and so persuade themselves that they only wear these to keep the cold at bay and not for inner warmth.)*

Furthermore, according to the Kabbalah, the surrounding light derives from God's wisdom, i.e., the intellectual aspect, as it were, of God's creative processes. This explains, says Phineḥas, why simple people or children find it so hard to get dressed. They have little wisdom, and wisdom is reflected in the surrounding light represented by clothes. The divine wisdom cares, as it were, for people's health, so that a sick person tends to throw off his clothes, representing again the surrounding light which is peripheral to the essential divine light.

III SHOULD PRAYER BE SILENT?

Midrash Pineḥas, p. 18, no. 51

Some people always recite their prayers with great force and in a loud voice. But, he said, it is stated in the Zohar that he who slays the dragon is given in marriage the king's daughter, that is, prayer. Consequently, a man must note whether or not prayer has been given to him (and he must not force the issue). He related how once a certain person came to him complaining that he was afflicted with idolatrous thoughts. He replied on the above lines. For if prayer is not given to man from Heaven and he wishes to take the hand of the king's daughter without permission, as above, it is sheer effrontery in the face of Heaven, and (even) where the honor of a mere mortal teacher is involved, there is a ban. Idolatry is called "banned thing" (*ḥerem*), as it is said: "for it is a banned thing" (Deuteronomy 7:26); hence he is afflicted with these thoughts and the rabbi instructed that man to agree to be placed under the ban (as a penance). The Zohar, he explained, suggests that one should recite his prayers only after adequate preparation and with due deliberation. Especially on Rosh Ha-Shanah, when the Holy One, blessed be He, is referred to as King, one must be very careful to observe this. He explained that "slaying the dragon" means that a man should see himself as really nothing at all, and then the king's daughter will be given to him. The indica-

tion of whether prayer has been given to him is when tears flow from his eyes. For twice the numerical value of *dimeah* **("tear") is** *Raḥel* **(Rachel), the daughter of** *Malkhut* **(Sovereignty), as is well known. He related, too, how a great man once stayed in his house and that man complained that his associates never seemed to pray along with him, one studying, the other sleeping. He said to him: "You will observe that when I say my prayers they all pray together with me," and so it was indeed. "For you pray," he said to the man, "before your prayer has really been given to you, but when prayer has been given from Heaven and is called "the king's daughter," representing unification on high, there is unity here on earth." Understand this.**

In this passage Phineḥas differs from the Baal Shem Tov and many of his followers, who prefer prayer to be recited in a loud voice and with violent gestures. Phineḥas does not believe in trying to storm Heaven. Rather his approach is that of the passive, mystical way in which the worshipper prepares himself to receive an influx of the divine grace. The prayers he recites are God's gift to him and owe little to his own efforts except those involved in making himself ready. Phineḥas quotes a saying from the Zohar to make his point. The motif of the hero who slays the dreaded dragon and receives the hand of the princess is, of course, a very familiar one, but is applied by the Zohar to prayer. Phineḥas understands it to mean that true prayer is a divine gift, from which it follows that it must not be snatched at will, any more than the hero is allowed to take the princess by force. To do so is sheer effrontery (ḥutzpah)*, and the penalty for one guilty of* ḥutzpah *to a scholar, say the Rabbis, is for him to be placed under the ban* (ḥerem)*, i.e., to be ostracized for a time. If this is the penalty where the honor of a mere human is at stake, how much more so where God's honor is at stake. Now the term* ḥerem *in the verse from Deuteronomy is used of idolatry. Hence the man guilty of taking Heaven by storm is afflicted with idolatrous thoughts.*

Thoughts of idolatry in Phineḥas's time can only mean thoughts that Christianity might be true. But why should a devout Jew have the thought that Christianity might be true, of all times, during his prayers? Perhaps Phineḥas means that because that man was vaguely dissatisfied with the spiritual experiences afforded him by Judaism, the thought enters his mind that Christianity might serve him better in this respect. Phineḥas attributes this to his effort to take Heaven by storm, to force the pace. If only he could learn quietly to await the divine grace, not demanding, but patiently making himself ready to receive, he will not be bothered by such thoughts any longer. On Rosh Ha-Shanah, the New Year festival, God is especially hailed as "King" in the liturgy.

Phineḥas then elaborates on the theme of passivity by introducing the typical Ḥasidic idea of self-annihilation. This means stilling the ego, or, in stronger terms, killing it. When man has become as "nothing," demanding nothing for himself, then the divine grace can freely flow down to him. When that happens his experience is completely authentic and uncontrived, and so his tears of joy or of sorrow flow automatically.

Phineḥas now introduces a kabbalistic idea. There are ten Sefirot, *powers or potencies in the Godhead. The lowest of these is known as* Malkhut *("Sovereignty") because it is through this that God's dominion is exercised. Now this aspect of Deity is also known as the* Shekhinah *("Divine Presence"), conceived of in feminine terms. There are two further aspects of* Malkhut, *one known as Leah, the other as Rachel, after Jacob's two wives. Thus Rachel is the "king's daughter," and authentic prayer comes from this aspect of Deity as a gift. Now the word for "tear"* (dimeah) *is formed from the letters* dalet, mem, ayin, hey, *the total numerical value of which is 119* (dalet *= 4,* mem *= 40,* ayin *= 70,* hey *= 5). Twice 119 is 238.* Raḥel *also has the numerical value of 238* (resh *= 200,* ḥet *= 8,* lamed *= 30). At least two freely flowing tears are an indication of complete authenticity. One cannot easily contrive to have tears flow. Finally, union with the king's daughter represents unification in the realms above and here on earth. Hence where there is authentic prayer all pray together. But Phineḥas's visitor, great though he was, was too concerned with his own spiritual progress, enough at least to be bothered about why his associates failed to pray together with him. As a result he was always in a state of isolation in his prayers and was therefore quite unable to influence others.*

IV HOW CAN PRIDE BE OVERCOME?

Midrash Pineḥas, p. 25, nos. 20–21

I heard in his name, that they once asked him how to overcome pride, and he replied that man was sent into the world for the purpose of studying how to avoid the sin of pride. I once heard him say, whenever someone pays another respect, the recipient of the honor should realize that the man paying him the honor evidently imagines him-

self to be inferior and by that very token he is, in fact, superior. So how can he be proud?

Whatever is more significant in this world is more scarce. There are thus fewer scholars than ignoramuses, and saints (zaddikim) are even fewer, and as for those who know how to pray, they are very few indeed. This is because the spiritual worlds on high are unwilling to allow any extension of themselves on earth.

It is worth noting in this passage the particular Ḥasidic emphasis: scholars, saints, and, highest of all, those who know how to pray. It is reported that the Baal Shem Tov also declared that all the spiritual illuminations that were granted him were not because of his learning, but because of the way he offered his prayers.

CHAPTER 4

Meir Margoliouth of Ostrog

d. 1790

Attachment to the holy letters

Meir Margoliouth, Rabbi of Jaslo, Horodenka, and, from 1777, Ostrog, was a famed talmudist (known as Rabbi Meir Harif, "the Sharpwitted") and kabbalist. Meir came under the influence of the Baal Shem Tov in his youth and looked upon him as his master, although, in many ways Meir followed the more conventional patterns of Jewish piety. He cannot be considered at all to be in the mainstream of Ḥasidic expression, but he belongs nonetheless to the Ḥasidic galaxy. Meir's work Meir Netivim, *published in Pulnoyye in 1791–92 does not deal with Ḥasidic matters. The following is from Meir's ethical will, entitled* Sod Yakhin U-Voaz, *first published in Ostrog in 1794. The edition used is that of G. Schwartz (London, 1956). The curious title means "The Mystery of Jachin and Boaz"—Jachin and Boaz were the two bronze pillars in Solomon's Temple (I Kings 7:15–22). The passage is from chapter 2 of the work, pp. 6–8.*

ATTACHMENT TO THE HOLY LETTERS

Even though our sages of blessed memory say that a man should study the Torah even if his motives are unworthy, they go on to give the reason why this is permitted: because he will come to study the Torah out of pure motives (*lishmah*). A man must try to reach this stage (of study out of pure motives) as soon as he possibly can, for

who knows if, God forbid, this "coming" [i.e., coming to study out of pure motives] will not be anticipated by another "coming," namely: "The gadfly out of the north is *come*, it is *come*" (Jeremiah 46:20). And it is written: "One generation passeth away, and another generation *cometh*" (Ecclesiastes 1:4). And it is written: "The sun ariseth and the sun goeth down" (Ecclesiastes 1:5) (i.e., "cometh"). And King Solomon, on whom be peace, enjoins us to remember our Creator "before sun, and the light, and the moon, and the stars, are darkened" (Ecclesiastes 12:2). For the main aim of Torah study is for it to be *lishmah* ("for its own sake"), namely, to study the Torah in order to obey its laws, to keep them and carry them out. It all depends on the right intention, and this alone is the perfect manner of fulfilling this precept (of Torah study). This is hinted at in the verse: "they shall prepare that which they bring in" (Exodus 16:5). This means that before a man begins to study the Torah, he should think to himself clearly and honestly that he is making himself ready to study *lishmah*, without any alien thought. As my great teachers in Torah and saintliness (*ḥasidut*) have taught me, among them my dear friend the Rabbi and Saint (*Ḥasid*), Marvel of his generation, Our Master Israel Baal Shem Tov of blessed memory, that the correct intention for the study of the Torah *lishmah* is for the student to attach himself, in holiness and purity, to the letters (of the Torah), actually as well as potentially, in speech as well as in thought, so as to bind the portion of *nefesh, ruaḥ, neshamah, ḥayyah,* and *yeḥida* to the sanctity of the lamp, that is, the precept and the light that is the Torah, to the letters which make wise and through which there is an influx of illuminations and true and eternal vitality.

We have noted earlier how Ḥasidism places the greatest stress on the idea of Torah study lishmah, *"for its own sake." Meir here introduces, in the name of the Baal Shem Tov, a novel interpretation of this concept. As we have seen, according to the Kabbalah the very letters in which the Torah is written represent the divine creative processes. Consequently, a man must try to attach himself to these letters and so assist the divine grace to flow into all creation. According to the Kabbalah, there are five stages of the soul in ascending order:* nefesh, ruaḥ, neshamah, ḥayyah *and* yeḥidah. *When a man concentrates with all the power of his soul on the letters of the Torah, he attaches all the elements of his soul to the divine. Actually, such an approach to study tends to make it semimagical, though highly devotional, and is bound, so the opponents of Ḥasidism argued at least, to detract from a real understanding of the Torah texts studied. The true student, argued the Mitnaggedim, is expected to concentrate on the meaning of the texts he studies, not on the letters. It is interesting to note that while at the end of this section Meir does quote this definition of* lishmah, *at the beginning of the section he gives a far more conventional definition—that it means studying in order to keep the precepts. It is also worth noting that he refers to the Baal Shem Tov as his friend and as only one of his teachers.*

Now once a man is worthy of understanding the holy letters and once he knows how to attach himself to them he becomes capable of knowing, from these very letters, what will be in the future. This is why the Torah is referred to as "enlightening the eyes" (Psalms 19:19). The Torah enlightens the eyes of those who attach themselves to the letters in holiness and purity in exactly the same manner as did the Urim and Thummim. From the day, when young, that I came to know affectionately my teacher the Rabbi, Our Master Israel, mentioned above, may his soul be bound in the bundle of life, I knew with certainty that this was how he conducted himself in his great sanctity, separated from worldly things and wisdom. This saint lived by his faith so that hidden things were revealed to him. "It is the glory of God to conceal a thing" (Proverbs 25:2).

Meir develops the idea of the magical power of the letters. The Urim and Thummim were, the Rabbis say, in the nature of an oracle. On the breastplate of the High Priests were twelve stones each containing the name of one of the twelve tribes. These letters became illumined in miraculous fashion so as to provide an answer to whatever question was put to the High Priest. If, for instance, the advice was negative, the letters alef *and* lamed *would become brighter than all the other letters and could then be combined to form the word* lo, *"no." Meir believes that when the holy man studies the Torah "for its own sake," i.e., for the sake of attachment to its holy letters, these letters become illumined and an actual message shines forth. He believes further that the Baal Shem Tov had this gift and was able to see into the future through his attachment to the letters of the Torah. "Hidden things" were revealed to him, but he, and Meir after him, had to keep quiet about these experiences because "it is the glory of God to conceal a thing," i.e., to keep the secret.*

I was grieved at my inability to understand the meaning of the Rabbinic saying, "David's mind remained uneasy until he reached the chapter (of the Talmud) entitled, 'A virgin marries on the fourth day.' " It is true that I did manage to explain the saying homiletically yet, for all that, I said: Homiletics is all right in its place but I wish I could understand the real meaning of this saying. And I did eventually grasp its meaning through thoughts which came to me as I lay on my bed. We know that the letters of our holy Torah are all sacred, so that when a man studies the Torah for the sake of Heaven and so becomes attached to its letters, he is able to see into the future. David was grieved because he may have been guilty of "Thou shalt not covet thy neighbor's wife" when he took Bathsheba. David was wise enough to be able to bind himself to the letters when he studied the Written Torah and the Oral Torah. In his studies he came to the chapter "A virgin marries." In that chapter our sages of blessed memory deal with the incident of David and Bathsheba. They ask there why was she not forbidden to David and reply: "Whoever went out to the wars of David gave a bill of divorce to his wife," and in that passage there is a further amoraic discussion of the whole affair. So King David, on whom be peace, set before his eyes the beginning of this chapter, namely the letters of *betulah niseet le-yom ha-revii* **("A virgin marries on the fourth day"), and in fear and love he entreated the Holy One, blessed be He, to illumine the letters and so inform him whether or not he had been guilty of sin by taking Bathsheba. He was worthy that the letters did become illumined, just like the letters of the Urim and Thummim. These letters shone forth in such a way as to reproduce the saying of our sages of blessed memory in chapter** *Ḥelek*: **"Bathsheba was suitable for the son of Jesse from the seven days of creation." Thus to that which he had in mind when he put the question he received the reply through the illumination of the letters, at first one at a time and then by repetition, until the words in reply to his question were formed. (For although the Urim and Thummim contained all the twenty-two letters of the alphabet there were many letters which occurred only once and were not repeated. Therefore, in the reply, some letters shone**

out more than once and these were then combined to form the words. That is to say, the letters which shone at first faded and those letters required for the reply shone forth once again in the correct order so that their message was clear and unambiguous).

For the understanding of this curious passage it is necessary to appreciate that masters like Meir believed that the Torah transcended time, so that no incongruity was seen in King David studying, as part of the Torah, a talmudic passage not recorded until some fifteen hundred years after his death. He saw the whole passage in a vision of the future. The saying: "David's mind was uneasy . . ." is quoted by Meir as rabbinic, but is not, in fact, found in the rabbinic literature. It is one of a number of floating sayings sometimes attributed to the talmudic Rabbis. The meaning of the saying is undoubtedly that in the first chapter of tractate Ketubbot (which begins with the words: "A virgin marries," i.e., stating the laws and customs concerning the days on which marriages took place) the question of David and Bathsheba comes up for discussion, and in the course of this discussion David's action in taking Bathsheba is justified on the grounds that Uriah, Bathsheba's husband, had divorced her before he left for the war. (The reference is to tractate Ketubbot 9a–b.) Thus what the saying intends to convey is that David was not guilty of adultery, as the Talmud says in tractate Ketubbot. What set David's mind at rest was the realization that Uriah had divorced Bathsheba and the passage in Ketubbot is only quoted to show that this idea is found there.

Meir is not satisfied with this. True, David was not guilty of adultery, according to the Talmud, but he was guilty of coveting his neighbor's wife, since when David first wanted her she was still Uriah's wife. But in another talmudic passage (Sanhedrin 107a) in the last chapter of Sanhedrin, known, after its opening word, as Ḥelek, it is said that Bathsheba was "suitable," i.e., destined for David from the seven days of creation. (Actually, our text says "from the six days of creation," but Meir is evidently quoting from memory.) Now Meir takes it quite literally that David really studied tractate Ketubbot, and from the letters of the opening words of the chapter which happens to refer to David's sin, he found the oracle which told him that Bathsheba was destined to be his from the beginning and was not therefore his neighbor's wife at all but his, the one destined for him. Very brilliantly, though naively, Meir demonstrates that the Hebrew letters of "A virgin marries on the fourth day" are the same as those in the saying, "Bathsheba was suitable for the son of David from the seven days of creation." The importance of this whole passage is that it contains one of the very few references in Ḥasidic literature to the techniques of the Baal Shem Tov himself by an eyewitness, though one writing many years after the events he had witnessed.

Let us now revert to the subject with which we were dealing. If a man was deficient in worship while young let him increase the amount of divine worship. If it was his practice in his youth to study one chapter by day and another by night let him increase it, as it is said: "sound wisdom is manifold" (Job 11:6). So, too, in connection with almsgiving and benevolence, if it was his practice to distribute a certain portion of his income or a single dinar a day, let him give two each day now that he has grown older. It is written: "And precious silver unto thee" (Job 22:25). This refers to doubling and increasing the silver one gives to charity, and there is a hint that this precious silver one gives to charity is "unto thee," that is, for your own good, as the Rabbis explained the words said to Abraham: "Get *thee* out" (Genesis 12:1). It is "unto thee," it is really yours whereby your soul gains merit. It is otherwise with regard to the silver you keep for yourself, for who dares to claim that he knows the fate of such silver or what will become of it? Even when he is alive, to say nothing of when he has died, no man can know who will eventually have his money or how long it will remain in the possession of his son. You surely know this and by experience at that. It can be observed with our physical eyes that, both in former times and in our own day, very rich men, their houses full of gold and silver and all manner of good things, came in but a short time to a state of utter penury, in which they lacked everything, so hungry and thirsty that it seemed they were about to expire. Very rich men have left their riches to their heirs, and yet in a short space of time all that wealth vanished like a passing shadow, fleeting as a cloud, so that their children had to be supported from charity funds, begging at doors, God forbid. Man has nothing of all his toil except that which he distributes to charity and which he spends on good works. These will accompany him to the grave. These will form a graceful diadem to his head and a necklace around his throat. For he will wear charity like a coat of mail, each penny he has given becoming part of a grand total. Happy

is the man who reflects daily on the means of perfecting his soul and is anxious that he may be called upon to speed his preparations, for he does not know when he will be called to render an account of his life.

Here Meir resorts to conventional moralizing but this is no less noble in its way than his more mystical flights. Whatever a man gives away to others in need he really retains for himself because it has contributed toward the perfection of his soul.

At the very least from the age of fifty, which our sages of blessed memory declare is the age for giving counsel, this should be done. Such a man has seen and experienced much of the world's events, the days of childishness and the longing for pleasures have passed, and the human intellect has become refined. He is therefore at this age a suitable person to give advice to others. If he is suited to be a counselor of others when they ask his advice, it is obvious that he should take counsel with himself on how to perfect his soul, hewn from on high and because of his sins reduced many degrees from her elevated rank. He should prepare himself in deed and thought and take clear and sound counsel so as to be able to answer well when his Creator orders him to give an account of his life, just as a messenger whose time has come to give an account to the one who sent him on his errand.

Again the conventional moralistic tone Meir uses seems to owe much to his general studies. Normally the Ḥasidim were not overly concerned with the fate of their soul in the hereafter, but stressed the idea of self-negation, so that the Ḥasid is encouraged not to think of himself at all.

CHAPTER 5

Aryeh Leib, the Mokhiaḥ of Pulnoyye d. 1770

The cloven hoof
The vanity of scholars

*Aryeh Leib was a member of the Baal Shem Tov's circle, perhaps the first to become his disciple. He was the official town preacher (*mokhiaḥ*, literally, "Rebuker") at Pulnoyye, where he was succeeded by Jacob Joseph, author of* Toledot Yaakov Yosef. *But after the pattern of preachers in his day, he delivered sermons in other towns, and it is said that the Baal Shem Tov encouraged him to introduce the new Ḥasidic ideas into the sermons he preached in the towns of Galicia and the Ukraine. Aryeh Leib's teachings, based on the sermons he delivered, are to be found in the work* Kol Aryeh *(The Sound of the Lion), first published in Koretz in 1798. (The edition used here is that of New York, 1956.) The teachings are arranged according to the sidrot of the Torah together with comments on other parts of the Bible and on the Talmud.*

I THE CLOVEN HOOF

Kol Aryeh, Shemini, p. 37b

"These are the living creatures which ye may eat. . . . Whatsoever parteth the hoof, and is wholly cloven-footed, and cheweth the cud. . . . But these ye shall not eat of them that chew the cud, or of them that part the hoof; the camel . . ." (Leviticus 11:2–4). There is a

difficulty here. Why is it that at first the parted hoof is mentioned before the sign of chewing the cud and yet in connection with those it is forbidden to eat, chewing the cud is mentioned before the indication of the cloven hoof? The second difficulty is: Why it should be mentioned at all, since it is all explained later on in the verse? To my humble mind it seems that hinted to here are the four types of persons who frequent the House of Study. One goes and practices, etc. Now the cloven hoof hints at going to the House of Study, while chewing the cud refers to one who studies but either does not understand or does not practice. Now it is said that only when a man's fear of sin takes precedence over his wisdom will his wisdom endure, but not when his wisdom takes precedence over his fear of sin. Consequently, the first thing is the cloven hoof, namely, a man must first advance stage by stage in the fear of sin and then he can engage in study. We are now able to see the solution to our problem. For if he chews the cud first, namely, if his wisdom takes precedence, it does not endure. "The camel" (*ha-gamal*)**, this refers to one who studies with the motive of receiving reward for his studies. "And the badger," this refers to one who at times is a "man" with the fear of Heaven, and at other times his spiritual power is weak like the badgers who, as is well known, change their sex periodically**

*Aryeh Leib follows the methods of the preachers of his day: the building up of "difficulties" so as to lead to an ingenious solution intended to convey a particular moral and the homiletical interpretation of scriptural verses far removed from the plain meaning of the text. But he manages generally to introduce some Ḥasidic doctrine into his message. The verses he comments on here speak of the animals it is permitted to eat and those it is forbidden to eat, but Aryeh Leib finds that these verses "hint," as he puts it, at various types of scholars. He notes that in the "permitted" type the cloven hoof is mentioned first while in the "forbidden" type chewing the cud is mentioned first. In Ethics of the Fathers (Avot 5:18) it is said that there are four types of men in connection with attending the House of Study—*the Bet Ha-Midrash*—the place where the Torah is studied. One goes but does not practice, one practices but does not go; one both goes and practices (he is called a "saint"—*ḥasid*), and one neither practices nor goes. It is said further in Ethics of the Fathers (Avot 3:11) that when the fear of sin takes precedence over the acquisition of wisdom, then and only then can wisdom endure.*

Aryeh Leib proceeds to interpret the verse on the basis of all the above. "Going" to the House of Study means, for him, progressing toward the fear of sin by adequate preparation so that one is ready for study of the kind that endures. Only when a man goes in this sense, only when he is somewhat advanced on the spiritual path, will he study sincerely and for the sake of Heaven. Hence for it to be "permitted" or "clean," there must be both the "cloven hoof" (i.e., spiritual progress) and "chewing the cud" (i.e., learning, because one "chews it over" in the mind), and it has to be in this order, the "cloven hoof" first. But if one tries to "chew the cud" first without adequate spiritual preparation, it will not endure. Aryeh Leib now adds a further homiletical note. Among the unclean animals mentioned in the verses are the camel and the badger. Aryeh Leib applies these, too, following his scheme, to scholars. The word gamal *("camel") is connected with* gemul *("recompense"). This refers to the type of scholar only interested in what he can get out of it, who studies in order to receive some reward or benefit for himself. It was a widely held folk belief that badgers change their sex periodically. This refers to the scholar whose spiritual life is unstable. One day he is full of the fear of Heaven, as strong as a male in spiritual progress. But on another day he is as weak as a woman and displays no spiritual energy. Here is a typical early Ḥasidic critique of rabbinic scholarship, leadership, and learning. The early Ḥasidim could not deny the high position study of the Torah occupies in Jewish thought, but they emphasized that its value depends on spiritual purity and sincerity of motive. Both Aryeh Leib and his successor Jacob Joseph are extreme in their castigation of the rabbinic leaders of their day, whom they accused of a lack of spirituality as well as unconcern for the plight of the flock they were supposed to lead. Early Ḥasidism was certainly antiestablishment.*

II THE VANITY OF SCHOLARS

Kol Aryeh, Jeremiah, pp. 76a–b

"How do ye say: 'We are wise, and the law of the Lord is with us'? Lo, certainly in vain hath wrought the vain pen of the scribes. The wise men are ashamed, they are dismayed and taken; Lo, they have rejected the word of the Lord; and what wisdom is in them? Therefore will I give their wives unto others, and their fields to them that shall possess them; for from the least even to the greatest every

one is greedy for gain, from the prophet even to the priest every one dealeth falsely. And they have healed the hurt of the daughter of My people lightly, saying: 'Peace, peace,' when there is no peace" (Jeremiah 8:8–11).

All these verses present great difficulties, and the intelligent student finds it hard to grasp their meaning. To my humble mind it seems that they can best be understood on the basis of the rabbinic comment that the prophetic writings contain prophecies for later generations. For our sins, in this generation they all imagine themselves to be sages and men of understanding. Some of them dare to declare to those who rebuke them that the main thing in this world is to study industriously so as to become a quick-witted and expert scholar. The main thing is to give keen expositions. Through this alone one inherits the world to come and nothing else is required. In this they vaunt themselves and pride themselves over anyone who disagrees with their view and, all the more so, over one who refuses to go in their way; even if he be a man of fine character and sound conduct he is an object of scorn to them.

In my humble way I shall argue against them, so that they will be unable to refute me. The prophet Jeremiah declares: "For my people is foolish, and they know Me not; they are stupid children, and they have no understanding; they are wise to do evil, but to do good they have no knowledge" (Jeremiah 4:22). The difficulty here is in the repetition, "they are stupid and have no understanding," for one who is stupid obviously has no understanding, since to have understanding is to be even greater than a sage.

Now in my humble opinion it seems that the man who does have understanding is capable of deriving one thing from another. Nowhere do we find it stated that the capacity to understanding in this sense is limited to the great scholar. It is true that the Rabbis say that words of Torah must be sharp in the mouth, but it is clear from the context and the general tenor of their remarks that they mean a man should be able to reply to questions put to him concerning practice, namely, that which one should do and that one should refrain from doing. As the Rabbis of blessed memory say: "It is not theory that is

most important but practice," and they state further that some may be distinguished for their ability to preach, but fall short when it comes to practicing what they preach.

The word for "understanding" is tevunah. *The rabbinic interpretation is to connect it with the word* ben, *"from among," and therefore interpret it as referring to deduction, where the conclusion is derived "from among" the premises. For the scholars of Aryeh Leib's day the "deductions" were entirely in the realm of theory, each scholar seeking to outdo others, or at least this was Aryeh Leib's contention, in the application of logical or pseudological arguments to the talmudic dialectics. Aryeh Leib, following his teacher's stress on inwardness and spirituality, prefers to interpret "deduction" as the ability to derive rules of practice from the principles of Judaism laid down in the classical sources. The scholars were fond of defending their attitude by quoting the rabbinic injunction (Kiddushin 30a) that the Torah a man has studied should be "sharp in his mouth," that is to say, clear and unambiguous. The scholars stressed the term* sharp. *It is the glory of the scholar that he is alert and able to engage in "sharp" dialectics. But Aryeh Leib argues that the meaning is rather that he should be so familiar with the Torah that he is able to respond quickly, to give sharp and clear replies, to questions regarding conduct that are put to him. The statement implying that practice is more important than theory is in Ethics of the Fathers (Avot 1:17). The statement disapproving of those who do not practice what they preach is in tractate Yevamot 63b.*

For this (to know how a Jew should conduct his life) great intellectual ability is required, for one has to know everything recorded in the Talmud, the codes, and the moralistic works. Especially is this true of one whose personality is tainted by evil character traits, for the Talmud remarks that a man who studies the Torah but behaves badly to his parents and to others, commits a profanation of God's name. The moralistic work *Reshit Ḥokhmah* **deals with this subject at length. Of such a person Scripture says, "But unto the wicked God saith: 'What hast thou to do to declare My statutes, and that thou hast taken My covenant in Thy mouth?' " (Psalms 50:16). It is possible that this is what the prophet means: "They are stupid children," i.e., "children" refers to the scholars, as it is said: "And all thy children shall be taught of the Lord" (Isaiah 54:13); "and they have no under-**

standing," i.e., they fail to understand one thing from another—that is to say, how to grasp the real meaning of the words of the Rabbis of blessed memory when they said that a man should be sharp and quick-witted. This is why it says: "and have no understanding."

Thus Aryeh Leib explains why "stupid" is followed by "and have no understanding." The meaning is that they imagine they are wise and have understanding, but in this they "misunderstand" the meaning of understanding and so are "stupid." The passage about the profanation of God's name is in tractate Yoma 86a. The work Reshit Ḥokhmah *is a kabbalistic-moralistic work by the sixteenth-century kabbalist Elijah de Vidas of Safed. It is certainly a curious interpretation that Aryeh Leib gives—that the prophet castigates the people of the future for failing to understand the proper meaning of a talmudic passage, but, as in connection with Meir Margoliouth (Chapter 4), preachers like Aryeh Leib believed that such anachronistic interpretations were perfectly legitimate, since the Torah is beyond time. Note that in leading up to this comment, Aryeh Leib states that Jeremiah is prophesying for future generations, i.e., for Aryeh Leib's day. This is the idea behind the next paragraph, too.*

To my mind a further lesson can be derived from Isaiah. The prophet says: "Wash you, make you clean. . . . Learn well" (Isaiah 1:16, 17). If they rely on this verse, they should know that Rashi explains that the meaning is: "Learn *to do* **well," to improve one's conduct. Consequently, God has protected us from misinterpreting this verse. And perhaps this is what the prophet means when he says: "They are wise to do evil, but to do good they have no knowledge," that is to say, they do not know that the correct interpretation of the verse. In Isaiah, "Learn well" is, as Rashi says, to do good to others, but they take it literally.**

There are a number of puns here which cannot be adequately conveyed in translation. The main point is that Isaiah says: limedu *("learn")* heytev *("well"). Rashi, the famous French commentator of the middle ages (1040–1105), rightly supplies the words "to do" between* limedu *and* heytev *so that the meaning of the verse is: "*Learn to do *well." But the scholars take it to refer to study, not to practice, and they take literally the words: "Learn well." (Actually, the word* heytev *is connected with* tov*, "good," and the scholars were no doubt thinking of the Yiddish expression "gut lernen," i.e.,* *well-versed in learning.) Now Jeremiah says: "to do good they have no knowledge." The Hebrew for "to do good" is* le-hetiv, *which is virtually the same word that Isaiah uses. Hence Aryeh Leib's ingenious interpretation: They do not know the meaning of* heytev *in Isaiah. Here again is the anachronistic type of interpretation referred to in the previous paragraph. Jeremiah rebukes the scholars of the eighteenth century for failing to interpret Isaiah as Rashi does.*

However, one must only study those moralistic works that are based on sound rabbinic principles. I have heard people say, "Can all the rabbinic and later references to punishment and reincarnation really be true? If it were so, then you take away life from everyone and we are all doomed. Who can bear such a thing? The Rabbis only recorded these things in order to frighten and terrify people." To my mind, whoever says this and holds it to be true is a real heretic. According to his argument the Talmud and the holy books contain falsehood, and those who gave their approbation to the books allowed their pen to be false by approving of falsehoods. This is what the prophet says: "How do you say, 'We are wise'? Lo, certainly in vain has wrought the pen of the scribes," that is, the pen of those who gave their approbation to the books.

*Note the reference to reincarnation—*gilgul*—a belief shared by the kabbalists and the Ḥasidim. A sinner has to return to earth again in order to put right his offense. Later in this sermon Aryeh Leib interprets the prophet's remarks about their wives being given to another to mean that the Torah they have studied (so long that it has become attached to them just like a man's wife is attached to him) will belong to another incarnation, for they will have to come back to earth again when they will study the Torah for its own sake. Aryeh Leib seems to be influenced here by the hell-preaching of his day rather than by his teacher the Baal Shem Tov. There is no doubt that the Ḥasidim did believe in Hell, but there are surprisingly few references to it in Ḥasidic literature, and the Ḥasidic masters do not seem to have used this kind of threat in order to encourage their followers to lead the good life. There is, in fact, a Ḥasidic legend which tells how the Baal Shem Tov interrupted a preacher who dwelt on the sins of Israel.*

CHAPTER 6

Moses Ḥayyim Ephraim of Sudlikov
d. 1800

When all seems dark
Why was the Baal Shem Tov so important?
What happens on Judgment Day?

One of the most interesting features of later Ḥasidic life is is the emergence of dynasties of Ḥasidic masters. The Baal Shem Tov himself, however, oddly enough, did not become the founder of a dynasty. He did have a son called Zevi of whom little is known and who plays no part in the subsequent development of Ḥasidism. Ḥasidic legend has much to say, on the other hand, about Odel, the Baal Shem Tov's daughter who married Jeḥiel Ashkenazi, a similarly unknown figure. Odel and Jeḥiel had two sons. The younger son, Baruch, did eventually become a Ḥasidic master, and his teaching will be considered presently. The older son, Moses Ḥayyim Ephraim, was brought up under the tutelage of the Baal Shem Tov. In a famous letter to his brother-in-law, Gershon of Kitov, who was then in Israel, the Baal Shem Tov refers to Ephraim's forthcoming marriage and to the fact that he is fast becoming a good scholar. (This letter was first published at the end of Jacob Joseph's Ben Porat Yosef, *and dates from 1750.) Allowing for the fact that marriages took place at a very early age in those days, it nonetheless is obvious that Moses Ḥayyim Ephraim must have been born some time before 1740.*

Moses Ḥayyim Ephraim settled in Sudlikov and lived a retiring life. Unlike his brother, Baruch, he was never a Ḥasidic master. But his work on Ḥasidic doctrine became one of the most popular of Ḥasidic books and is a major source for the actual teachings of the Baal Shem Tov, which he introduces with the formula: "I have heard from my master, my grandfather." This book is entitled Degel Maḥaney Efrayim *(The Banner of the Camp of Ephraim, after Numbers 10:22). The title hints at the author's name,* Maḥaney *representing* Moshe Ḥayyim. *The Ḥasidim refer to Moses Ḥayyim Ephraim as "the Degel," after his book. The book was first published by Moses Ḥayyim Ephraim's son, Jacob Yeḥiel, in Koretz in 1810. Unlike many Ḥasidic works, which were recorded by the master's disciples, this book was actually written by the author, who is gifted with an easy, fluent style. The edition used here is that of Jerusalem, 1963.*

I WHEN ALL SEEMS DARK

Degel Maḥaney Efrayim, Va-yetzay, pp. 40–41

"And Jacob went out from Beersheba, and went toward Haran. And he lighted upon the place . . . and behold a ladder set up on the earth, and the top of it reached to Heaven; and behold the angels of God ascending and descending on it" (Genesis 28:10–12).

Contained in this passage is the mystery of greatness and smallness [of soul]. The saying of my master, my grandfather, his soul is in Eden, his memory is for a blessing, is well known, that "the living creatures run to and fro" (Ezekiel 1:14), and it is impossible for a man to remain always at the same stage, but he must ascend and descend. His descent is for the purpose of a further ascent. For when a man considers that he is in a state of smallness he prays to the Lord, as it is said: "But from thence ye will seek the Lord thy God; and thou shalt find Him" (Deuteronomy 4:29). The meaning of "from thence" is, from the place in which you find yourself, as my master, my grandfather, his soul is in Eden, his memory is for a blessing, has said.

The mystics speak of the "dark night of the soul" when man falls back after his ascent of soul and feels very remote from God. They urge him not to be dismayed, but to press on until new light illumines his soul. The Jewish mystics deal with the same problem, but the terminology they use is "smallness" (katnut)*, when all seems dark and narrow, and "greatness"* (gadlut)*, when all is bright and* *clear and man senses himself to be very near to God. In Ḥasidic thought the idea receives a special kind of emphasis. The Ḥasidic ideal is* devekut, *"attachment" (to God), a state in which God is always in the mind. But man, being what he is, cannot possibly live always at this stage. He falls from it from time to time, but as a result he reflects on his remoteness from God and, making an even greater effort to be near, he rises even higher. Thus his very descent is the means for a further, even higher ascent, and so it goes on. It is as if someone is slowly climbing a high mountain and has to step back occasionally in order to gain fresh strength for the ascent. This is the Ḥasidic interpretation quoted by Moses Ḥayyim Ephraim here of "the living creatures ran to and fro," i.e., they recoiled and then drew near to God and then recoiled again and they could not always be near. There is a further pun on the word* ḥayyot *("living creatures"). This word is read as* ḥiyyut, *"vitality." There is an ebb and flow in man's spiritual vitality. A further interpretation on the same lines in the name of the Baal Shem Tov is also quoted. "From thence" in the verse in Deuteronomy is interpreted to mean "from whatever place [i.e., spiritual state] man finds himself." Whether he is in the state of* gadlut *or that of* katnut *he has to seek God, and if he persists he will find God even in the state of* katnut *and thus rise again.*

Now this is hinted at in the verse: "And Jacob went out from Beer-sheba." This means that the zaddik sometimes falls from his high stage and is outside the influx of divine grace. It is well known that the *Shekhinah* is called Beersheba. Hence it says: "and went toward Haran," that is to say, he falls into the state of smallness. When he senses that this has happened to him then: "And he alighted upon the place," that is, he prays for it to the Place, blessed be He. "And he took of the stones of the place," that is to say, the place in which he finds himself, as above, "from thence ye will seek the Lord thy God," as we have said in the name of my master, my grandfather, his memory is for a blessing. And then: "And he dreamed and behold a ladder set up on the earth, and the top of it reached to Heaven." This means that the descent, "set upon the earth," is really a ladder by which one can ascend to an even higher stage, as is well known that descent is for the purpose of an even higher ascent. Therefore, it says: "and the top of it reached to Heaven," namely, he will attain to an even higher stage.

The zaddik is the "righteous man," the "saint," but the term is used in the Ḥasidic literature especially to mean the "holy master." According to the kabbalistic doctrine of the ten Sefirot, there are ten powers or potencies in the Godhead, the lowest of which is known as Malkhut (Sovereignty). This is known as the Shekhinah (Divine Presence) conceived of in feminine terms, because it is, as it were, the passive principle in the Godhead. Of the ten Sefirot three are thought of as having to do with the divine thought and the other seven having to do with the divine emotions. Malkhut is the lowest of these seven and into it flow the light of the other Sefirot to give it vitality, and so enable it to pour out the divine grace upon those below.

Thus, in a sense, the other Sefirot can be said to give birth to Malkhut; but Malkhut, in turn, then pours out the divine flow to all creatures. For this reason Malkhut can be called a "daughter" (of the Sefirot) and it can also be called a "well" (from which creatures derive their sustenance). If Malkhut is itself counted as one of the seven lower Sefirot as well as being the recipient of their flow, Malkhut can be called Beersheba (interpreted as "the daughter of the seven"). Beer means a well, hence the interpretation of Beersheba as "the well of the seven." Jacob emerges from Beersheba, i.e., he falls into the state of katnut and so is outside the flow of the divine grace from Malkhut. He then goes to Haran (which is read as ḥaron af, "wrath," "anger," "sternness"), that is to say, he falls from his high spiritual stage, in which he is the recipient of divine grace, into the state of katnut. In rabbinic literature a name for God is Makom, "the Place" (interpreted as "the Place of the world"), so that Jacob's alighting upon the place is said to mean that he prayed to God. Thus Moses Ḥayyim Ephraim interprets the verse to mean that when Jacob saw that he had fallen from grace he entreated God to help him rise again and in his new ascent took of the very stones of the place into which he had fallen. Therefore, the vision of the ladder was shown to him. This ladder, with its feet on the ground, suggests the descent of the zaddik, but its head reaches to Heaven, since the very descent provides the means for raising the zaddik to even greater heights.

"And behold the angels of God," i.e., he sees that this happened to all the zaddikim, they all are in a state of "ascending and descending on it," they all fall, but this very fall is for the purpose of an even higher ascent, as it is said of Abraham that he went *up* **out of Egypt, and so of Isaac and so of others.**

The "angels" represent the zaddikim who lead holy lives. No one should be too distressed when he descends because this is the normal pattern of the spiritual life and is to be observed even among the zaddikim. Of Abraham and other biblical heroes Scripture says that they went up out of Egypt. Now Egypt is the symbol of spiritual bondage and darkness, but their ascent was occasioned by their previous descent. They went up out of Egypt, i.e., as a result of first being in Egypt.

II WHY WAS THE BAAL SHEM TOV SO IMPORTANT?

Degel Maḥaney Efrayim, Be-shallaḥ, pp. 100–101

"The children of Israel went out with a high hand" (Exodus 14:8). The Targum renders *be-yad ramah* **("with a high hand") as** *be-resh geluy* **("with uncovered head"). Now the holy Zohar states: "Through this book they will go out of exile," and the explanation is given that when the Zohar is revealed they will go out of exile. This is hinted at in our verse: "The children of Israel go out" of exile, as above,** *be-yad ramah,* **the Targum of which is** *be-resh geluy.* **The letters of** *be-resh* **are the initial letters of** *R*abbi *Sh*imon *b*en *Y*o**ḥai, and** *geluy* **("uncovered") means "revealed." Hence the meaning is that when his holy book, the Zohar, will be revealed they will go out of exile. Understand this.**

*The Hebrew for "went out" (*yotzeim*) can mean "go out," and Moses Ḥayyim Ephraim finds a mystical "hint" at the process of Israel's redemption from exile. The Targum is the ancient Aramaic paraphrase of the Bible. The Targum translates* be-yad ramah, *which is idiomatic, as* be-resh geluy, *"uncovered head," a similar idiom for freedom, without fear of the Egyptians over their head. Moses Ḥayyim Ephraim takes* geluy *as "revealed" and* be-resh *as the initial letters of Rabbi Simeon ben Yoḥai, the traditional author of the Zohar, who lived in second-century Israel. (Modern scholars understand the Zohar to be a much later work—see the section on the Zohar in Volume 2 of this series.) Now the Zohar was only known from the end of the thirteenth century, when it was "revealed" by Moses de Leon, in Spain. From that time onward, the Kabbalah, the mystical doctrine expounded in the Zohar, helped Jews to become more holy and hence more worthy of redemption from exile. Thus the children of Israel go out (are engaged in the process of redemption from exile) from the day that Rabbi Simeon ben Yoḥai's book, the Zohar, was revealed.*

Or one can say: The holy Rabbi Lipeh of Chmielnik said, and it is also found in the holy letter of my master, my grandfather, his memory is for a blessing, printed in the holy book of the Rabbi of Pulnoyye, on whom be peace, that he [i.e., the Baal Shem Tov] asked the Messiah: "When will your honor come?" and the Messiah replied, "When your teachings will be revealed and when your fountains will be distributed to all." Consult that letter. We can say, therefore, that this is hinted at in our verse: The children of Israel go out of exile *be-resh geluy*. **The letters of** *be-resh* **are the initial letters of** *R***abbi** *Y***israel** *B***aal** *Sh***em, and** *geluy* **means that when his doctrine will be revealed and his fountains distributed, then they will go out of exile. Understand this.**

In his famous letter to which we referred at the beginning of this section the Baal Shem Tov describes what happened in an "ascent of soul," i.e., when his soul ascended to Heaven, where he saw a vision. There he conversed with the Messiah, and the Messiah, in reply to the question of when he will come to redeem Israel from exile, stated that it will be when the Baal Shem Tov's teachings become very widely known. Note the parallel here with that of Rabbi Simeon ben Yoḥai in the previous paragraph. There is a recognition that the Baal Shem Tov, like Rabbi Simeon ben Yoḥai, is the instigator of a new mystical tradition. Rabbi Lipeh of Chmielnik was a close associate of the Baal Shem Tov.

III WHAT HAPPENS ON JUDGMENT DAY?

Degel Maḥaney Efrayim, pp. 282–83

The following is among the sayings which Moses Ḥayyim Ephraim records as having heard personally from his grandfather. These are in addition to the many sayings of the Baal Shem Tov recorded in the body of the book.

I once stood before him after Rosh Ha-Shanah had gone out and he related what happens up there. He related how the Patriarchs of the world stand there in the presence of the King of Judgment (I am not sure whether he said all the Seven Shepherds together with Abraham, Isaac, and Jacob) and they declare the merits of Israel. Moses our teacher, on whom be peace, also stands there. He acts like a broker, turning this way and that, skillfully and in a roundabout way bringing

in the merits of Israel and seeing to it that no accusers and sinners should enter there, God forbid. This is the gist of what he said, though I have not reported it exactly in his own pure words. Afterward he said to me, "Was it not a good tale that I have told you?"

Rosh Ha-Shanah, the New Year festival, is judgment day. The Baal Shem Tov describes to his grandson, who must have been a little boy at the time, how Moses and the Patriarchs plead on behalf of Israel. This motif of interceding on behalf of Israel is prominent in Ḥasidic life and thought. It helps explain the rapid rise of Ḥasidism which brought hope to the suffering masses of Jews in the lands in which Ḥasidism was taught. The Seven Shepherds (based on Micah 5:4 and tractate Sukkah 52b) are Adam, Seth, Methusaleh, David, Abraham, Jacob, and Moses.

I heard that a man is guilty of sins he had committed in a previous incarnation. But when he prays on behalf of sinners, his sins, too, are put right. And the words of a wise man's mouth are gracious. Understand this.

As we have noted earlier, the Ḥasidim believed in gilgul, *"reincarnation." A further typical Ḥasidic idea, based on the Kabbalah, is that of* tikkun, *"putting right," i.e., making good the sins one has committed and thus restoring harmony in the soul and in all creation in which sins make "flaws." The Baal Shem Tov is here reported as saying that even the man who knows that he has not committed any serious sins may nonetheless be guilty of sins he had committed in a previous incarnation. But if he is sufficiently generous and compassionate to pray even on behalf of sinners, God is similarly compassionate to him and pardons all his sins. Here is another typical Ḥasidic motif, the zaddik's regard for all, even for sinners.*

He explained further an apparent contradiction in the Zohar. In one passage the Zohar expresses disapproval of those who beg for their sustenance like dogs who bark for their food, but in another passage it states that whoever does not pray for his sustenance daily is lacking in faith. This is how he resolved the contradiction. Whenever a man lacks anything it is the vital part within him that feels the lack. It follows that whenever a man prays for his needs to be satisfied—when, for example he prays for his sustenance—it is the vital force

which senses the need, and this force derives from the *Shekhinah.* **Therefore, he should pray for the pain suffered by his vital force—in reality, the** *Shekhinah.* **This is how the above contradiction is resolved.**

The vital force in man derives from God. In Ḥasidic thought this means that it is especially connected with the divine, that it is, in fact, the Shekhinah *itself. Thus whenever man is in need, it is the* Shekhinah *that is really in need. Ḥasidism is none too happy about men petitioning God for their needs, since this can be an exercise in pure selfishness. The Ḥasidim do not urge men to give up petitionary prayer, but to engage in it with the motive of fulfilling God's will. Thus when he prays, the Ḥasid is saying, "I do not ask it for myself, but in order for God's will to be carried out, in order to fill the lack the* Shekhinah *experiences." This is how the Baal Shem Tov resolves the contradiction. Those who pray only for themselves are compared by the Zohar to the barking dogs, but it betokens lack of faith not to pray at all. The true Ḥasid does offer petitionary prayer, but it is an unselfish prayer and for the sake of the* Shekhinah. *This idea of prayer for the sake of* Shekhinah *occurs repeatedly in Ḥasidic literature; the idea, as can be seen from this passage, dates back to the Baal Shem Tov himself.*

CHAPTER 7

Baruch of Meziboz

1757-1810

Hints in Scripture
External versus internal piety
How can God be served when man eats and drinks?
A playful comment
What is the role of the zaddik?

Baruch, the younger brother of Moses Ḥayyim Ephraim, held a Ḥasidic "court" in the town of his grandfather, the Baal Shem Tov. He was a boy of three when his grandfather died, and his main teacher in Ḥasidic doctrine appears to have been Phineḥas of Koretz, though, apart from numerous legends, we have no indication of how Baruch received his training. Because Baruch conducted his court with great splendor—he even had a court jester, Hirshel Ostropoler—and because he appears to have been the first zaddik to make it a policy to receive large sums from his supporters, Baruch has been treated very unsympathetically by the historians of Ḥasidism, especially Hordetzky and Dubnow. He is certainly no profound thinker compared with some of the other Ḥasidic masters, but the facts are that he became a highly revered figure in Ḥasidic lore, the Ḥasidim always referring to him as the Rebbe Reb Baruch. He left no writings, but the book Botzina Di-Nehora *(Candelabrum of Light) contains his teachings as recorded from time to time by an associate whose identity is unknown. (The term* Candelabrum of Light *is used as a* *title of honor in the Talmud and is found in the Zohar in the sense of mystical light.) The book was first published in Lemberg as late as 1880. (The edition used here is that of Reuben Margaliot, Lemberg, 1930.) Dubnow (*Toledot Ha-Ḥasidut*, p. 395) is somewhat skeptical about the book's claim to be the authentic teachings of Baruch, but at all events the book has been accepted as authentic by the Ḥasidim, and, as Dubnow admits, it does seem to contain a hard core, at least, of historical truth.*

I HINTS IN SCRIPTURE

Botzina Di-Nehora, Bereshit, p. 53

He remarked that the zaddikim utter words of Torah and rebuke and link their ideas to Scripture by means of vague hints which barely touch the text. This is because Scripture says: "and the spirit of God hovered over the face of the water" (Genesis 1:2). "Water" refers to the Torah, and the Rabbis understand the word "hovered" to mean that it barely touched the water.

A common rabbinic interpretation of the scriptural references to "water" is that it means the spiritual water of the Torah. Thus the spirit of God which infuses the discourses of the zaddikim "hovers" over Scripture. Baruch is evidently aware of the farfetched nature of much of Ḥasidic exegesis. The verses the zaddik quotes in support of his ideas cannot possibly mean what the zaddik says they mean. (We have many instances of this peculiar method of interpretation in the sayings of the Ḥasidic masters quoted in this book.) Baruch defends it on the grounds that even though the spirit only "hovers" over the Torah, what emerges from the exposition is still part of the Torah. There is here, too, the implication that the zaddik's words are divine inspired. They are infused with the spirit of God. This was a widely held Ḥasidic belief and is why the classical Ḥasidic works are called by the Ḥasidim "holy books."

II EXTERNAL VERSUS INTERNAL PIETY

Botzina Di-Nehora, Ekev, p. 58

He said: It is written: "And at Taberah, and at Massah, and at Kibroth-hattaavah, ye made the Lord wroth" (Deuteronomy 9:22). This means that even a man who serves God by studying the Torah and praying to Him can still cause a flaw to be made, God forbid, if he is insincere

in his worship. And the same applies to Kibroth-hattaavah, even when a man shatters his desires he can still make the Lord wroth. The main thing is for man to worship God in sincerity without any ulterior motive, God forbid.

The three places mentioned are interpreted homiletically (see the comment on the previous paragraph). Taberah *means "burning," hence prayer offered with burning enthusiasm.* Massah *means "testing," hence studying the Torah in order to arrive at the truth.* Kibroth-hattaavah *means "burying desire." Thus the verse is made to yield the thought that it is possible for a man to conduct himself like a saint, studying the Torah, praying to God and leading an ascetic life and yet still be guilty of making God angry because he is puffed up with pride at his attainments or does it all for reasons of self. The reference to the "flaw"* (pegam) *is to the kabbalistic doctrine that when a man sins he brings about a flaw in the heavenly realm. It is the opposite of* tikkun, *"putting right," mentioned by Moses Ḥayyim Ephraim in Chapter 6.*

III HOW CAN GOD BE SERVED WHEN MAN EATS AND DRINKS?

Botzina Di-Nehora, Ki tetze, p. 59

"If a man have two wives, the one beloved, the other hated, and they have born him children, both the beloved and the hated, . . . he may not make the son of the beloved the first-born before the son of the hated, who is the first-born; but he shall acknowledge the first-born, the son of the hated, by giving him a double portion. . . ." (Deuteronomy 21:15–17).

He, blessed be his memory, explained this as referring to two different categories of divine worship. A man may serve God only by studying the Torah and praying to Him. This is the category of the beloved wife, for whoever sees this type of worship admires it. But there are zaddikim who serve God even when they are engaged in worldly matters, when they eat and drink and attend to their other physical needs and they elevate all the holy sparks in all earthly things. This is the category of the hated wife, for not everyone is capable of appreciating how there can be service of God in these matters. Most people imagine that the zaddik attends to his physical needs without any intention for the sake of Heaven but just like all the common

people, and it is consequently in the category of the hated wife in the eyes of the world. But Scripture says: "He may not make the son of the beloved the first-born, . . . but he shall acknowledge the first-born, the son of the hated, by giving him a double portion." For the service of the zaddik when attending to his physical needs is considered in God's eyes to be twice as valuable as the service of the beloved.

A kabbalistic idea, that of the "holy sparks," became very prominent in Ḥasidic thought. The doctrine runs that when God began to engage in the creative process there took place a cosmic catastrophe known as the "shattering of the vessels," i.e., the containers of the divine light were unable, at first, to confine it within themselves and they were broken. As a result, "holy sparks" were scattered into all things and these have to be reclaimed for the holy and restored to their Source. This is done when man attends to his physical needs in a spirit of purity. When, for example, man eats not to satisfy his hunger alone or in order to indulge himself but as an act of divine worship, then the holy sparks in the food he eats are redeemed. Thus there developed the typical Ḥasidic idea that God is not only to be worshipped by Torah study and prayer, but He can be served by man even when man eats or drinks or carries out other physical acts. Baruch carries this to extremes by arguing that the zaddik who worships God in this way is superior to the one who "only" prays and studies the Torah. Since the zaddik is Baruch himself, students of Ḥasidism hostile to this zaddik have seen in this a crude attempt by Baruch to justify his nonascetic life and his lack of great knowledge of the Torah. Baruch is only too well aware that people criticize the zaddik when they see that he behaves just like anybody else and enjoys material things as much as others do. They expect the zaddik to be a holy man, which, for them, means leading a severely ascetic life and denying oneself the good things of this world. Because they fail to appreciate that the zaddik's mind is on God in whatever he does, they find his conduct repellant. This is how Baruch meditates on the law of the two wives and their offspring. The "offspring" are the deeds which result from the different types of worship engaged in by the two types of zaddikim. These are referred to as their "wives" because the zaddikim are wedded to the way they have adopted. Thus the verse tells us that contrary to general opinion, according to which the zaddik who engages in worldly things is "hated," his deeds deserve special praise. He has the rights of the first-born, and a double portion is due to him. Naturally, this whole idea was anathema to the Mitnaggedim, who accused the Ḥasidim of reducing the study of the Torah to a lower scale in the hierarchy of Jewish values.

IV A PLAYFUL COMMENT

Botzina Di-Nehora, Tehillim, 22, p. 61

"I am a worm, and no man" (Psalms 22:7). A playful explanation. Some people, if they have the slightest suspicion that there is a worm in the fruit they are about to eat, will throw away the fruit uneaten in order not to offend against the prohibition of eating worms. But when these same people are angry with someone else, they will victimize him in body and spirit until they devour him. Therefore, King David, on whom be peace, said: "I am a worm, and no man." You are so careful, he said to his enemies, not to devour any worms, so treat me at least as a worm and I will be spared.

"Playful" though this comment is, Baruch is here castigating the unethical conduct of those who are so very scrupulous in avoiding the slightest infringement of the dietary laws and yet careless about the more serious offense of wronging their neighbors. For all its emphasis on the mystical life and the purely religious aspects of Judaism, Ḥasidism is profoundly concerned with sound ethical conduct.

V WHAT IS THE ROLE OF THE ZADDIK?

Botzina Di-Nehora, Tehillim, 30, p. 61

"I will extol Thee, O Lord, for thou hast raised me up" (Psalms 30:2). He explained *dillitani* **("Thou hast raised me up") in four different ways: (1) I extol Thee in that Thou hast made me a door** (*delet*) **and a gate for all Israel. For whoever wishes to pray to God, to entreat Him, and to repent of his sins, I open a door for them and a gateway to the Lord. (It is possible to explain on these lines the verse: "This is the gate of the Lord—the zaddikim"—Psalms 118:20.) So the word** *dillitani* **is understood as derived from the word** *delet* **("door"). (2) Or** *dillitani* **can be connected with** *deli* **("bucket"). This means: I praise God for having made me like a bucket for all Israel. The illustration is of a deep well full of living water. A bucket is required to be attached to a long rope in order to draw the living water from the well, and**

without it no one can draw the water, the well being so very deep. In the same way all the world requires the zaddik to bring down the flow of divine grace, bringing all good things from the Fountain of Life, and he is like a bucket. (3) Or *dillitani* **may be from the word** *dallut* **("poverty"). He praises God in that he knows how little he is worth, for the zaddik is always in a state of lowliness and he despises himself. (4) Or the meaning may be, quite literally: "Thou hast raised me up, and hast not suffered mine enemies to rejoice over me."**

Baruch's fourth explanation is, in fact, as he says, the plain meaning of the verse. But he suggests three other explanations and, evidently, sees these, too, as implied in the verse. His other three (from delet, *"door,"* deli, *"bucket," and* dallut, *"poverty") are farfetched, but Baruch seeks to defend the philosophy of zaddikism. First, he sees the zaddik as the door through which people can come to God. (The interpretation of* This is the gate*—zaddikim is, of course, very fanciful. The verse says: "This is the gate of the Lord, the zaddikim [righteous] shall enter therein." But Baruch detaches the word zaddikim from the end of the verse to yield the thought that the zaddik is the gateway to the Lord.) The second interpretation is that the zaddik is attached to God and so is able to bring down the flow of the divine grace. In the first interpretation the zaddik brings man to God, in the second he brings God to man. According to both, the zaddik's mediation is required, a source of great offense to the Mitnaggedim, who taught that Judaism does not know of any intermediary between God and man. But the zaddik, says Baruch, must not pride himself on his tremendous role. He must always be aware of his spiritual poverty and think little of himself. Hence in the third interpretation the zaddik gives thanks to God for enabling him to see how lowly he is.*

CHAPTER 8

Naḥman of Bratslav

1772-1811

Why are hindrances essential?
Why should good men be persecuted?
Why should one force himself to rejoice?
What are the virtues of solitude?
Should one plan for the morrow?

The Baal Shem Tov's granddaughter Feige, sister of Moses Ḥayyim Ephraim of Sudlikov and Baruch of Meziboz, married Simḥah the son of Naḥman of Horodenka, an associate of the Baal Shem Tov. Naḥman, the son of Feige and Simḥah, named after his paternal grandfather, was thus born into the "royal family" of Ḥasidism. Yet this most original of the Ḥasidic masters had little use for mere traditional loyalties and sought a way of his own. His thought, in Jewish garb, bears some resemblance to his contemporary, the Danish thinker Kierkegaard. Indeed, Naḥman is the most "existentialist" of the Ḥasidic masters in his emphasis on personal commitment and the complete subordination of reason to faith. After a stormy period in which he was involved in controversies with other Ḥasidic teachers, Naḥman settled in the town of Bratslav in the year 1802, and although he went to Uman in 1810, where he died and is buried, he is generally known by the Ḥasidim as the "Bratslaver" and his Ḥasidim as the Bratslaver Ḥasidim. Naḥman believed strongly in his own special role. Many of the references to the "true zaddik" in his works seem to refer to Naḥman himself. There is evidence, too, that he had messianic pretensions.

Naḥman's disciple, Nathan Sternhartz, was his scribe and Boswell, recording his master's teachings and writing his biography. The most interesting feature of Bratslaver Ḥasidism is that Nathan did not succeed him as the zaddik, and to this day the Bratslaver Ḥasidim have only one "rebbe," Naḥman himself, as if he were still alive. The other Ḥasidim tended to look askance at Bratslaver Ḥasidim, calling them "the dead Ḥasidim" because they had no living master. Most of the present-day Ḥasidim of Bratslav live in Jerusalem.

Nathan Sternhartz wrote down most of Naḥman's teachings in a number of works. It would seem from Nathan's references that Naḥman did record many of his ideas in writing, but that Nathan put them into the form they now have. Naḥman is the author (but not the final recorder) of, among other works, a number of fairytales, like that of the seven beggars, into which the Ḥasidim read all kinds of mystical ideas. There is a vast literature on Bratslav. The late Professor J. G. Weiss devoted his life to an elucidation of Naḥman's thought. Weiss believed that Naḥman was the most profound religious thinker produced by Jewry these past few hundred years. According to Weiss, Naḥman's personality was such that reason and faith were locked in unendurable conflict in his soul; the only way he could find relief was to reject totally one or the other. He came down on the side of faith, hence the antirationalism of a good deal of his thought and his opposition to philosophy and even to the great medieval Jewish philosophers. He dared to criticize Maimonides for his philosophical learnings, not an uncourageous thing to do in his age.

The main work on Naḥman's teachings is Likkutey Moharan *(The Collected Teachings of Our Master Rabbi Naḥman), first published in Ostrog in 1806, with another series (*Likkutey Moharan Tinyana*) published, after Naḥman's death, in Mohilev in 1811. Subsequent editions contain both parts in a single volume. (The edition used here is that of Bene Berak, 1965.)*

I WHY ARE HINDRANCES ESSENTIAL?

Likkutey Moharan, no. 66, 4, pp. 83d–84a

Naḥman has described the thought processes of man. He observes that all thinking is done in words and that for ideas to be well defined *the words must be clearly enunciated in thought. This means that vague ideas only become clear when, in the language of Naḥman, the vowels (*nekudot*) must be added to the consonants. (In Hebrew only the consonants are written as letters, the vowels are represented by* nekudot*—vowel points.) Naḥman here goes on to develop this idea and states that the desire for something is the cause of it being clearly realized in the mind—of the consonants receiving their vowel points.*

The way to attach the vowels to the consonants is by way of yearning and longing, the yearning and longing of a Jew to perform a *mitzvah* or some other holy thing. This is the category of "points of silver" (Song of Songs 1:11), for through longing and desire the points are formed. Nothing can be achieved without desire. For instance, when a man speaks he can only do so because he has a desire to speak, and so unless a man had a desire to do something, he would not in fact do it. Consequently, when a man has to carry out some holy task—journeying to a true zaddik, for instance, or some other holy task that he is required to carry out—he is first given the desire to do it so that he will in fact do it.

Naḥman puns on the word kesef*, "silver," in the verse from the Song of Songs. He connects it with the word* kisufim*, meaning "longings." Hence his maxim:* nekudot kesef*, "[vowel] points [are produced by] longings." Note how Naḥman gives as the illustration of a holy task journeying to a true zaddik.*

The strength of desire is mainly brought about when obstacles to its realization are presented. For when a Jew has to do something for his Judaism, especially when he has to do something so important that the whole of his Judaism depends on it—to journey to a true zaddik for instance—he is presented with obstacles to its realization. These obstacles are presented in order to awaken his desire, in order that he should have an even stronger desire to do it than when there are no obstacles to be overcome. For whenever a man is prevented from doing something, his desire to do it becomes much stronger. For example, when a child is shown something he wants and that thing is then immediately taken away from him and hidden, the child runs after the man who has hidden it and begs him to give it to him, and his desire for it is all the greater. It follows that the child's desire is

caused mainly by the very fact that the thing has been snatched away and hidden from him. In the same way, obstacles are placed in the way of a man who needs something so that his desire for it will be increased. This is the category of "Bread eaten in secret is pleasant" (Proverbs 9:17). The meaning is that the more a thing is hidden from man, the more obstacles it presents, the more does he desire it and the more pleasant it is when he attains it.

Naḥman interprets the verse in Proverbs to mean that when bread is secreted, i.e., when it is hard to get, it is all the more pleasant to engage in the search for it and enjoy it once one has found it. Note again his reference to the true zaddik.

This is why there is so strong a desire to commit sinful acts, may God save us from them! Since these acts seem impossible for man to do, for we are commanded and enjoined and instructed not to do them, it follows that there is a great obstacle to their realization, and for this very reason the desire to do them becomes all the more powerful, as above, in the category of "Bread eaten in secret is pleasant."

Naḥman refers here to the subtle lure of the verboten, that which is forbidden, which is desirable precisely because it is forbidden.

The same applies in matters of holiness. Whenever there is a difficulty, the greater the desire, and the more important the thing desired, the greater the obstacles that are presented. For there is a desire, there is one who desires, and there is a thing that is desired. That is to say, there is the man who has the desire, there is that for which he has the desire, and there is the desiring itself. The strength of the desire must be in proportion to the value of that which is desired. It follows that where the worth of that which is desired is very high, it is essential for the man who has the desire for it to have a very great desire for it, and he must therefore be presented with more powerful obstacles to its attainment, since there will then be an even greater desire for it. As we have said, the greater the obstacles the stronger the desire to overcome them and realize the desire. Consequently, when a man experiences many obstacles to the realization of some holy task, he should realize that this shows the importance of the thing desired. It must be a thing of great value

if the obstacles are so great. This applies especially when one wishes to journey to a true zaddik. For there are many zaddikim, but there is the category of the point of truth among the zaddikim. And when a man wishes to draw near to such a one, for on this everything depends, many great obstacles present themselves to him and from this very fact he should realize how great, as above, is that which is desired.

Naḥman seems to be saying that the whole of the Ḥasid's Judaism depends ultimately on whether he approaches the "true zaddik," namely, Naḥman himself. He does not use the plural zaddikim, but refers here and also in similar contexts to "the true zaddik." It is not unknown in religious writings for saints to have a very high opinion of themselves, partly because they saw their attainments as being purely a gift of God for which no thanks were due to them in any personal way, so that their self-praise was as if they were praising another. Nevertheless, Naḥman's attitude does present something of a psychological puzzle.

This is the general rule. Every obstacle is presented only for the sake of increasing desire so that once a man has a great desire to do something he will carry it out, converting the potential into the actual. For it is through desire that the vowels are formed, and it is by means of these that the actual emerges from the potential, as we have seen. For desire shatters all obstacles. For since, as we have said, the obstacles are chiefly presented in order to increase desire, it follows that once a man has come to desire the thing even more because of the obstacles, these latter are shattered automatically.

It should be noted that the references to obstacles "being presented" mean, of course, presented by God. It is typical Ḥasidic doctrine that nothing happens on earth unless the hand of God is directly involved. Naḥman thinks of hindrances to the good life as being intentionally presented by God in order to increase man's desire by provoking the need to overcome obstacles.

II WHY SHOULD GOOD MEN BE PERSECUTED?

Likkutey Moharan, Tinyana, no. 13, p. 144c

When people disagree with a man they tend to persecute him and he then flees for protection to God, so that the more they disagree

with him the nearer he comes to God. For God is everywhere, in the category of: "If I ascend up into heaven, Thou art there; If I make my bed in the netherworld, behold, Thou art there" (Psalms 139:8). So wherever he flees it is to God that he comes. This is the category of: "Pharaoh drew nigh" (Exodus 14:10), which, the Rabbis say, means that Pharaoh drew the people nearer to their Father in Heaven, for because Pharoah pursued after them he brought them nearer to God.

Naḥman's philosophy of suffering. The man who is persecuted has no one to whom he can turn, but God is there and so he throws himself on God's mercies. Here, too, Naḥman is no doubt thinking of his own experiences when many of the zaddikim of his day "disagreed" with him and positively persecuted him.

III WHY SHOULD ONE FORCE HIMSELF TO REJOICE?

Likkutey Moharan, Tinyana, no. 24, p. 146b

The general rule is that a man must try with all his might always to be joyful, for by nature man is drawn toward melancholia and sadness because of the events which befall him, and all men are full of suffering. It is, therefore, essential that man force himself with all his strength to be joyful always and to use every means to make himself rejoice, even if he has to resort to silly things. It is true that it is also very good for man to have a broken heart, yet this should only be in a certain hour. He should set aside an hour each day to break his heart and pour out his speech to God, blessed be He, as we have explained. But for the rest of the day he should only be in a state of joy. For it is easier to be led into melancholia from the state of brokenheartedness than it is to stumble, God forbid, through joy so that one is led to frivolity, God forbid. For it is easier to come to be melancholic as a result of having a broken heart. Consequently, a man should always be in a state of joy and should only practice brokenheartedness during the hour he sets aside.

Naḥman believes that the risks which stem from joy are less than those which stem from misery. Here we have a typical Ḥasidic emphasis on simḥah, *"joy." The theological background is that for the Ḥasidim God pervades all, so there is no room for a sad approach to life. But it is worth noting that Naḥman makes a clear distinction between simḥah, the joy with a strong religious connotation, and frivolity, which is simply a lack of proper seriousness.*

IV WHAT ARE THE VIRTUES OF SOLITUDE?

Likkutey Moharan, Tinyana, no. 25, p. 147a

In this passage Naḥman defines the ideal of hitbodadut, *"being alone" with God, "solitude." This is a general ideal among the mystics and the Ḥasidim generally, but it is stressed particularly by the Bratslaver Ḥasidim.*

To be in solitude is a supreme advantage and the most important ideal. This means that a man sets aside at least an hour or more during which he is alone in a room or in the field so that he can converse with the Maker in secret, entreating and pleading in many ways of grace and supplication, begging God to bring him near to His service in truth. This prayer and supplication should be in the vernacular, namely, in these lands, German [i.e., Yiddish]. For it is difficult for a man to express himself adequately in the holy tongue [i.e., Hebrew], and his heart cannot be in it to the same event, for we do not normally converse in Hebrew. But it is easier to have a broken heart when one speaks in Yiddish, the language of our daily conversation. In Yiddish a man expresses everything he wishes and he should say to God whatever is in his heart, relating to him both how sorry he feels for his past misdeeds and his desire to repent of them and his prayer for the future that he be brought nearer to Him from that day onward in truth, and so forth, each according to his spiritual stage. He should take great care to carry this out daily at a special time, as above. But during the rest of the day he should be in a state of joy, as above. This habit is exceedingly important and is the way that is most beneficial in order to draw nearer to God, for it is a counsel that embraces all others. He should tell God all that he lacks with regard to the worship of Him or how far he is entirely from the worship of Him. Even if it happens to be the case that he finds himself incapable of opening his mouth to speak to God at all, yet this is good in itself, namely, the very preparation in which he makes himself ready to speak to God although he cannot actually do so, yet since he wishes to do so, this in itself is very good. And he

can make up a prayer and carry on a converation with himself regarding this very thing. Regarding this very thing he should cry out in prayer that he has become so remote from God that he finds himself unable even to speak to Him. And he should entreat God and beg for Him to open his mouth so that he can converse with Him. Know that very many of the great and famous zaddikim related that they only attained to the stage they did as a result of this habit. The intelligent will understand himself the great advantage of this habit which ascends very high indeed, and, moreover, it is something that is possible for all, great or small. For they are all capable of engaging in this practice, through which they will reach a high stage. Happy is he who grasps this ideal.

It is also good to make up a prayer from the Torah one has studied. That is to say, after one has studied the Torah or heard some exposition of the Torah from a true zaddik, he should turn it into a prayer, namely, he should offer supplication to God for all that he has heard in that exposition, saying how remote he is from it and when he will reach it, and begging God to allow him to realize all that is implied in that exposition. The intelligent man who desires the truth will be led by God in the way of truth. He will be able to work out for himself how to follow this practice, so that whatever he says is gracious and with proper pleading how to persuade God to draw him near to His service in truth. This idea of speaking to God ascends to a very high place. Especially when a prayer is made from the Torah one has studied there is an exceedingly great delight on high.

This practice of talking to God as one would talk to a friend is typical of Bratslav. It is, in a way, a very unsophisticated approach to prayer, but Naḥman would say that in religious matters simple faith is the only way to God and that the highest degree of religious sophistication lies in lack of sophistication.

V SHOULD ONE PLAN FOR THE MORROW?

Likkutey Moharan, Tinyana, 272, p. 119c

"Today, if ye would but hearken to His voice!" (Psalms 95:7). It is a great rule for the service of God that a man should only have in mind the day in which he is. Both with regard to his business affairs

and his needs, where, as the holy books say, he should not think today of what tomorrow will bring, and with regard to God's service, where he should only have in mind that day and that hour. For when a man wishes to begin to serve God it appears to him to be a burden too heavy for him to carry. But if he thinks only of that which he has to do that day it will not be burdensome at all. This also implies that he should not put it off from day to day, saying, Tomorrow I shall begin; Tomorrow I shall pray with concentration and put my strength into the prayers as I should, and so in connection with other types of worship. For all man has in the world is the day and the hour where he is, for the morrow is an entirely different world. "*Today,* **if ye would hearken to His voice!"** *Today.* **Understand it well.**

A typical "existentialist" approach. Too much planning, too much thought for the morrow, is not desirable even so far as worship is concerned. God wants man as he is. Tomorrow something else will be demanded of him.

CHAPTER 9

Dov Baer, the Maggid of Meseritch d. 1772

God is in all
The role of the zaddik
How can man influence the Divine?
How is God like a father?
Rules for saints

Dov Baer is, next to the Baal Shem Tov, the most important figure in Ḥasidism. We have seen at the beginning of this book how Ḥasidic legend treats the influence of the Baal Shem Tov on the Maggid (Dov Baer). Yet the Maggid is always reported as referring to the Baal Shem Tov by name and with great respect, but never as his teacher, unlike Jacob Joseph of Pulnoyye. It is also worth noting that the two great theoreticians of Ḥasidism, Jacob Joseph and the Maggid, never refer to one another. The conclusion seems to be that the relationship between the Baal Shem Tov and the Maggid was not that of master and disciple but of associates of equal rank, although the Ḥasidim do generally speak of the Maggid as the disciple and successor of the Baal Shem Tov. The Maggid gathered around himself a number of gifted men who later became Ḥasidic masters, and there is no doubt that the rapid spread of Ḥasidism was largely due to his organizing abilities. In a sense the Maggid is the real founder of Ḥasidism. He is the most profound of the early masters, and his doctrine differs in some important respects from the more simplistic teachings contained in the aphorisms of the Baal Shem Tov.

In his youth Dov Baer studied under the famous talmudist Jacob Joshua Falk, author of the Talmud work Peney Yehoshua. *At first Dov Baer was a poor teacher in a little village, but later on he became a maggid ("town preacher") in a number of towns, among them Rovno and Meseritch. He is known by the Ḥasidim as "the Rebbe Reb Baer" or "the Meseritcher Maggid."*

The Maggid left no writings of his own, but his doctrines are to be found in the works of his disciples, who quote him frequently. The most important collection of the Maggid's sayings and ideas is that of his disciple Solomon of Lutzk, made with the Maggid's approval and entitled Maggid Devarav Le-Yaakov *(He Telleth His Word To Jacob) or* Likkutey Amarim *(Collected Sayings). This work was first published in Koretz in 1784 and then again in Koretz in 1797 and in Zolkiew in 1792 and 1797. (The edition used here is that of Jerusalem, 1962.) Israel Klepholtz has published an anthology of all the references to the Maggid's teachings in the works of his disciples, under the title* Torat Ha-Maggid *(The Doctrine of the Maggid) (Tel Aviv, 1969), in two volumes.*

I GOD IS IN ALL

Solomon of Lutzk, introduction to the doctrine of the Maggid, the second introduction to Maggid Devarav Le-Yaakov, *pp. 9–11. Solomon of Lutzk offers this as a key to the teachings of the book.*

The first thing one has to know is that God fills all worlds and that no place is empty of Him and that He is in all worlds, etc. That this is so can be observed from experience. For in all things there inheres the vital energy of the Creator, blessed be He. It is obvious that things have taste or smell or appearance or love, that is to say, there are things that are loved or are feared or are beautiful and so with regard to the other attributes. Now if one strips away the material aspect of things to concentrate solely on the spiritual aspect in itself —the taste or the smell and so forth—it becomes quite obvious that this is not something tangible or apprehended by the senses but by man's vital force, by his soul. It follows that it is a spiritual thing, the energy of the Creator which resides in this material thing just as the soul resides in the body. And so it is in connection with all things and all forms of motion. As the author of *Ḥovot Ha-Levvavot*

remarks: "All thy movements depend on the Creator's will." In all things there are sparks of spiritual energy which come from the Creator, blessed be He, who is the *Bundle of Life,* **the** *Light of Life, The Fountain of Life,* **and the** *Life of Life,* **and from Him, blessed be He, there derives the vitality of all, from the highest of the high down to the lowest down here below. This is the meaning of "He concentrated His** *Shekhinah,*" **that is to say, "He resides among creatures down here below." Each spark comes from its own world. For example, when something is loved, that love comes from the world of love. That is to say, it is obvious that there is a source and root from which love comes to everything that has love.**

A key word in the Lurianic Kabbalah (see the section on the Kabbalah in Volume 2 of this series) is tzimtzum, *used in our passage a number of times. This means both "concentration" and "withdrawal" (the two are really two sides of the same coin, for when one concentrates on something one withdraws from concentrating on anything else). The basic idea is that God "withdrew from Himself into Himself," as it were, in order to leave room for the emergence of that which is not God, the fine world and the creatures who inhabit it. In the process He "concentrates" Himself, as it were, into particular things so that one assumes this form, one the other. The Ḥasidic interpretation of* tzimtzum, *in the Maggid's understanding of it, is that God really pervades all things in the universe. This is the doctrine of* panentheism, *that all is* in *God and God is* in *all.* Tzimtzum *does not really involve a complete withdrawal of God, for nothing can possibly exist when God is totally absent.* Tzimtzum *only means, in this view, that God's power is concentrated on particular things and is thereby limited. But beneath the appearances of particular things there is only the "simple unity" of God. Solomon of Lutzk uses a typical Platonic notion, the "idea," i.e., all things on earth have a prototype in Heaven. For example, in Platonic thought (the Kabbalah and much of medieval Jewish philosophy have been strongly influenced by Neoplatonism) all elephants are simply instances on earth of the "idea" of the elephant, which is their prototype on high. Thus Solomon of Lutzk in the name of the Maggid here points out that everything on earth is but a pale reflection of some spiritual force on high. Food, for example, is only coarse matter in itself, with no "energy" in it. What makes it attractive and vital is its taste or its pleasant smell or its fine appearance. Now one cannot get hold of a taste or a smell or an appearance. These are experienced by man's soul, as Solomon of Lutzk would say. The idea mentioned here has often been compared to modern scientific views on how matter is constituted. A table, for instance, is now seen to be not the solid mass it appears to be, but ultimately a characteristic pattern of energy states. (Though it has to be appreciated that Solomon of Lutzk, when he uses the term* ḥiyyut *("energy" or "vitality"), is thinking of a spiritual force which, he would no doubt say, cannot be measured in the laboratory.) This spiritual energy of which Solomon of Lutzk speaks is thought of in terms of God's concentration, and Solomon is leading up to the view that beneath the appearance of things there is only God, the only true Reality. This leads to the special emphasis of the Maggid, though to some extent already present in the less systematic thought of the Baal Shem Tov, that man's task is to gaze beyond appearances to see only the divine vitality which influences all things and maintains their existence. The* Ḥovot Ha-Levvavot *is the famous medieval work on religion and morals by Baḥya ibn Pakuda (see the first section in Volume 2 of this series).*

In order to make this slightly more acceptable to the mind, we should notice that the idea of the root of love is nothing else than the divine energy concentrated, as it were, so that it is experienced in the category of love. For it is obvious that there are other forms of energy and spirit that are not experienced in the category of love but in other categories—fear, beauty, and so forth. All these, as above, are all pure energy and spirit, but each is experienced in a different way from the others, since it has been concentrated into a different concentration, i.e., a different experience. But in their inner essence they are all the same, as above, all pure energy and spirit, since they are all derived from a single Root in which there is no multiplicity at all.

The multiplicity of things is only apparent, not real. Beneath all appearances there is only the simple unity of the divine, but this simple divine light is concentrated in many different ways so that in experience it is differently apprehended by creatures. Thus the multiplicity of things is really in the eye of the beholder. He sees love as one entity and fear as another and so forth, but what he really experiences is the simple divine energy and spirit. In a word, all experience is really an experience of God if only man can learn to gaze beneath the surface. In the next paragraph Solomon will read this idea into the Tikkuney Zohar. *(For this supplement to the Zohar see the section on the Kabbalah in Volume 2 of this series.) In the following paragraph the reference to the female aspect alludes to the fact that the* Sefirot *enjoy their existence only as a result of the divine action and are therefore, in relation to the Root of Roots, like the woman who is passive in relation to the man, or, better, the act of concentration which produced the* Sefirot *is in this relationship.*

This is why the *Tikkuney Zohar* says: "And through it all supernal forms are seen," namely, through the divine concentration, as above. The feminine form is used (*bah*, for "it," literally, "she") for it (concentration—*tzimtzum*) is in the category of the female in relation to that which is even higher, the Root of Roots. And He who understands will understand. That is why they (the *Sefirot*) are called *olamot* ("worlds"), namely, because the Creator's energy is hidden (from *neelam*, "hidden") and concentrated into one particular form of experience. They are also called "measures" (*middot*) because they are experienced in a measured way, that is to say, in this way and not in another. But in reality each one of them includes all the others. For emanation began in the Root of Roots because of His lovingkindness in His desire to benefit His creatures. He needed, therefore, to concentrate, as it were, of Himself no more than a thin line and spark into each quality. But this is from the energy and splendor of the Creator Himself, blessed be He, as it is written: "And breathed into his nostrils the breath of life" (Genesis 2:7). Whosoever blows out his breath blows it out from his very self. It was theoretically possible for it to continue ad infinitum, as in the verse, "a great voice that did not cease" (Deuteronomy 5:19), but this would not have brought about the purpose intended so that, for His splendor to be revealed, it was necessary that it be measured. Yet these matters are extremely profound and the most elaborate exposition is required if we are to see how the principle operates in each world. "For one higher than the high watcheth, and there are higher than they" (Ecclesiastes 5:7).

The Tikkuney Zohar *is speaking of the ten* Sefirot, *to which reference has already been made in this book (and see the section on the Kabbalah in Volume 2 of this series). All creation, according to the*

Kabbalah, proceeds by a process of emanation. The Sefirot are derived, by the emanation process, from En Sof (the Limitless), God as He is in Himself, the "Root of Roots." Among the names given to the Sefirot are olamot ("worlds") and middot ("measures"). Solomon of Lutzk applies this to the doctrine of tzimtzum. He connects the word olamot with a root meaning "to hide." God has hidden Himself from the Sefirot, i.e., He had to withdraw His full power from them so that they could exist as independent entities, to be "measured." This is because God in His goodness requires creatures whom He can benefit, and this involves the existence of a world apart from God in all its multiplicity. Consequently, He arrests the flow of the divine and infinite energy and causes it to be channeled into the ten Sefirot, each different from the others. These are, in turn, the source of all division and multiplicity here below, love deriving from one of the Sefirot, fear from another, and so forth. The quotation about breathing out is sometimes said to be in the Zohar. It is not found in our editions of that work, but is quoted by the medieval kabbalists such as Naḥmanides. God breathes His spirit into all, from His very essence, but the flow of love cannot remain uncontrolled, for if it were it would engulf all creatures in its splendor, and then they could enjoy no independent existence.

From the Sefirot downward, all has to be measured, controlled, confined, limited. Solomon adds that there are many of the most profound ideas here, but that he cannot elaborate on these in what is no more than a brief introductory essay into the thought of the Maggid. Dov Baer takes the verse from Deuteronomy to mean "great voice that did not cease." Our translations say "a great voice that did not continue," an opposite meaning. Like many preachers, Dov Baer used the text as he willed.

I can only be brief since my sole aim is to provide an introduction to the study of this holy book, *Likkutey Amarim*. Let us now revert to what we were saying. As above, there is nothing without a root on high. That is why Hebrew grammar knows of the basic root of the verb and its active and passive forms. The root of the verb represents its root on high, as above. The active form of the verb represents man, whose activities draw down the influence from that root on high. Take joy, for example. There is a world of joy, namely, the energy of the Creator, blessed be He, channeled through the quality of joy.

This is the root. The man who rejoices is the active element in that he actualizes the joy and draws it down from the world of joy when he rejoices after having been previously in a state other than joyous. The joy itself is, as above, the passive element.

This is Solomon's interpretation of experience as taught by the Maggid. What happens when a man suddenly feels joyous? The explanation is that he has drawn down the joy from the world of joy on high. There are thus three elements: (1) the root of joy on high, the world of joy; (2) the man who experiences the joy; (3) the joy itself, the actual experience. And the implication is, of course, that through joy man is attached, as it were, to the world of joy and through that world to God, who is its Source.

In the same way a man should reflect on his own qualities, whether love or fear or other qualities, and so, too, he should reflect on his speech and the sounds he utters and on his voice and his thoughts, coming to realize that they are all energy and of the spirit and that each derives from its Root and Source on high. This means, whenever there is love this love is drawn to creatures from the Root of love, and so with regard to fear and the other qualities, and so with regard to the world of speech, from which speech comes for all creatures who speak and, indeed, for all other creatures. For in all things there are the words of the Holy One, blessed be He. For His energy, blessed be He, is like the voice and the clothing of that energy in concentrated speech and provides a limit for the voice. And he who understands will understand.

The meaning of the reference to speech and to the voice is that God's creative energy before it is limited and is still all-pervading is like a bare voice or sound, but when particular things have been created it is as if that voice had been "garmented," had been given the limited but articulate expression that is typical of speech. When a man speaks he emits certain sounds to form words. Precisely because he limits the bare sound he is able to communicate with others. God's boundless energy can only converse with His creatures, can only bring them into being, in fact, by limiting itself to the particular.

It follows that if a man has a heart and the ability to see with his mind's eye, then, even though the spark he sees with the eyes of

flesh is very small in quantity, when he strips away the material aspect which envelops it he will depict in his mind only the divine energy which derives, as we have said, from the supernal root so that its light will be of infinite greatness. For in spirit and energy it is all attached to the Source and he will see the Root and Source on high of all things. It is possible that this is the meaning of the verse, "I rejoice, I will rejoice in the Lord" (Isaiah 61:10). This means that when I rejoice it is in the Lord that I rejoice because I recall that the holy spark derives from Him, as we have said, and I am therefore attached to the world of joy. This is also the meaning of "Thou shalt surely give him, and thine heart shall not be grieved when thou givest unto him" (Deuteronomy 15:10). The meaning is: When you give and come to realize that by so doing the source of giving on high has been affected, you will not grieve. And he who understands will understand.

Thus all joy is connected to God, so that the true Ḥasid rejoices always in the Lord. And he is never grieved when he has to give alms to the poor, for he realizes the magnitude of his act. He is not only giving away some money, but is setting in motion the source of all giving on high (the world of giving, as Solomon would say) and thus assisting the divine grace to flow through all creation. Every good deed has a cosmic significance. The Baal Shem Tov, as we have seen, has expressed similar ideas, but in the Maggid's thought it is all developed systematically.

This is the meaning of "By the word of the Lord were the heavens made" (Psalms 33:6). And in the same way there is a root of thought in the world of thought as above. When a man reflects on this and comes to realize that it is so, there will undoubtedly fall upon him a great dread and he will be abashed in the presence of God, blessed be He, who resides in all his movements. As the *Ḥovot Ha-Levvavot* says: "Do not rebel against your Master for He sees you." For how can a man possibly behave contrary to God's will when he realizes that his very capacity for so doing derives from Him? He will be attached constantly to God in wondrous attachment and will know that through his worship of God and through his attachment to God he is able to elevate all worlds. For since every quality he possesses, and his speech and thoughts, will become attached to that Root from

which all creatures are derived, it is obvious that all creatures will then be attached to him and he will be then attached to the Creator, blessed be He. This is what the Rabbis mean when they say that the whole world rests upon a single pillar and its name is that of zaddik.

*The rabbinic saying about the pillar is in the talmudic tractate Ḥagigah 12b. The Rabbis no doubt mean that the world endures because of the merits of the righteous. In Ḥasidism, however, as we have noted, the zaddik is the saint who is in a constant state of attachment (*devekut*) to God. Thus he is in touch all the time with the Source of all being and hence with the essential spirit of all creatures. Thus the zaddik by his holy life and attachment to God raises up the whole of creation, elevating all creatures to God.*

It is possible that this is the meaning of the saying in the Mishnah: " 'With all thy might' (Deuteronomy 6:5). With whatever quality He measures out to you be exceedingly grateful to Him." The difficulty that presented itself to the author of the Mishnah was that the verse should simply have said, "With all might." Why "With all *thy* might," implying that there are many "mights"? Consequently, he explains the verse to mean: "With whatever quality, etc." That is to say, on the face of it all men's qualities are very small in quantity, as above. But when a man uses them in God's service and attaches them to God, realizing, as above, in thought and intention that each is attached to its source, then each becomes exceedingly great. Therefore, it says: "With whatever quality He measures out to you be *exceedingly* grateful," namely, when you are grateful to Him by attaching each quality to Him then each becomes exceedingly great. Remember this rule. Do not forget it. Then you will be able to study this pure and holy work with confidence. The good Lord will not withhold His goodness from those who walk uprightly. Amen. Selah.

*The Mishnah is in Berakhot 9:5 and contains a number of puns—*meod*, "might,"* middah*, "measure" or "quality,"* modeh *"give thanks" or "acknowledge," and* meod *"exceedingly." Solomon's interpretation is that each of man's emotions and thoughts, insignificant in itself, assumes cosmic proportions if it is attached to God.*

II THE ROLE OF THE ZADDIK

Maggid Devarav Le-Yaakov, p. 16

The Talmud says that the acts of the zaddikim are greater than the acts of creation of Heaven and earth. The meaning is that the act of creation involved the emergence of something out of nothing, whereas the acts of the zaddikim involve the turning of something into nothing. For in whatever they do, even if it be a physical thing like eating or drinking, they raise on high the holy sparks in that food and so in all that they do they convert something into nothing.

The talmudic passage is in tractate Ketubbot 5a. Here again the "zaddikim" means, for the Maggid, the holy men. The Talmud probably means that the deeds of the righteous are more significant even than the creation itself, since these deeds are the purpose of the creation. But the Maggid interprets the saying to accord with the Ḥasidic doctrine of bittul ha-yesh, *"annihilation of the self" or "annihilation of the somethingness of things." God as He is in Himself is called* Ayin, *"Nothing," because no thought can ever grasp the essential nature of God, and "nothing" can be said about this aspect of Deity. In the previous statement of Solomon of Lutzk we have noticed the idea that behind all things there is only God, the true Reality, so that the "somethingness" of things (*yesh, *"that which is") is only an appearance and the only Reality is the divine Nothing. In the medieval Jewish philosophical literature* creatio ex nihilo, *"creation out of nothing," is* yesh me-ayin, *"that which is from that which is not," "something out of nothing." For the kabbalists this means that the "somethingness" of things emerges from the divine Nothing, and this thought is given a further subtle twist by the Maggid so as to mean that the somethingness of things, that which gives them their own separate identities, is really only the result of the contraction and concentration of the divine energy, as above in the statement of Solomon of Lutzk. The zaddik who engages in worldly things in attachment to God sees only the divine energy which sustains all things and he restores this to its Source. Consequently, he repeats the creative process in reverse. God has made something out of His Nothing, and the zaddik converts that something back into the divine Nothing. He thus fulfills the purpose of creation, and his acts are therefore greater than the original act of creation.*

III HOW CAN MAN INFLUENCE THE DIVINE?

Maggid Devarav Le-Yaakov, pp. 25–26

"And I, I taught Ephraim to walk, taking them into My arms" (Hosea 11:3). A parable. A father has a little child who is too small to climb into his arms, so he lifts him up. When the child is firmly settled he plays with his father's beard. So, too, man is unable to attach himself to God, so God causes the love and fear of Him to enter man's heart. These are called "hands" on the analogy of the hand one gives another to help him up. Worship without love and fear cannot fly upward, but when men do serve God in love they cause grace to flow through all worlds. For when man becomes attached to the Holy One, blessed be He, in love and fear, then He causes, as it were, His attributes of compassion and graciousness to be realized. These attributes are called "beard" and "hair," meaning "measures," for they are superfluous. They are inessential because He is God even without any attributes. It is only that the worlds require Him to be compassionate and gracious, otherwise they could not endure. Hence they are only needed for the sake of the worlds and are called superfluities.

*In the parable the child is unable to climb up unaided onto his father's lap. So, too, finite man could never become attached to God were it not for the fact that God gives him a hand by supplying him, in an act of pure grace, with the love and fear of Him. These are God's "hands," the means He uses to draw men near to Him. The result of sincere worship in love and fear is attachment to God, and when the zaddik is attached to God he can bring down to earth the flow of divine grace. This is on the analogy of the child who pulls his father's beard once he has become settled on the father's lap. The Hebrew for "hair"—*saarot*—is fancifully connected with* shiur, *"measure," which it resembles. The reference is to the divine attributes, the* Sefirot, *which, as Solomon of Lutzk has reminded us, are "measures." The reason these are called the hairs and the beard is because a man is still a man even if he has no hair. Hair is not an essential element in being a man. In this sense hair is superfluous. By analogy, God does not need in Himself His attributes of compassion and grace and so forth. These only have meaning for God in His relationship to His creatures, to those for whom He can express His compassion and His grace. For God as He is in Himself they are superfluous, but they are needed if all worlds are to be kept in being.*

Thus without the aid of God the zaddik could have no contact with Him. But once God has put the love and fear of Him into the zaddik's heart, the zaddik can, in turn, influence God in His relationship to the world by assisting the expression of divine compassion and grace.

IV HOW IS GOD LIKE A FATHER?

Maggid Devarav Le-Yaakov, p. 83

"Draw me, we will run after thee" (Song of Songs 1:4). A parable. A father sees his son playing childish games with his companions. The father goes up to them and allows the child to see him. When the child sees his father he leaves his games and runs to his father, shouting, "Father!" When the father sees that the child is running to him, he walks away, and then the child calls out even louder, "Father! Father!" and runs quickly toward him until he reaches his side. Now when the father first allowed his child to see him it was so that the child would leave his childish games and run to him. The father is hugely pleased that his child is cleaver enough for nothing to matter so much to him as his father's love. But when the father notices that the child has left his childish games behind him he pretends to ignore the child so that the child should have an even greater distaste for the childish games and yearn all the more to be near to his father. When that happens the father's joy is even greater and great feelings of compassion stem from it in addition to the joy the child has. It follows that the great joy the father experienced and the resulting joy of the child would not have been possible were it not for the father's retreat (*tzimtzum*) when he pretended to walk away. When that happened the child, too, retreated from his games because of the love he had for his father and the result of it was the even greater joy we have mentioned. It follows that the idea of retreating operated both for the father and the child. Now it is obvious that the whole being of the worlds were present in the Primordial Thought. The process was as follows. At first the thought arose, "I will reign," and then, when the measurements and limitations were made, for there can be no king without subjects, He retreated from His glory, blessed be He, so that the worlds could contain it. It follows that the first thought, "I will reign," was in order to produce greatness and delight, and without the retreat this could not have been possible. Afterward, we now

magnify His name by retreating from childish things. For when we attach ourselves to things down below and to temporal pleasures we are as nothing to Him. But when we have the strongest distaste for worldly pleasures when we compare them to our love for Him, we cause, as it were, great joy to God, blessed be He. Hence the verse says: "Draw me, we will run after Thee." This means that first God should show Himself to us and then we will run after Him as it was His intention from the beginning. Mark it well.

The Song of Songs is interpreted as a dialogue between God and man. Man has to find God when God hides Himself. But God only hides or retreats so that man can run after Him. The Maggid touches here on the question discussed earlier of gadlut *and* katnut*, smallness of soul and greatness of soul. Man should not despair when God seems very remote from him. God had once appeared to him. The rest is up to him. He should seek God with greater effort and then the very remoteness will be the cause for the even greater delight in God that will be the result of his quest. Note how the Maggid qualifies it by saying, "as it were," because, of course, we cannot really speak of God in such anthropomorphic terms. But the Maggid would no doubt go on to say that all human phenomena have their source in God, and so the father-child relationship must somehow reflect a part of ultimate reality so that it can be used as a paradigm for the divine-human encounter.*

V RULES FOR SAINTS

The following consists of paragraphs from the list of rules drawn up by the Maggid and found in the writings of his disciple Ḥayyim Ḥaike of Amdur. The selection is from the list as published in Torat Ha-Maggid*, volume 1, pp. 9–11.*

These are the things a man should train himself to do in order to refine his soul that it should not turn to temporal vanities but only to God, blessed be He, and that his thoughts should be pure and then the pure can be joined to the Pure.

As soon as a man rises in the morning he should realize that the Creator has been good to him by restoring the soul to him and the soul now fills his body. By this means a man sanctifies himself, as it is said (Jeremiah 2:3). "Israel is sanctified to the Lord at the be-

ginning" (of the day). For (when a man wakes up) it is the first thing he thinks about (that matters) when his thought has not as yet been distracted. He should also first sanctify each limb of his body, his gazing, his listening and his speech. That is to say, before using his eyes he should draw down his Creator, blessed be He, to his eye, and so with regard to listening, understanding and speaking. When all the deeds he does that day will be sanctified, as it is said: "Declaring the end from the beginning" (Isaiah 46:10) and he will then have a good ending (to his day).

He should always be very careful about his thoughts. Whenever the thought of love enters his mind, he should at once bestir himself to love the Creator, blessed be He; whenever the thought of something he hates or is angry about enters his mind he should at once bestir himself to fear the Creator, blessed be He; and whenever the thought of beauty enters his mind, he should at once sit down to study the Torah, which is called Beauty; and if the thought of getting the better of someone enters his mind, he should at once try to get the better of himself by carrying out some act of self-discipline or of benevolence, whether in speech, thought or deed. And if, God forbid, some anxiety or trouble afflicts him he should know for certain that it derives from *Hod* **(Splendor—one of the** *Sefirot*), **and when he gives thanks to God for it he will certainly find that it has been converted from** *Davah* **(Pain) into** *Hod*. **The rule is, he should do nothing, great or small, until he first reflects on the quality from which it derives and on how he can use this to give satisfaction to his Creator, blessed be His name. He should do this, too, in connection with physical matters in order never to cease from rejoicing in his Creator and being attached to Him, blessed be He, who is exalted over all intelligences.**

The letters of Hod *(*hey, vav, dalet*) are the same as those of* Davah *(Pain), but in reversed order. When a man accepts his troubles as being from God and accepts them in love he converts the Pain into Splendor. There is no doubt that the Maggid really believed that this would happen if a man was truly sincere. A similar saying is attributed to the Baal Shem Tov. The letters of the word for "trouble" (*tzarah*) are the same as those of "light" (*tzohar*). If a man bears his sufferings in love, God provides him with light. The task of man is to convert* tzarah *into* tzohar *or* Davah *into* Hod.

He should see to it that he becomes attached to the zaddikim who limit their bodily pleasures for the sake of the honor of their Creator, blessed be He. How can a small pleasure be compared at all to infinite delight? He should, therefore, give up all pleasures. Even though this is very hard at first: "For though thy beginning was small, yet thy end should greatly increase" (Job 8:7). The main thing is for him to discipline himself to drive out from his heart the false idea that it is self-frustrating to give up pleasures, for the real form of self-expression is to serve God in truth. Man's energy and his soul are not his own, and even when he bestirs himself to worship God it is not his own doing, but because God has pity on him that he be not rejected. For there is no lasting happiness in the things of this world. A parable: A man had a precious stone, but it became so grimy that it no longer shone at all and everyone forgot that it was once so bright and it was thrown away onto the rubbish heap. A sage who saw it lying there took it and polished it until it shone. Those who did not know what it looked like previously were glad to see it shine, but those who knew how brightly it once shone could not be satisfied until it was so polished that it shone as brightly as before. The application is obvious. It is a refutation of pride and of showing off to others. And he takes no notice of the physical pleasures of the world, for he is not of this world at all and his sole aim should be to delight in the Holy One, blessed be He.

The ascetic note sounded so prominently in this passage is more typical of the Maggid than of the Baal Shem Tov or of Ḥasidism generally, though it should be noted that the Maggid does not approve of self-mortification and only decries pleasure because it leads away from God.

He should see to it that he is alone in thought with his Creator daily and he should draw down into his being the fear of the Creator, who is so great. He should practice this until it becomes second nature for him never to forget his Creator, even when he converses with other human beings.

This is the Ḥasidic ideal of devekut *("attachment"), of God being always in the mind even when man appears to be conversing with others on worldly matters.*

He should take care to recite his prayers daily with proper concentration and if he has no time to do it in every prayer of the day he should see to it, at least, that he says one benediction or one paragraph with concentration in the heart as he speaks to Him.

He should set aside daily a period in which he studies the Bible and the Mishnah and for the rest of the time he has he should engage in inwardness. He should not converse overmuch with people who are not attached to the Creator, blessed be He. When he is studying he should pause from his studies from time to time in order to remember his Creator, blessed be He.

"Engage in inwardness" probably means contemplating God. The Ḥasidic ideal of devekut *is really at odds with the traditional Jewish emphasis on the study of the Torah. How can one adequately master the texts one studies if the mind is not on their meaning but on God? This was, in fact, one of the complaints of the Mitnaggedim against the early Ḥasidim. The Maggid deals with the problem by limiting study to a fixed period each day and by demanding regular pauses for* devekut *even while studying.*

CHAPTER 10

Abraham ben Dov Baer, the "Angel"

1741-1776

The man too good to be a leader

Abraham, son of the Maggid of Meseritch, is one of the most mysterious figures in the history of Ḥasidism. He led an extremely ascetic life, departing from the way of both the Baal Shem Tov and his own father. The latter, as we have seen, did have a negative approach to worldly pleasures, but did not agree that it was right for the zaddik to forgo worldly things entirely or to lead a hermitlike existence. On the contrary, the Maggid stressed the Ḥasidic ideal of reclaiming the "holy sparks" which reside in food and drink and other things of the world. Abraham, too, does not deny his father's philosophy so far as others are concerned, but he departs from it for personal choice. Ḥasidic legend has it that when his father rebuked him, Abraham repudiated Dov Baer, saying that he has only one father, his Father in Heaven. Because of his way of life, remote from the world, the Ḥasidim refer to Abraham as "the Angel" and tales are told of his terrible appearance, so frightening that he was obliged to keep his face hidden. Abraham died young. He left a son, Shalom Shachna of Probishtch (d. 1803), who became a Ḥasidic zaddik of the conventional type and was succeeded by his son Israel of Ruzhyn (d. 1850), the founder of the famous Ruzhyner dynasty. Abraham's ideas are found in the little book Ḥesed Le-Avraham, *which first appeared in Tchernowitz in 1851 (edition used here; Jerusalem, 1954).*

THE MAN TOO GOOD TO BE A LEADER

Ḥesed Le-Avraham, introduction, pp. 14–15

The matter of Saul having pity on Agag who is Amalek (1 Samuel 15:9) is as follows. There are two types of zaddikim. The first is the elevated zaddik who is unable to lead his generation; he is so spiritual that his generation cannot tolerate him. Saul was such a type: "from his shoulders and upward he was higher than any of the people" (1 Samuel 9:2). This means that his power of comprehension was so profound that his generation could not tolerate him for he was in touch with the supernal wisdom and was unable to descend to his generation down beneath in order to raise them up. The truth is that Saul was not suited to be a king and belonged in a different rank, as it is written: "Is Saul also among the prophets?" (1 Samuel 10:11). The difference between the rank of prophecy and that of royalty we learn from Moses, the father of the prophets, who said of himself: "and what are we?" (Exodus 16:8). This means that Moses reached such a high degree of fear that, for him, no partition existed at all, and the Holy One, blessed be He, remained alone, His glory filling the world so that there was no darkness whatsoever. Such was the great fear that Moses had. Saul, in reality, reached through this degree to such an elevated rank that his generation could not tolerate him. He attained to the stage of compassion, boundless and unlimited.

The truth is that Saul was not suited to be a king, and royalty was only given to him on borrowed terms. That is to say, at first, there was no king in Israel, so that when they wanted to appoint a king it was necessary, for sovereignty to find its expression, to realize it at first through the physical existence of a great zaddik gifted with profound wisdom. And the truth is that he was sent to occupy the throne until David and Solomon were able to realize the idea of sovereignty. But Saul was incapable of leading his generation for, as above, "from his shoulder and upward he was higher than any of the people."

He had the quality of compassion, as it is said: "and lay in wait in the valley" (1 Samuel 15:5), which the Rabbis explain as referring to the law of the valley (Deuteronomy 21:4), and his sole intention was for the sake of Heaven, as it is said: "to sacrifice unto the Lord thy God" (1 Samuel 15:15). But the truth was otherwise. For just as the quality

of compassion is necessary, so is the quality of cruelty. Just as the Creator commanded us to have compassion when compassion is demanded, so did He command us to be cruel when circumstances demand cruelty. The illustration is from the rite of circumcision. The Creator, blessed be He, could have created man in such a way that there would be no need to remove the foreskin, yet He did create the foreskin, only He commanded us to cut it away. But Saul's degree was so much higher, that of boundless compassion, that he took pity on the sheep. For he belonged to the stage of the Messiah. He wished to raise the sparks from Amalek in such a way that it would not be necessary to cut them off, but they would cease to be of their own accord and then the sparks would automatically ascend on high. This, however, is impossible before the coming of our righteous Messiah. At the present it is necessary to cut them away until they die and then will the holy sparks ascend on high. But he was of such a high stage that he wished the holy sparks to ascend on high automatically. That is why he had pity on them. This is the stage of our righteous Messiah. May he come speedily in our days. Amen.

This very remarkable statement, though clear on the whole, does require some elaboration for it to be fully intelligible. In the first book of Samuel we read that King Saul was commanded to destroy Amalek (the symbol, in the Jewish tradition, of sheer, unbridled cruelty) but failed to do so, sparing Agag the king and the sheep of Amalek. The Rabbis (Yoma 22b) comment on the verse which says that Saul lay in wait in the valley, *[saying that] he pondered over the law of the heifer that was to be beheaded* in the valley. *This Deuteronomic law provides the rite of the heifer as an atonement for the murder of a victim whose murderer cannot be found. Saul argued: If the Torah has such compassion on even a single victim, how could he be so cruel as to slay so many innocents? The reference in the passage to the "physical existence" means: In medieval Jewish literature the Greek term* hyle *is used for the basic substance of things, for the stage at which a thing begins to emerge from the potential to the actual. In the thought of the Maggid and his son this stage is said to belong to God's Wisdom. Before a wise plan can be realized, there must be the basic flash of insight which suggests how it is to be realized. This is fleeting and insubstantial, having no permanence, but without it there could not be later realization—indeed, no plan at all. (This is, on the deeper level, the idea we have encountered when considering the thought of the Maggid, of all things deriving from the divine* Nothing.*) Now at this stage, all evil, limitation, sternness have not as yet emerged. All is mercy, grace, and pure compassion.*

We are now in a position to follow Abraham's exposition. A leader has to be one of the people, in the sense that he is fully aware of the needs of the hour, living in a real world in which there is evil as well as good, in which cruelty has to be shown to the totally wicked and evil, otherwise good will be vanquished. Saul's spiritual degree was far too high for him to have such qualities of leadership. He was not really suited to be a king at all. His true role should have been that of prophet. Moses, the prototype of the prophet, said, "what are we?"—i.e., he saw himself and the whole of creation as "nothing," and the partition between God and the world was dissolved so far as he was concerned. Saul, really a prophet, similarly could not see the world as really enjoying any existence at all. He reached that stage in which evil is nonexistent and only God's pure compassion holds sway. Such a man cannot be a king, who, in the nature of things, has to grapple with real problems in the real world. Why, then, did God allow him to become king? The answer is that for the idea of royalty to be realized it was first necessary to have as its representative an ideal figure, too ideal for permanence, in fact, but one who would set the standards and give the institution its impetus. Only later, after the idea had been given expression in too elevated a manner and had therefore failed, was David and then Solomon able to establish the kingdom.

Saul had pity on Amalek and on the sheep belonging to Amalek. As the man of infinite compassion he could not bear the waste of human and animal life. (He did not look upon the sheep to be sacrificed as a waste because the animal is "elevated" when it is offered as a sacrifice to God.) The only role suitable for such a man is that of the Messiah. In the messianic age evil will be completely overthrown. In the premessianic age a leader requires an element of hardness, even of cruelty, in his makeup, since circumstances may demand, as they demanded of Saul, that he destroy the evil which threatens the life of his people. In the language of the Kabbalah, the "holy sparks" which reside even in evil men and things can only be raised by the actual destruction of evil.

It is ironic (perhaps Abraham was subconsciously aware of this) that the whole of what he says was applicable to "the Angel" himself. The aim he had set himself was too high for him to succeed as a

Ḥasidic master. He remained "shoulder high" above his followers, who were unable to "tolerate" him. They required not an angel but a human being with human weaknesses who would be able to appreciate their problems, spiritual and material. In fact, Abraham's son and grandson were zaddikim of this type, living in regal splendor and demanding total allegiance from their followers. In fact, later Ḥasidism refer to the dynasty of Ruzhyn as that of Malkhut (Sovereignty). Perhaps implied here, too, is the thought that David and Solomon would have been altogether too ruthless were it not that Saul had first established standards of regal conduct that were, to be sure, too difficult to live by, but which nevertheless kept the ideal always before his successors. And by the same token, zaddikism in the person of "the Angel's" successors may have completely lost its spiritual aim had it not been for the "impossible" standards of spirituality and otherworldliness he had set from the beginning.

CHAPTER 11

Menaḥem Naḥum of Chernobyl

1730-1787

How can God's mercy and His justice be reconciled?
What are the virtues of humility?

Menaḥem Naḥum was born and educated in Lithuania but came under the influence of the Baal Shem Tov in his youth. After the death of the Baal Shem Tov, Menaḥem Naḥum became a follower of the Maggid of Meseritch, and it is to him and not to the Baal Shem Tov that Menaḥem Naḥum generally refers as his teacher. Menaḥem Naḥum's official position was that of preacher (Maggid) in Chernobyl, where he found it extremely difficult to eke out a living and was obliged, after the pattern of those days, to become an itinerant preacher. He was succeeded as Maggid in Chernobyl by his son Mordecai, but the latter, unlike his father, became a famous Ḥasidic master, living in great style supported by the lavish gifts of his followers. Mordecai is the head of the Chernobyl dynasty of Ḥasidim, his eight sons all becoming Ḥasidic masters in towns of the Ukraine. The best known of these was David of Talnoye, of whom it is said that he sat on a silver throne on which was engraved the words: "King David lives for ever." Menaḥem Naḥum is known either as "Reb Naḥumke Chernobyler" or, after his major work, "the Meor Eynayim." Mordecai is known by the Ḥasidim as "Reb Mottele Chernobyler."

Menaḥem Naḥum's exposition of the Torah, sidra by sidra, is found in the work Meor Eynayim *(Illumination of the Eyes), first published in Slavita in 1798. In the same year in Slavita a smaller work of Naḥum,* Yismaḥ Lev *(Let the Heart Rejoice), on the aggadic passages of the Talmud, was also published. Later editions have both these works printed together in a single volume. (The edition used here is that of Jerusalem, 1968.) Menaḥem Naḥum did not write these books himself. The work was done by his disciple Elijah ben Zeev Wolf with the approval of the master, to whom he showed the manuscript before receiving permission to have it printed. Thus, although the words are not Menaḥem Naḥum's own, the ideas contained in these works certainly are and they can be seen to be greatly influenced by the thought of the Maggid of Meseritch.*

I HOW CAN GOD'S MERCY AND HIS JUSTICE BE RECONCILED?

Meor Eynayim, Pineḥas, pp. 163–64

It is well known that the ten sayings by means of which the world was created (Ethics of the Fathers 5:1) are the ten qualities (*middot*) which the holy books call the *Sefirot*. The creation of the world was by means of these ten qualities. For the Creator, blessed be He, is good and it belongs to the nature of the good to be benevolent to others. He wished, therefore, that there be creatures who could recognize His attributes and deeds, and that He be called "Compassionate," "Gracious," and "Long-suffering." Now all this could only have been realized in a world in which there are creatures, and it was His will to create such a world so that creatures could recognize His greatness. However, since God, blessed be He, is *En Sof* (Infinite, the kabbalistic name for God as He is in Himself), it was impossible for men to have any apprehension of Him, since He is Infinite. Consequently, He decreed in His wisdom that the world be created by means of these *middot* (which also means "measures"), so called because, as it were, the Creator, blessed be He, emerged in limited measures so that His creatures could have some slight apprehension of His unity, knowing that there is a Creator and a Ruler and that He, blessed be He, is Infinite and has brought all things into being.

Menaḥem Naḥum here describes the kabbalistic doctrine of tzimtzum *(the divine "withdrawal" and "concentration") as understood in the school of the Maggid of Meseritch. Since it is the nature of the All-Good to be good to others, God, in order to realize Himself, as it were, has to have creatures who will be the recipients of His bounty.*

But how can the Infinite produce the finite? The answer is that God "reduces" Himself, as it were, to make room for the finite world. This is furthered by a process of emanation in which the full, infinite divine splendor is successively reduced (or, as Menaḥem Naḥum puts it, "measured") into one Sefirah *after another, one bringing the other into being by a cause-and-effect process. God thus becomes apprehended through His "measures" or "qualities," and these, being to some extent limited, can serve as the link between God and finite man. Menaḥem Naḥum in the next passage goes on to explain the sefirotic process. The highest of the* Sefirot *(see the section on the Kabbalah in Volume 2 of this series) is* Keter *(Crown). This is so near to* En Sof *that it cannot be apprehended at all and is therefore called "Nothing,"* Ayin. *The lowest quality or* Sefirah *is Malkhut (Sovereignty), so called because it is at this stage that the link between the Godhead and the finite universe is completed, and it is therefore an expression of God's sovereignty, of His desire to rule over His creatures. It is the "gateway" through which the righteous can enter in order to know God.*

He measured Himself out, as it were, from quality to quality. For the highest quality of all is called *Ayin* ("Nothing"), for it represents a stage of which, as yet, there cannot be any apprehension. He then measured Himself out, as it were, from quality to quality, by a chain process of cause and effect, down to the tenth quality called *Malkhut* (Sovereignty). For through this tenth quality creatures are able to recognize the majesty of His reign, that He is King over all the earth and created everything out of nothing. As the verse says: "This is the gate of the Lord; The righteous shall enter into it" (Psalms 118:20). For this quality is the gateway and doorway through which everyone who desires to worship his Creator and take upon himself the yoke of His kingdom, blessed be He, has to pass. It is well known that there is no other means of entrance than through this quality. It is the final *hey* of the special divine name and it represents the five modes of articulation, providing man's mouth with the power of speech so that he can become attached to the Creator, blessed be He.

According to the Kabbalah, the special divine name of four letters— YHVH*—the Tetragrammaton, represents the* Sefirot, *and the final* hey *represents the* Sefirah Malkhut. Hey *has the numerical value of 5 and represents, too, the five modes of articulation (i.e., by means of the* *gutterals, the palatals, the dentals, the labials, and the sibilants). It is through* Malkhut *that the Infinite God is able to converse with His finite creatures, is able to "speak" to them, and it is through* Malkhut *that man is endowed with the gift of speech so that He can engage in dialogue with his Maker.*

All this is by the grace of the Creator, blessed be He, so that His creatures might comprehend His sovereignty and lordship. He concentrated Himself (*Tzimtzum*), as it were, from quality to quality down to the final quality, as we know from the holy books. Every man in Israel—since, as we have stated on a previous occasion, Israel is an actual portion of God—has in himself something of these ten qualities, which, as is well known, are His divinity. The more a man proceeds from stage to stage once he has entered this gate, as above, the more he will recognize and the more he will comprehend of the greatness of His divinity as expressed in His supernal qualities, and the stronger will be these qualities as they are firmly fixed in that portion of his own soul which derives from these supernal qualities.

Menaḥem Naḥum refers here to the very radical doctrine, taught in some schools of Ḥasidism, that deep in the recesses of the human psyche there is a portion of God. (The Ḥasidim, however, unfortunately limit this to the souls of Israel.) This is the Ḥasidic interpretation of: "For the portion *of the Lord is His people" (Deuteronomy 32:9). It follows that man can come near to God through the* sefirotic *processes as mirrored in his own soul. Man's contemplation of the divine is in reality a contemplation of the divine in himself. He must begin with the lowest stage of all, that of* Malkhut *and then as he advances higher and higher he comprehends more and more. It follows, too, that every one of man's thoughts and emotions has its source in one or other of the* Sefirot. *Whenever he experiences anything he should reflect on its source on high and thus "restore" it to God whence it came.*

However, it was really impossible for the supernal qualities to become awakened within man, since he is clothed with the coarse garment of his material body. How, therefore, could there be awakened in man the love of the Creator, blessed be He, a love so refined, or how could he ever come to fear God or to realize any of the other quali-

ties? The physical nature of man in the body would not have allowed him ever to be awakened to such pure spirituality. Consequently, God, blessed be He, caused His qualities also to be concentrated in the material, in such things as the love of physical pleasure in this world of matter and external fears, such as the fear of punishment and fear men have for one another. This process was by stages, the supernal qualities expanding by means of cause and effect until they came down into extremely low things. All this was for one purpose only: that as a result of his physical nature which desires physical pleasure there will be awakened in man the quality of love that is inherent in the things he loves. Once a man is sufficiently intelligent and sufficiently a man of faith, to see that this is really the quality of love—that the Creator, blessed be He, has measured out and concentrated Himself into this quality in this world, expanding until it reached the thing that is loved solely for the purpose of awakening that quality in man for him to grasp—then he will tremble and will seize hold of the love that has been awakened in him and will begin to love the Creator, blessed be He, with a most powerful love. There will then be increased for certain his love for spiritual delight, since the Rabbis say (Yoma 39a) that God helps man once he tries to be pure. It will be easy for him, since the quality of love has already been awakened in his soul. Understand it well.

*Man would be utterly incapable of loving God, who is incomprehensible to him. But since all love derives ultimately from the quality of love on high, which is, as it were, God Himself in "concentration," then whenever man has a love experience in the material universe he is really experiencing the love of God in concentrated form, as it were, and he must allow himself to appreciate what is happening to him, directing the love that has been awakened not to its object here on earth, which is only a very pale reflection of the divine, but to the source of love in God. Thus Ḥasidism, as taught by Menaḥem Naḥum and in the school of the Maggid of Meseritch generally, urges man to use his own physical nature to lead him on toward the nearness and love of God. Martin Buber, in his writings on Ḥasidism, seems to understand this doctrine to mean that all love is in itself the love of God. As Professor Gershom Scholem (*The Messianic Idea in Judaism, New York, 1971, pp. 227ff.*) has shown, this is completely to misread Ḥasidism. Worldly things, the Ḥasidic masters say, are the means by which the divine qualities* *in man's soul are awakened, but man is eventually expected not to remain in the worldly stage but be led on to the purely spiritual love of God.*

II WHAT ARE THE VIRTUES OF HUMILITY?

Yismaḥ Lev, Avot, pp. 353–54

"Be exceedingly lowly of spirit before every man" (Ethics of the Fathers 4:12). The main thing is humility. A man must be lowly of spirit before every man, that is to say, even before one who seems to be inferior. For a man can know his faults from his virtues themselves. For example, if he sees someone inferior to him in knowledge of the Torah so that he is the greater scholar, he should think to himself, That man is better than I am. For not only have I failed to achieve anything worthwhile, as commanded by the Creator, blessed be He, with the Torah I have studied, but it is almost certain that I have done wrong by studying with ulterior motives, God forbid, or merely in order to acquire fame and a reputation for myself, God forbid, as is well known. Whereas that man, whom God has not endowed with my intellectual gifts, serves God according to his lights. If a man is wealthy he should think to himself, Have I used my wealth as the Torah wants me to do, in a spirit of integrity, faith, and trust, and have I given proper tithes and been sufficiently generous with my wealth? And so it should be with regard to all other good qualities a man happens to possess. Even if, thanks to God, he serves God, blessed be He, studying the Torah for its own sake and praying to God in love and fear, yet he should consider himself to be inferior to others. For he can do more harm by merely gazing (*at something at which he should not gaze*) **than others by actual sinful deeds** (*since more is expected of him*). **The proof of this is from Moses our Teacher, on whom be peace. He was possessed of every good quality and was far more spiritually advanced than anyone else in Israel, and yet he said: "And what are we?" (Exodus 16:8). On the face of it, it is hard to see how Moses could have thought this. How he could have been so convinced that it was so, since surely he must have been aware that it was to him and to no other that God had spoken and that he was the Teacher of all Israel? But it has to be understood on the principle that whoever has one hundred wants two hundred** (*i.e., the more a* *man has the more he wants*). **For whoever has only a little lacks only a little, but whoever has much lacks much. Therefore, Moses, precisely because he was so superior to all of them, felt more than any of them how much he lacked. This is a great truth. Understand it. For no one is really a scholar or a sage. As Scripture says: "The Torah of the Lord is perfect" (Psalms 19:8), which the Baal Shem Tov, his soul is in high Heaven, interpreted to mean: The Torah is perfect because no man has even begun to understand it and it remains whole** (*taking "perfect" in the sense of "whole," "untapped," no one has really been able to take anything away from it*).

Shiflut, *"lowliness," "humility," is one of the great Ḥasidic ideals. Menaḥem Naḥum explains that it does not mean that a man should be guilty of self-delusion by imagining himself to be more inferior than he really is. It means, rather, that however superior one is there is no cause for pride. The more a man is spiritually gifted, the more conscious is he of his unworthiness, because the standards by which he measures himself are so high. This should be compared with Naḥmanides' letter on humility in Volume 2 of this series, but Menaḥem Naḥum gives the idea a more Ḥasidic turn.*

CHAPTER 12

Menaḥem Mendel of Vitebsk

1730-1788

How can man attach himself to God?
The zaddik is not a miracle worker

Menaḥem Mendel was born in Vitebsk. It is said that he met the Baal Shem Tov in his youth, but he is regarded as the disciple of the Maggid of Meseritch. Menaḥem Mendel had a congregation of followers in Minsk and later near Vitebsk. He is called by the Ḥasidim "Reb Mendele Vitebsker." Menaḥem Mendel was involved in the struggles between the Ḥasidim and the Mitnaggedim and eventually, together with his colleague Abraham of Kalisk, another disciple of the Maggid, he set out for Israel where he became the leader of the Ḥasidic group that had established itself there. The Ḥasidim in Russia considered it their holy task to send financial contributions to the Ḥasidim in the Holy Land. Menaḥem Mendel's teachings are found in the little book, Peri Ha-Aretz *("Fruit of the Land"), so called because it contains letters Menaḥem Mendel sent when he resided in the Holy Land and many of his other doctrines were also given fuller expression there. The work was first published in Kopys in 1814. (The edition used here is that of Jerusalem, 1965, which is a photocopy of the Zhitomer edition.)*

I HOW CAN MAN ATTACH HIMSELF TO GOD?

Peri Ha-Aretz, Ki tissa, p. 34

In this passage Menaḥem Mendel defines the Ḥasidic ideal of devekut, *"attachment" to God, as he had learned it from his teacher the Maggid. Naturally, the particular way in which this subtle doctrine is expressed is Menaḥem Mendel's own.*

The meaning of *devekut*. There can only be attachment when everything that separates has been removed. The Baal Shem Tov gave this illustration. When two pieces of silver are to be soldered together it is only possible to do so after the silver itself has first been scraped clean at the place where they are to be joined if the join is to take adequately. If there is tarnish or any other dividing matter on the silver, the join is bound is to be ineffective. Hence the verse says: "If thou seek her as silver . . ." (Proverbs 2:4). Attachment to God, blessed be He, must follow the same pattern. A man must first scrape away something of his self so that there is no tarnish nor anything else to act as a partition. Then can *devekut* be achieved. But as long as anything else is held onto there can be no real attachment. It is well known that attachment to material things means that there is pleasure in these things. Man's pleasure in having them is so strong that it permits no distraction of the mind from them, his thought being constantly occupied with these things. This applies to every kind of pleasure. For instance, when a man loves money more than himself, all his thoughts are of money and so it is with regard to all such matters.

The general principle is that all a man's Torah and all the precepts he carries out avail him nothing, God forbid, without the *devekut* we have mentioned. It depends on each man's particular circumstances, but it is demanded of man that his attachment to God be of the same order as his attachment to whatever material thing happens to attract him. Man must cleave to God, for this is the whole duty of *man*. For it is the mind and the emotions and the ability to be attached to something that constitutes man's basic humanity, his being a *man*. For man's body is called only "the flesh of man." Therefore, that which constitutes his humanity, as above, must be directed to the Creator, blessed be He, who is eternal, and then his humanity will remain with him for all eternity, even after the death of the body, and he will then be able to make use of all that he has comprehended, and he will delight in the Lord for ever. It is otherwise if he has trained himself in the way we have mentioned, but took his

pleasures during his lifetime only in material things which decompose and vanish. When such a man has been separated from material things and his body has decomposed, what is there left to be blessed? And how can such a one even begin to use his delight and his potentialities, as above, unless he has known the way of the living and eternal God while still alive? This is the meaning of the biblical references to the soul being "cut off." Since that soul had no attachment to spiritual things and to that which is eternal, it is destroyed once the body has decomposed.

When the silver is scraped, a little bit of the silver itself has to be removed if the tarnish is to be removed. The spiritual "tarnish" has to be removed from the self, and this involves some giving up of the self, but it is for the sake of realizing the true self, the silver being attached to silver. Implied here is the radical doctrine, elaborated on especially by Menaḥem Mendel's younger colleague, Shneur Zalman of Liady, that when man's soul is attached to God it is like meeting life (the "silver" meeting "silver"). This is because, in this view, deep in the recesses of man's soul there is a portion of the divine. Note Menaḥem Mendel's extreme statement that without devekut *all man's Torah is worth nothing, a statement the Mitnaggedim found particularly offensive. Menaḥem Mendel gives a novel interpretation of the biblical punishment of* karet. *For Menaḥem Mendel this is not so much a punishment as a natural result of the unspiritual man's life. He has become so attached to material things that his soul powers have not been developed in any other way. When he dies he is not "punished" by being "cut off." It is just that he has virtually lost his soul.*

II THE ZADDIK IS NOT A MIRACLE WORKER

Peri Ha-Aretz, Letters, no. 2, p. 60

This is a letter Menaḥem Mendel wrote to a follower and supporter in Russia who had demanded that Menaḥem Mendel pray for him to have a child. Menaḥem Mendel declares that he is not that kind of a zaddik and that only the Baal Shem Tov was great enough to have his prayers answered in this way. Menaḥem Mendel himself prefers to see his role as that of spiritual mentor.

Many greetings to our beloved and faithful friend, his honor the scholar Rabbi Jacob, may his light shine. His great love and affection

has been expressed in his deeds. Happy is he. Fine are his merits. How good is his portion, how pleasant his lot. Peace be in his ramparts, tranquility in his tents, until Shiloh comes.

We are glad to inform you of our happiness that our yeshiva is so successful in this city that it is a fortress to us. All the members of the college rejoice and delight in doing God's will. I have heard how hard you prayed and have seen that you have begged me to pray on your behalf and, indeed, I remember you in all my prayers. May God hearken to them and answer you. Amen. You refer in your letter to your tremendous efforts at all times. Even though for the time being your reward has not been adequate, it will increase of its own accord in time without you having to ask any sages to intercede on your behalf.

However, I am unable to do anything in connection with your main request, that God give you children. I am most embarrassed when I observe how great is your prayer and how you demand that I pray for you because you have done so much for us. But "am I in God's stead?" (Genesis 30:2). The word of God was in the hands of the Baal Shem Tov. He decreed and it came to pass. But he was unique. There was no one like him in former times and who can arise in his stead upon earth? Even though many of the zaddikim of our generation do have a mouth (wherewith to pray) and they make great promises that their blessings will be fulfilled, I cannot behave in this way. But what I can do is to tell you the truth and record it in writing.

Menaḥem Mendel's saying about the uniqueness of the Baal Shem Tov is often quoted in later Ḥasidic literature. His remark that even among those of former times there was none like the Baal Shem Tov in having his prayers answered is an illustration of the way in which the early Ḥasidic masters regarded the Baal Shem Tov. The saying about the Baal Shem Tov issuing a decree and God fulfilling it became for some of the later zaddikim a maxim of practical application in their own careers as Ḥasidic masters, believing that they, too, could order God, as it were, to do their bidding. Naturally, this, too, was a source of offense to the Mitnaggedim.

You carry out your business affairs with all your heart and soul in any event, and your needs and sustenance are adequately provided for in

any event, so why not do it all for the sake of Heaven as well? I do not mean that you should make the "for the sake of Heaven" element secondary. On the contrary, make it primary and the attainment of your material ambitions secondary. If you train yourself to do this you will undoubtedly become a true supporter of the Torah. So far as I am personally concerned, what am I? But so far as you are concerned you are allowed to believe that we are righteous men (zaddikim) and that we do occupy ourselves in the study of the Torah under the gate of Heaven. Then your motive will truly be for the sake of Heaven and we shall try to serve God sincerely. Now I agree that it is true that there can be no possibility of any man attaining to the World to Come unless he has children. You will be blessed with children. The Rabbis of blessed memory say: "Whoever brings merit to many, no sin will come through him, so that he should not go down to Sheol and his disciples inherit Paradise." How much more is this so with regard to those who support the Torah in truth. It is certain that such persons become one in soul with the scholars. The supporters of the Torah are called by the Zohar, in a comment on "he touched the hollow of his thigh" (Genesis 32:26), the "feet" of the Torah. Consequently, it cannot be possible for the soul itself to be in Paradise and part of it, the feet, to be in Sheol. So God will surely give you children. And this is sufficient for one who understands.

The saying about the disciples in Paradise is in Avot De-Rabbi Nathan, *a comment on Ethics of the Fathers (Avot 5:18). Menaḥem Mendel evidently believes that without children a man cannot go to Paradise(!) but argues that since the true supporter of the Torah must be in Paradise like those he has supported, then God will give him the means of getting there and will bless him with children. Or he may be hinting that even if eventually children are not given by God the Torah patron has enough merits to get him into Heaven.*

I am confident that there is no need for me to urge you to attend to your affairs, the affairs of Heaven, diligently because we all know how loyal you have been until now in supporting our yeshiva and our followers. If to you it is a small thing, for us it is a great thing. We remember you always because you are engraved on the palms of our hands. Our innards are moved to pray unto the Lord on your behalf

and on behalf of your household [your wife], that you should be given a child. Once you have sanctified your soul and body only for the sake of Heaven to be among those who support the Torah in the land of the living [i.e., the Holy Land], I am confident that the Life of Lives will revive you and give you strength sevenfold and you will have the merit of having children who will survive, as well as sustenance and life all the days of Heaven. May the Redeemer come to Zion and to Jerusalem. Amen. Written and sealed here in the city of Tiberias, may it be built up and established. The truly lowly Menaḥem Mendel son of the Rabbi, our Teacher Rabbi Moses of blessed memory.

The threefold blessing of children, life, and sustenance—i.e., progeny, good health, and the means of earning of living—are the three blessings the zaddikim especially were said to bring to their followers.

CHAPTER 13

Elimelech of Lizensk

1717-1787

How can men have the Holy Spirit in an unholy age?
How can false modesty be avoided?
Rules for saints

Elimelech and his brother Susya of Anipol were among the foremost disciples of the Maggid of Meseritch, although Elimelech refers to him as the Maggid of Rovno, evidently coming under his influence when he was maggid in that town. On the death of the Maggid the town of Lizensk in Galicia, where Elimelech resided, became a new center of Ḥasidism; Elimelech is the father of the movement in Galicia. Before coming to Ḥasidism Elimelech led an ascetic life, and even after his conversion to the ideas taught by the Baal Shem Tov and the Maggid about reclaiming the holy sparks in material things there still existed a strong ascetic tendency in Elimelech's thought. It is even reported that Elimelech used to engage in acts of self-mortification such as prolonged fasts and flogging himself with stinging nettles. There is a full-scale but somewhat uncritical biography of Elimelech by Bezalel Landau, Ha-Rebbe Rabbi Elimelekh Mi-Lizensk *(Jerusalem, 1963). Elimelech is known among the Ḥasidim as the "Rebbe Elimelech."*

Elimelech's work Noam Elimelekh *(The Pleasantness of Elimelech) is one of the major and most popular Ḥasidic works. It was first published by Elimelech's son in Lemberg in 1788 and subsequently in numerous editions. (The edition used here is that of Jerusalem, no date.) The book is in four parts: (1) expositions of the Torah* sidra *by* sidra; *(2)* Likkutey Shoshanim *(Bunches of Roses), brief comments on other biblical verses and talmudic passages; (3) letters of Elimelech, his son, and his disciple; (4) two lists of religious exercises. In some editions these latter are printed at the beginning of the book. The* Noam Elimelekh *is a paean of praise to the zaddik. Although the central role of the zaddik had been affirmed by the Baal Shem Tov, Jacob Joseph, and the Maggid, it is in this work of Elimelech that the role of the zaddik as an intermediary (Dubnow says, not without justification, a "broker") between God and man is developed. The status of the zaddik is described in such exaggerated terms that the Mitnaggedim held the book to be blasphemous. The work deals at length with the training of the zaddik, his role as intercessor, his holy life, and the way he can transmit his sanctity to others, especially to his children.*

I HOW CAN MEN HAVE THE HOLY SPIRIT IN AN UNHOLY AGE?

Noam Elimelekh, Va-yeshev, p. 21a

Elimelech here seeks to meet the objection that the claims made for the zaddik would have been extraordinary even in the days of the great prophets.

I have heard a sweet parable from the mouth of our Master and Teacher the Rabbi the Maggid of Rovno, the memory of the righteous is for a blessing. We see that now that we are in the bitter exile some people are gifted with the holy spirit far more easily than in the days of the prophets when, it is well known, they were obliged to engage in conjurations and remain in solitude for lengthy periods before they could attain to prophecy and the Holy Spirit. He gave this fine and sweet parable. When a king is in his palace with full regal honors paid to him, he will be annoyed if a friend invites him to have a meal in his house, for it is beneath the king's dignity to leave the splendor of his palace to visit someone. This is so even if the repast prepared for the king is exceedingly lavish. It is quite impossible for anyone to get the king to consent to be his guest unless he first makes due preparations and begs those close to the king to intercede on his behalf. But when the king is on a journey and wishes to stay

overnight in a certain place, he will be prepared to stay even in the village inn provided that it is clean. The application of the parable is obvious. When the Temple stood and the glory of the *Shekhinah* resided in the Holy of Holies, great effort was required if a man was to succeed in drawing down the Holy Spirit, as we find in connection with the ceremony of rejoicing at the Water Drawing, when they drew down the Holy Spirit. But now in the bitter exile the holy *Shekhinah* is in exile with us and, for our sins, wanders from place to place and is prepared to dwell with any man who is free from sin. And the words of a wise man's mouth are gracious.

The ceremony of the Water Drawing took place in Temple times during the festival of Sukkot, and the Rabbis say it was a time when the holy men, after due preparation, were able to draw down into themselves the Holy Spirit. The contemporary zaddik, says Elimelech, can easily achieve that which was hard even for the prophets because in exile the Divine Presence is ready, as it were, to accept any lodging provided it is clean. The "King" cannot be choosy, as it were, because if the zaddik will not "let Him in," no one will.

II HOW CAN FALSE MODESTY BE AVOIDED?

Noam Elimelekh, Likkutey Shoshanim, p. 101a

"And to walk humbly with thy God" (Micah 6:8). It is necessary to grasp the meaning of this verse. For it should have been put in the second person: "walk humbly with thy God" (in the imperative), as the verse concludes: "with thy God" (in the second person). But the meaning is as follows: A man has to be extremely careful to avoid the blandishments of the evil inclination. Even if his good deeds are performed away from men, nevertheless, since he himself is aware that he serves God, that he studies the Torah and is charitable and benevolent and so forth, he can have the ulterior motive of pride even in the most secret places. Anyone who looks into himself will see that what I have just said is true. It is therefore essential that a man should never think of his good deeds, and they should be hidden from him so that he is unaware of them at all and on the contrary, nothing he does should be considered to be good. That is why the verse says "to walk," in the infinitive, which is impersonal. This hints at the thought that even walking humbly should be in a

spirit of humility. That is to say, even when his deeds are hidden from men, they should be hidden also from himself so that he is unaware that he has achieved anything. This is the meaning of: "thou shalt love thy neighbor as thyself" (Leviticus 19:18). For God is called "thy neighbor" as in the verse: "Thy neighbor, and thy father's neighbor, forsake not" (Proverbs 27:10). Scripture says: *Thou shalt love*, **namely: the way to attain complete love, to love God who is called "thy neighbor," is impossible unless you behave "as thyself," that is to say, it is** *as if*, **that you yourself are unaware that you have done anything and it is only** *as if* **you have done it. Understand this well, for this is a basic principle and a great root in the worship of the Creator, blessed be He.**

Elimelech's novel interpretation of "thou shalt love thy neighbor as thyself" is: "thou shalt love God by behaving as thyself," i.e., by looking upon all your good deeds as if they were performed by another. Humility, for Elimelech, does not only mean that a man must avoid "showing off." For if he is content with this he will find himself "showing off" to himself and taking pride in not being the sort of person who "shows off." The only antidote to the "evil inclination" is for a man to forget himself completely, so that he is never aware of his self but only of as himself.

III RULES FOR SAINTS

Noam Elimelekh, Hanhagat Adam (Conduct of Man)

"The Conduct of Man" comprises rules printed at either the end or the beginning in the editions of the book. This is one of the two lists of religious exercises in which a fantastic piety is held up for emulation. Elimelech no doubt recorded these in the first instance for himself and then, possibly, for the guidance of his disciples.

These are the things a man must do to live.

[1] First a man must study the Talmud together with the commentaries of Rashi and the Tosafists, according to his ability, and afterward he should study the Codes, giving preference to the Shulḥan Arukh Oraḥ Ḥayyim. He should pray to God to enable him to arrive at the truth, for the sins of his youth, of the man he was formerly, blind his eyes so that even when he is able to engage in dialectics

and declare the law to others, he himself forgets and does not really keep the laws. Consequently, a man must express his deep remorse over his sins. He should be in solitude before daybreak, for then it is an acceptable time to weep many times over the exile of the *Shekhinah* **and he should shed tears. He should be in solitude also during the day (from time to time) and then his sins will be before him. He should remember his sins, his iniquities, and his transgressions, as high as the hills, which, if he did not behave in this manner, he would never have remembered. So should he do, not once nor twice nor a hundred times, until Heaven will take pity on him. He should pray to God to lead him in the right way so that his life should not be wasted. Then God, in His mercy and great compassion, will illumine his eyes in the holy Torah, and he will grasp the essence of the matter to keep it and to establish it.**

[2] He should guard himself against flattery, falsehood, frivolity, slander, envy, hatred, competition, anger, and pride, and gazing at women and from gossiping even with his own wife, especially when she has her periods.

[3] He should always reflect on the day of his death. He should never interrupt his studies so as not to offend against the rabbinic prohibition of interrupting Torah studies. And he should pray to God to be worthy of studying the Torah for its own sake.

[4] Each day he should study in the moralistic literature, such as the *Reshit Ḥokhmah*, **the** *Shelaḥ*, **and the** *Ḥovot Ha-Levvavot.*

The Reshit Ḥokhmah *is the sixteenth-century moralistic work by Elijah de Vidas; the* Shelaḥ *is by the seventeenth-century author Isaiah Horowitz; the* Ḥovot Ha-Levvavot *is Baḥya ibn Pakudah's* Duties of the Heart. *For these see Volume 2 in this series.*

[5] Occasionally he should study in a little fear of the writings of the Ari of blessed memory, but it must be in fear and dread and in awe of God. In former times men's souls were holy and they would take care in their youth not to commit any sins or transgressions and their souls were equipped to study this science [the Kabbalah]. But nowadays, for our sins, when we have a course body and are of gross

matter, a man must first refine his soul and wash it clean from every taint of sin. The test a man can apply to see whether he is clean is that the evil inclination no longer entices him to folly and stupidity as it did beforehand. Then he may study the Lurianic writings from time to time. God will reward him if he has purified his soul, by opening up for him the gates of wisdom contained in the writings of the Ari of blessed memory, which cannot be for as long as he is enveloped in the physical lusts of temporal vanity when this subject will be exceedingly difficult for him, God forbid.

The Ari ("the Lion") is Isaac Luria, the famous sixteenth-century kabbalist. Elimelech is no doubt thinking of the Shabbatean movement in which the study of the Lurianic Kabbalah led to a casting off of the discipline of the Torah. He is saying that the Kabbalah will be misunderstood unless it is engaged in by men who have made the effort to lead holy lives.

[6] The way of purification in this matter is to study the Talmud and the rabbinic Aggadah, which has the special property of refining the soul.

[7] He should keep himself far from sin and evil thoughts in all circumstances.

[8] He should guard himself against hating any Jew, except for the wicked for whom no excuse can be found. But where there appears to be such, even the wicked should be given the benefit of the doubt.

"Loving Israel" is an ideal stressed by all the Ḥasidic masters. An important ingredient in the success of the movement was precisely because of the encouragement it gave to ordinary Jews and the assurance that they mattered to God.

[9] He should not engage in any conversation at all, not even a single word, before prayers, because it is a hindrance to concentration during prayer.

[10] He should see to it that he relieves himself before prayer and before meals so as not to offend against the prohibition of being disgusting in one's person.

[11] He should see to it that his shirt and drawers are always perfectly clean.

Ḥasidism stresses that bodily cleanliness is an aid to spiritual refinement.

[12] He should never act as a tyrant in his home, and no one and no thing should ever give him offense. He should blame the offense on his own sinfulness. In this way he will succeed in subduing the evil inclination and breaking its hold over him.

[13] He should pray to God to help him repent of his sins and that he should not die unrepentant, including his own prayers with those of other repentant sinners and asking pardon together with the pardon granted for all Israel.

[14] He should speak gently to all men. Whenever men praise him he should go away energetically and should be distressed, saying to himself "How they do praise me without knowing what I am really like? If only they were aware of how inferior I am, of my folly and my evil deeds! And how can I raise my face to the Creator, blessed be He, who knows and sees my deeds at every moment and all times and yet He has compassion upon me in all that I do?"

[15] He should think to himself that a man is always standing beside him, never ceasing from looking at his deeds, so that if that man saw him commit an ugly deed he would be so ashamed that he would try to hide in a mousehole. How much more so, then, when it is God who stands over him and sees all his deeds all the time and from Him it is impossible to hide.

[16] When anyone insults him he should be very happy that God has sent him such a man so that his bad deeds should be exposed. Every person should seem to him to be his superior.

[17] He should keep far away from anything that is not essential to keep his body healthy for the service of God, whether it be food or drink or any other pleasure.

[18] The main thing is to keep from intoxicants, for this is a great malady and brings a man to a very inferior stage. The Rabbis say, "Do not become drunk and you will not sin."

[19] He should take care never to utter God's name in vain.

[20] He should take care never to utter or to think on holy things in an unclean place.

[21] He should never engage in conversation in the synagogue, not even on matters of morals or religion, lest it lead to profane talk.

This list of Elimelech and the other list printed in the book were widely studied by the Ḥasidim. These two lists have been printed in some prayerbooks so that the worshippers could read them daily.

CHAPTER 14

Zeev Wolf of Zhitomer

d. 1800

A critique of zaddikism of the wrong kind

Zeev Wolf was a disciple of the Maggid of Meseritch and is known to have been one of the most prominent zaddikim of the eighteenth century, but the details of his life remain obscure. His book Or Ha-Meir *(The Shining Light) was first published in Koretz in 1798 (edition used here; Jerusalem, 1968) and is a major source for the ideas of early Ḥasidism. The book has an unusually attractive Hebrew style and is disfigured by none of the awkward formulations and half-Yiddish expressions that seem to have affected the majority of Ḥasidic works. Some later Ḥasidim questioned whether the book was actually written by Zeev Wolf, but there are no real grounds for this suspicion and it seems to be based solely on the fact that, as in the passage quoted, the author is severely critical of some of the zaddikim of his day. As early as the end of the eighteenth century, less than forty years after the death of the Baal Shem Tov, zaddikism had become an established institution with its own abuses, to which the* Or Ha-Meir *calls attention. From the beginning Ḥasidism believed in the right of the zaddik to be assisted by his followers even in material things, but as zaddikism developed many zaddikim were not content with the mere necessities of life but journeyed from city to city so that the masses, impressed with their sanctity, would contribute generously to their support. Their excuse was that their journeyings were in order to elevate the "holy sparks" wherever these were to be found, an idea which Zeev Wolf does not repudiate in itself, although he is skeptical as to whether this is the true motive. The Ḥasidim generally refer to Zeev Wolf, after his book, as "the* Or Ha-Meir."

A CRITIQUE OF ZADDIKISM OF THE WRONG KIND

Or Ha-Meir, Tzav, pp. 95d–96d

"And the priest shall put on his linen garment, and his linen breeches shall be upon his flesh" (Leviticus 6:3). Rashi comments that the linen garment is the shirt and the reason it is called *middo* (literally, "his measure") is because it has to fit him. It seems to me that hinted at here is a moral lesson for this generation in which so many ambitiously pride themselves on their great name so that they journey all over the place and give themselves rest neither by day nor by night until they obtain sufficient for their needs. They experience no shame in using the Torah to support their families. Whoever heard of such a thing, whoever saw it in the generation before ours, when our fathers, the zaddikim, went hungry and thirsty and even had no clothes to wear and yet they did not travel around to act as teachers, saying openly, "Let me be your leader for I have no bread in my household and no garments," as they do in this generation? The majority of them no sooner feel that they are too poor than they gird their loins like a mighty man to cross the boundaries and give away all their pleasant things, that is, the Torah which is called "a pleasant thing," for the sake of food. Oh, the shame of it! They never stay at home, but are always on the move, rejecting entirely the ideal of solitude. We are unable to stop this ugly behavior and can only be apprehensive about whether it will be rectified in the coming generation, at least. For our eyes see that they have removed the mask of shame from their faces.

Zeev Wolf uses many scriptural allusions and clever puns which cannot be reproduced in translation, but this paraphrase is close to the author's meaning. A line or two has been omitted where the author refers to a comment in another part of the book. The early Ḥasidic teachers taught the value of solitude as a means of spiritual advancement. Zeev Wolf states here that he fails to see how this ideal can be furthered if the zaddikim are always on the go.

I once explained the verse about Samuel: "And his return was to Ramah, for there was his house" (1 Samuel 7:17) on the lines of an interpretation I heard from the Baal Shem Tov of the verse: "It is of the Lord that a man's goings are established; and he delighteth in his way" (Psalms 37:23). The Baal Shem Tov observed that this verse speaks of those who travel great distances in order to sell their wares, but God's thoughts are not theirs. They imagine that the sole purpose of their journey to distant lands is in order to obtain much gold and silver in exchange for the goods they sell and it is for this reason that they go to so much trouble. But God knows otherwise, for He knows how to shape man's destiny. There may be a loaf of bread in a distant land that belongs in the category of a particular man so that he has to eat that loaf in that particular place and in that particular time or he has to drink his fill of water in that place. It is with this intention that man's goings are established, that he should have to journey over hundreds of miles in order to perfect his soul through eating that particular loaf of bread or through drinking that water, whether little or much. It may even be that his journey is not brought about for his own benefit, but for that of his Hebrew servant for whom that loaf or that water is waiting. Since the servant could never afford the cost of the journey to such a distant place, it is determined that his master journey there, but it is solely for the sake of the servant who has to fill his stomach with the bread he has to eat there or the water he has to drink there. For, by the decree of God's wisdom, blessed be He, all is ordered for the sake of the perfection of a man's soul. This is hinted at in the verse: "It is of the Lord that a man's goings are established." When he undertakes a journey to a distant place it is all by a divine decree for the sake of the soul's perfection through one of the means known to God. But man thinks otherwise and he sees it differently. He "delighteth in *his* way," that is to say, in his own way, to journey to distant places in order to sell his wares and so forth, and in the process he forgets God.

The meaning of the Baal Shem Tov's saying has to be understood on the basis of the doctrine of the "holy sparks" we have encountered more than once. According to the Baal Shem Tov each person was sent into the world to redeem particular holy sparks. These belong to the "root of his soul," and until he redeems them his soul remains imperfect and unfulfilled. It is possible, for instance, that the "sparks" in a particular piece of bread or glass of water have to be redeemed by a particular man and by no other and in one particular place. God then arranges things so that the man journeys to that place, imagining that he is motivated by reasons of his own, but in reality he is simply the agent of the divine, cosmic plan of total redemption of the holy sparks. There are many Ḥasidic tales with this as their motif, a man finding himself in a completely unexpected situation and coming to realize that he has been placed in it for the sake of redeeming the holy sparks. This is the motif behind the legends about the strange wanderings of Eliezer, the father of the Baal Shem Tov. Zeev Wolf means to suggest that planning long journeys for business purposes is really futile because if there are sparks to be redeemed in those distant places to which he journeys, God will get him there somehow whether he plans it or not. All events are really part of a vast plan too mysterious for man to grasp. As Zeev Wolf goes on to say, it is too much to expect ordinary merchants to see it in this way, but one expects the zaddikim to see it thus and not waste their time by traveling about for the sake of gain.

Now so far as these folk are concerned, it is not so surprising since, after all, not all those with large business activities are necessarily wise enough to understand God's ways. But what is astonishing is that men learned in the Torah should wear out their feet traveling from city to city and country to country for the sake of bread and refuse to stay at home. They cannot have the excuse that it is, as above, for the sake of that loaf of bread and that glass of water, since each of them knows himself his true motive for undertaking these journeys. He imagines that the whole world was created for his sake, so that he can say, "Mine is the gold and silver," as our eyes see it is with regard to the majority. Each one wants all the honor available to be paid to him alone. He sees no danger in counting large amounts and refuses to count small amounts [of money given to him]. . . . If only their heart would let them see how ugly is their character, they would perhaps be shamed into improving it. It is perhaps possible to find this hinted at in the verse which tells of how Samuel returned to Ramah. For among those who journey from place to place, there are two types. The good type is of those who sincerely go in the way of the Lord. They have the advantage in that they put things right on their journeys so that the very ways themselves beckon to them to

come, for these wise men achieve great things all along the way in their eating and drinking and sleeping and the things they talk about, binding all these to the Torah and divine worship, doing it all in attachment (*devekut*) to the Creator, blessed be He. The motive of such men is to raise up all things to the Creator, blessed be He. Yet I have noted that men of this type are very few, and not everyone who claims to be among their number is justified is so doing by declaring that he, too, can put things right as he journeys on the way. It would be enough if he would put himself right when he sits alone in his house. Never mind putting others to right by journeying afar for many miles.

The reference to "putting right" is to the doctrine of tikkun, *the kabbalistic idea we have noted earlier in this book. Zeev Wolf does not deny that there are some zaddikim who are able to redeem the holy sparks on their journeys and so engage in* tikkun, *in promoting the harmony of creation. But he does not believe that many are of this elevated stage, and so far as the others are concerned it were better for them if they stayed at home.*

If you see such a person with no power to put many to right, as we have said—for since he cannot observe his own faults, how can he put right those of others?—and yet the soul of that man desires him to be constantly on the move from city to city, you can know for sure that it is because it has been destined that he come under the wheel of fate according to which unfortunate beggers have to find their sustenance by traveling from village to village and city to city. The principle here is that one of two things is possible. Either his journeyings belong to a high (*ramah*, "high") stage, in which he puts right and elevates the holy sparks wherever he goes, as above, or else his journeyings belong to the mystery of the wheel of fate, like the poor and needy who can only find their sustenance through these means. That is why it says of Samuel that his "return," his wanderings from place to place, was "to Ramah," namely, they belonged to this high degree since Samuel, a well-established prophet, obviously had the capacity to put right and elevate [the holy sparks] wherever he was, just as he was able to do in his own home. His wanderings were undoubtedly in the category of *ramah* and were most elevated. But there is also the type of journey that belongs solely to the mystery

of the wheel of fate. For those in this stage there is no ability of elevating the sparks on their journey, and they are simply like beggers who go begging from door to door in accordance with the mystery of the wheel of fate.

Samuel was a prophet, and only the very few zaddikim of his rank dare to suggest that they travel about solely in order to raise the holy sparks. The others ought to recognize that their behavior, far from denoting a high spiritual degree, is neither better nor worse than that of the common begger. Some people are fated to obtain their sustenance through begging at doors, but let them not pretend, says Zeev Wolf, that they are engaged in some sublime task of cosmic restoration.

The principle which emerges from all that has been said is that a man should be on his guard not to lose his high rank. He should walk humbly, allowing himself to be a prisoner in his own house where he can sit in solitude as in former times. This may well be his consolation, providing rest for body and soul, that he sincerely worships his Creator and refuses to follow the ugly habits of this generation. Let each man help his neighbor without embarrassment. And now we must revert to the verse with which we began: "And the priest shall put on his linen garment." This is an admonition for the zaddik who wishes to draw near to the innermost sanctuary of holiness, to be among those who serve God, blessed be He, in truth and with a perfect heart. For it is well known that the "priest" is one who worships God. The first thing the Torah teaches us is that the priest should put on himself only the garment that fits him. As Rashi says, it is the shirt that is referred to, and it is called *middo* **because it has to fit him. This means: Let him be content with as little as possible. Let him loathe luxuries in food, drink, and clothes, having only that which is essential, such as a shirt. And even this should "fit him" so that there is nothing between him and his garment. For there is no worse form of division than that which keeps man apart from his Maker. If the priest "wears this," acquiring this good quality (of contentment with what he has), there will certainly be no need for him to go on journeys, to wear himself out wandering from city to city for the sake of his sustenance. The hint is that the word** *middo* **is formed from the initial letters of** *me-avor derekh u-gevulim* **["from crossing ways and**

boundaries"], which suggests what we have said. And may the Lord in His mercy make us of those who sincerely trust in Him. Amen. Selah. For ever and ever.

The priest's shirt has to fit him. It must not be too big for him. Hence Zeev Wolf's homiletical interpretation. The true zaddik must be content with the bare necessities of life, as if all he requires is a shirt for his back. And he should not long for anything else as if the shirt did not fit him properly. Zeev Wolf seems also to be punning on the word for "linen," bad, *which he seems to connect with a word meaning "alone." Thus* middo bad *is the "measure" (of contentment;* middah *also means an ethical quality) that enables a man to remain in solitude and prevents him from wasting his time traveling. Finally, Zeev Wolf says that the letters of* middo *comprise an acrostic representing thought: "Stay at home and do not cross pathways and boundaries in search of luxuries."*

CHAPTER 15

Levi Yitzḥak of Berditchev

d. 1810

How to serve God without thought of self
What is true humility?
Can man have an influence on the Divine?

*Levi Yitzḥak of Berditchev, called by the Ḥasidim the "Berditchever" or the "Berditchever Rov" (he was one of the few Ḥasidic masters to serve as a town rabbi), is one of the most lovable figures among the Ḥasidic masters. He has become part of the folklore of the Jewish people, not only among the Ḥasidim, for his mighty pleading with God in behalf of his people. Levi Yitzḥak became a disciple of the Maggid of Meseritch in 1766 and remained one of the foremost exponents of the Ḥasidic way in his writings and by his life. A distinguished talmudic scholar, Levi Yitzḥak was appointed Rabbi of Zelechov, where he met with strong opposition on the part of the Mitnaggedim for his Ḥasidic views. Eventually he had to leave his post, and the story was repeated during his rabbinate in Pinsk. He finally settled in Berditchev in 1785. There are Ḥasidic tales, which seem to have a basis in fact, which tell of Levi Yitzḥak, suffering for a period, as a result of his bitter experiences and the strains he had to live under, from "smallness of soul," i.e., he had a nervous breakdown, but he recovered and continued to teach and to pray with the burning (*hitlahavut*, as this is called by the Ḥasidim, from *lahav*, "a flame") that was typical of him. Levi Yitzḥak's special company of followers* *who traveled around with him from town to town in order to win souls for God is also celebrated in Ḥasidic tales and seems, too, to have basis in fact.*

Levi Yitzḥak's book of Ḥasidic doctrine on the sidrot of the week, the festivals, and the talmudic Aggadah is entitled Kedushat Levi *(The Holiness of Levi). The first part of the book was published in Slavita in 1798 and the second part in Berditchev in 1816. Later editions contain both parts plus later additions in a single volume. (The edition used here is that of Jerusalem, 1964.)*

I HOW TO SERVE GOD WITHOUT THOUGHT OF SELF

Kedushat Levi, Va-yishlaḥ, p. 60

"I have seen God face to face, and I am spared" (Genesis 32:31). A man can serve God, blessed be He, in order to receive all good things from Him as a reward for his worshipping Him. But there is a higher category than this, when a man serves the Creator, blessed be He, because He is the mighty Ruler, and such a man has no thought of serving God for the good he will receive from Him. The second category is called "face to face." When man serves the Creator, blessed be He, because He is the mighty Ruler, then the Creator, blessed be He, turns toward him, as it were, face to face. But the other category is called "face to back." The Creator, blessed be He, turns to face him, as it were, but man serves only for the sake of the good he receives from God. Hence our verse states: "I have seen God face to face," referring to the second category of worship. This is hinted at in the words "and I am spared." "Spared" here means "separation." The meaning is that it never entered his head to serve God for the sake of anything that concerned himself, namely, in order to receive good from God, blessed be He. Hence it says: "and I am spared," that is to say, he was spared from having his thoughts on his "I." This category is that of *lishmah* **("for its own sake") while the other category is** *she-lo lishmah* **("not for its own sake").**

When two people are in accord they can be said to face one another. But if a man is friendly with another only because of what he can get out of him, he does not really face his friend but, figuratively speaking, turns his back on him. His motive is what is behind *the friendly activity, namely, how it will benefit him. So is it, says Levi Yitzḥak, in connection with man's relationship to God. The worshipper who believes that God will reward him and worships solely for this reason is not really a worshipper at all. Rather, he is a self-worshipper. God turns His face toward him while he turns his back on God. The true worshipper is in awe of his Creator and forgets himself entirely. The "I" of such a man is "spared," it has been allowed to escape; his thoughts being only on God. Again we have here the particular Ḥasidic emphasis on* lishmah, *worshipping God with no ulterior motive whatsoever, not even that of winning God's blessings.*

II WHAT IS TRUE HUMILITY?

Kedushat Levi, Shir ha-shirim, p. 191

"I am black, but comely, O ye daughters of Jerusalem, As the tents of Kedar . . ." (Song of Songs 1:5). It is well known that the main spiritual stage man has to reach is to be aware of his lowliness. When he stands in the presence of the high and exalted King, seeing His greatness and exaltedness, and how all the seraphim on high stand in dread and fear, trembling and terror seizing hold of them, his own unworthiness becomes immediately apparent. It is written: "Now the man Moses was very meek, above all the men that were on the face of the earth" (Numbers 12:3). This hints at the category we have just mentioned. Moses was the meekest of men, and the verse tells us how he reached a stage of humility that was greater than all men. It was because they were "men that were on the face of the earth," while Moses' holy and pure intellect soared in the upper worlds, seeing how all the seraphim on high stand in awe and dread, and it was as a result of this that he reached the degree of humility we have mentioned.

This stage is that of the true zaddik, the holy man who has reached the stage of humility as a result of his contemplation of the great majesty of the Creator, blessed be He. As the Rabbis (Pesaḥim 8a) say: "To what are the zaddikim like in the presence of the *Shekhinah*? To a lamp in front of a burning fire." For a man may be humble as a result of his reflection on his own unworthiness. But with regard to the true zaddik it is because of his profound contemplation of the great majesty of the Creator, as we have said. It is because of this that

there resides in him the quality of humility when he sees how bright is the greatness of the One above. That is why the Rabbis speak of a lamp in front of a burning fire. As Rashi explains it, the brightness of the burning fire is so great that there seems to be no brightness at all in the lamp. The scientists illustrate it in this way. When a man stands in front of the sun his face becomes dark and sunburned. Now the sun is, in reality, light, and yet it makes others dark. But the reason is that when any brightness is confronted by the sun, the source of all light, that brightness returns to its source in the sun so that the light is not discernable at all. So it is when a man gazes at the brightness of the Creator, blessed be He. Everything reverts to its Source and man forgets his ego and is no longer aware of his selfhood at all.

Levi Yitzḥak's illustration from the sun is a little curious. He says that the fierce brightness of the sun darkens the skin of any person exposed to it. So, too, any true zaddik is exposed to the fierce brightness of God's spirit and realizes that though he had been proud of the brightness of his own soul, that it really is dark before God's brightness. In the same way the true zaddik, when he contemplates the realization that God is all, transcends his ego and sees only God. This is the Ḥasidic doctrine of self-annihilation, bittul ha-yesh. *Note the difference between the ideal of humility as taught by Menaḥem Naḥum of Chernobyl (Chapter 11), and that of Levi Yitzḥak. For Levi Yitzḥak true humility does not mean that a man thinks little of himself, but that he does not think of himself at all. For Levi Yitzḥak humility is, in fact, not so much an ethical ideal as a religious virtue. It involves the complete forgetfulness of self when confronted by the majesty of the Creator.*

This is the quality of humility that is praiseworthy and beautiful. Happy the man who attains it. This is the meaning of our verse. "I am black," that is to say, my blackness is the result of my humility. But do not say that my blackness is due to the fact that I really am an inferior type of person so that, knowing my unworthiness, I am humble. It is not so, since I am "comely" in good deeds. If then, you ask, whence comes my humility? The answer is: "as the tents of Kedar." This means that just as the tents of Kedar are blackened through being in the sun, because they face the source of brightness, my blackness, too, is the result of my contemplation of the tremen-

dous brightness and greatness of the Creator, blessed be He, so I automatically forget my self. This is the degree of my humility. This is also the meaning of the following verse: "Look not upon me, that I am swarthy, because the sun has tanned me" (Song of Songs 1:6). The meaning is: When you see that I am swarthy, do not see it as meaning that I am really swarthy in my disregard of the *mitzvot*. **It is rather that the swarthiness you see is because the sun has tanned me, as above, that is to say, because I have contemplated for so long on the greatness of the Creator, blessed be He, and His brightness that my self has automatically been transcended.**

It might seem odd for someone to praise himself and yet claim to be humble, but, as he has said, Levi Yitzḥak does not think of humility as mere lack of pride but rather as forgetfulness of self in the presence of God so that it is possible at other times for a man to be aware that he had achieved this state.

Of course, the "tents of Kedar" are not black because they are in the sun. They are made of black sheep's wool. But Levi Yitzḥak allows himself a poetic liberty.

III CAN MAN HAVE AN INFLUENCE ON THE DIVINE?

Kedushat Levi, Naso, pp. 206–7

"And the Lord spoke to Moses, saying: Speak to Aaron and to his sons: Thus shall you bless the children of Israel. Say to them: . . ." (Numbers 6:22–23). This is the general principle. The Baal Shem Tov always used to rebuke people by quoting the verse, "The Lord is thy shadow" (Psalms 121:5). Just as a man's shadow does whatever he does, so the Creator, blessed be He, does, as it were, whatever man does. Consequently, a man must perform good deeds, giving alms and showing compassion to the needy, so that the Creator, blessed be He, too, will bestow His goodness. This quality is called: "Thus." For the meaning of the word *Thus* **is "like this." That is to say, just as a man does, so the Creator, blessed be He, does.**

This is a typical Ḥasidic idea. The midrash to the verse in Psalms uses the illustration of the shadow, but the Baal Shem Tov interprets it in a more mystical way. God's goodness to His creatures depends on the way they conduct themselves. All good deeds have a cosmic significance because God's grace can only flow if man behaves graciously. Consequently, God is like man's shadow. When a man moves his hand his shadow's hand moves too. When man is benevolent this brings about an increase, as it were, in the flow of divine grace. Levi Yitzḥak says that this is the meaning of "Thus," namely, as you do, so God does. He goes on to say that God needs, as it were, to benefit His creatures because it is the nature of the All-good to be good. But He cannot do this unless man first gives Him the power to do so by practicing benevolence. Hence man's worship is an act of assisting God, as it were. The remark to follow about the cow and the calf is a rabbinic saying, applied to the teacher of the Torah, who wishes to teach more than the pupil wishes to learn from him (Pesaḥim 112a).

It is well known that the Creator, blessed be He, wants to bestow goodness upon His people Israel. For more than the calf desires to be fed the cow wishes to feed it. Whenever a man stands before the Creator, blessed be He, in prayer, reciting the eighteen benedictions or other supplications, his sole intention should be so that the Creator, blessed be He, will have delight. As the Mishnah (Avot 2:8) puts it: "If you have studied much Torah, do not ascribe any merit to yourself, because for this you were created." The meaning is that the sole motive of man for doing good should be for the delight of the Creator.

The Mishnah really means that a man should not be proud of the good deeds he has done. He should not "ascribe any merit to himself." But this phrase, literally translated, is: "keep not the goodness for yourself"—which Levi Yitzḥak understands as meaning: "Do not think of your own goodness, but think only of the delight God has from your good deeds, not because He needs these good deeds, but because it enables Him to bestow His bounty on His creatures and this is His delight."

Now, when a man prays for himself he is called a recipient. When a man wishes to receive something he holds out his hand with the palm upward and the back of the hand downward. But when a man prays only for the sake of the delight that the Creator, blessed be He, will have, that man is a giver—he gives to God, as it were. A giver holds his hand with the palm downward and the back of the hand upward. The priestly blessing has to be recited with the hands up-

lifted, that is to say, the priests hold the hands with the palm away from themselves, as does one who is a giver. This is the meaning of "Thus shall you bless the children of Israel." It means, bless the children of Israel with the intention of giving delight to God and then you will be as givers to the Creator, blessed be He, as it were, and then the Creator, blessed be He, will bestow all His goodness and blessings upon Israel, as we have said. For this quality is called, "Thus." Whatever Israel does, so, as it were, God does and He bestows upon His people Israel goodness, blessings, life, and peace. Amen.

The priests when they recite this blessing (this is the priestly blessing) place their hands with the palms outward because their intention is to give to God. They are endowing God, as it were, with the capacity to be good to His creatures. In turn He will increase the flow of blessing. This is the Ḥasidic idea of man's participation in God's goodness.

CHAPTER 16

Shneur Zalman of Liady

1745-1813

How can man rejoice in the Lord?
How can Schadenfreude be avoided?
What is the extent of man's generosity?

Shneur Zalman is the founder of the intellectual movement in Ḥasidism, the systematic exponent of the basic ideas of Ḥasidism with a strong emphasis on theory, contemplative prayer, and detailed study of the kabbalistic principles in their Ḥasidic interpretation. The movement he founded within Ḥasidism is known as Ḥabad, a word formed from the initial letters of Ḥokhmah, Binah, Deah *(Wisdom, Understanding, Knowledge). These are technical terms referring in the first instance to the* Sefirot *of these names, and then to the intellectual processes in man which mirror the processes on high.*

Shneur Zalman was born in Liozna in Russia. From the year 1760, when he journeyed to the Maggid of Meseritch, whose fame as a spiritual leader had spread to distant Russia, Shneur Zalman became a member of the Maggid's circle of close disciples. He became the particular target of the Mitnaggedim after he had become a Ḥasidic master in the town of Liady. Accusations were brought against him that he was plotting the downfall of the tsar, and in 1798 he was arrested and imprisoned in Saint Petersburg. He was acquitted on the nineteenth day of the month of Kislev (December 1798), and to this day yat Kislev *("the nineteenth day of Kislev") is celebrated as a major festival by the Ḥabad Ḥasidim.*

Shneur Zalman was succeeded by his son Dov Baer (whom he named after his teacher, the Maggid of Meseritch) in the year 1813. Dov Baer became the head of the movement with his center in the town of Lubavitch; hence the Ḥabad Ḥasidim are called the "Lubavitcher Ḥasidim." Dov Baer was succeeded by his son-in-law and nephew (the son of Shneur Zalman's daughter), Menaḥem Mendel of Lubavitch (1789–1866). The Ḥabad Ḥasidim call Shneur Zalman the "Alter Rebbe" ("the Old Rabbi"), Dov Baer the "Mittler Rebbe" ("the Middle Rabbi"), and Menaḥem Mendel, after the title of his magnum opus, "the Tzemaḥ Tzedek." The Ḥabad dynasty has many ramifications, and an immense literature has been produced by the various masters of the group. The present Lubavitcher Rebbe in New York is the great-great-grandson of Menaḥem Mendel.

Shneur Zalman's major Ḥasidic book is Tanya *(It Has Been Taught). The meaning of the title is that the book begins with the word* Tanya, *quoting from a passage in the Talmud, and books were frequently called after the opening word or words. Another name for the book is* Likkutey Amarim *(Collected Sayings), i.e., an anthology of Ḥasidic ideas. The first part of the book was published in Slavita in 1797. A third part, called "The Letter on Repentance"* (Iggeret Ha-Teshuvah) *was added in Shklov in 1806. Finally, the fourth part was added:* Iggeret Ha-Kodesh *(The Holy Letter), letters of the rabbi, in the Shklov edition of 1814. The standard edition of the* Tanya *was published repeatedly by the famous printing house of Romm in Vilna, 1900, etc. This is the edition used here. So high is the regard of the Ḥabad Ḥasidim for the* Tanya *that many of them keep it in the same bag as their* tallit *and study it regularly. One of Shneur Zalman's contemporaries is reported to have said when he read the book, "What an achievement, to contain such a great God in such a small book!"*

I HOW CAN MAN REJOICE IN THE LORD?

Tanya, part 1, chapter 33, pp. 82–85

Here is another way to make the soul glad, especially when a man senses, from time to time, that his soul needs to be refined and illumined by rejoicing in the heart. He should then engage in deep contemplation, depicting in his mind and understanding the idea of God's true unity, blessed be He. That is to say, He fills all worlds, those on high and those beneath them, and even the fullness of this

earth is His glory, blessed be He. In relation to Him everything is really nothing at all. He alone is actually in the upper and lower worlds, just as He was alone before the six days of creation.

Shneur Zalman gives here his typical Ḥabad *exposition of the Maggid's views on the immanence of God. His grandson Menaḥem Mendel states in one of his works that the idea of God's unity has passed through three distinct stages. In the Bible and Talmud the unity of God means, chiefly, that there is only one God and that there are no other gods. For the medieval Jewish philosophers the doctrine of God's unity meant not alone that He is one but that He is unique, that none of His creatures can in any way be compared to him. The disciples of the Baal Shem Tov deepened the idea still further, teaching that the unity of God means that God is the only ultimate reality, that there is no world at all because all is God. In that case, why do we see a world, and how can we ourselves exist? The* Ḥabad *answer is that the divine light is screened so that we* appear *to enjoy existence, and so does the world. But the man who contemplates long on this version of God's unity comes to realize that, in reality, God is the same, "filling all," even now that there seems to be a world, just as He was "before the six days of creation." Shneur Zalman is here developing the thought that this idea brings joy into the soul.*

Even in the space into which this world was created, heavens and earth and all their hosts, He alone fills this space. And even now He alone is, without any change whatsoever, because all creatures are annihilated in Him just as the letters by means of which speech and thought take place are annihilated in their source and root. That is to say, in the real being and essence of the soul, its ten aspects of *Ḥokhmah, Binah, Deah*, **and so forth.**

We have seen in a previous chapter that the ten Sefirot *(in* Ḥabad *and other kabbalistic systems,* Deah *is one of the ten) are mirrored in man's soul and that therefore man's nature can be used as an analogy for God's relationship to the universe. The* Sefirot *in man's souls are the potential means of all expression, the pure thoughts and emotions of man. For these to be actualized man has to think or speak, thus bringing his thoughts and feelings into play. For speech (and thought, because one thinks in words) letters are required which are formed into words. These letters are the "garments" of the ten aspects of the soul. But although from one point of view they have a separate identity, from another there are no such things. This is because the letters are simply the means of expressing and were it not for the forces in the soul requiring expression, letters and words would be unimaginable. In Shneur Zalman's analogy, the letters are "annihilated," i.e., lose their identity in the forces which resided in the soul and which brought the letters into being. In the same way, God is really all. The world is only the word He uses to express His goodness, and in relation to His Being there is no world because it is "annhilated in Him." Now Shneur Zalman goes on to illustrate this idea by means of another analogy.*

We have also given elsewhere an illustration taken from the physical world for this idea. The shining and the light of the sun are annihilated in the sun itself in the heavens. For without doubt up there, too, its light shines and extends even more so than it extends and shines in space below. Only there it is annihilated in its source and enjoys no existence at all. So by analogy is the total annihilation of existence of the world and the fullness thereof in relation to its source, which is the light of *En Sof*, blessed be He.

The rays of the sun shine on earth. Logically, there must be sun rays in the sun itself, but so bright is the light of the sun, the source of the rays, that in the sun itself the rays fade into total insignificance. By the same token the whole world is only the ray of the light of En Sof. *Now since He is beyond space and time and is present always, this really means that the world and its creatures only enjoy existence by being remote from God to some extent. When man contemplates long on this theme he comes to see that he and the world he inhabits are like the rays of the sun in the sun itself and there is total "annihilation."*

Now when a man contemplates on this idea very profoundly, his heart leaps in joy and his soul is glad, there is abundant joy, and in this belief there is gladness and song, with all the heart and all the soul and all the might. For this is to be near to God quite literally. This is the whole purpose for which he and all worlds were created, that God should dwell among those down below. . . . How great is the joy of an ordinary, inferior person who draws near to a king who has agreed to be his guest and to live with him in his house! How

much more so, then, when man is near to the King of the kings of kings, the Holy One, blessed be He, who dwells with him! As it is written: "For who is he that hath pledged his heart to approach unto Me? saith the Lord" (Jeremiah 30:21). This is why it was ordained that we should say each morning when praising God: "Happy are we. How good is our portion and how beautiful our heritage." This means that, just as a man rejoices when he is left an inheritance of a very large amount of money for which he has not toiled, so, and even more so, should we rejoice over the heritage our fathers have left us, namely, the doctrine of God's unity in truth, that even on this earth down below there is none else beside Him, and this is the meaning of His dwelling down below.

The verse in Deuteronomy (4:35) says: "Unto thee it was shown, that thou mightest know that the Lord, He is God; there is none else beside Him." In the context, the verse means that there is no other God beside Him. But Ḥabad *understands it to mean that there is only He, there is none else beside Him, i.e., apart from Him, no worlds and no creatures.*

This is why the Rabbis (Makkot 23b, 24a) say that 613 precepts were given to Israel, but Habakkuk came and reduced them to one great principle: "The righteous shall live by his faith" (Habakkuk 2:4). This means that it is as if a man only had a single precept to carry out, that of faith, for through faith on its own a man will come to carry out all the other precepts. For when a man's heart leaps for joy in his belief in the unity of God, with limitless joy, as if the only command he had been given was this one and that this is the whole purpose for which he and all worlds were created, then this joy he experiences will endow him with such strength and such vitality that he will be able to rise far, far above all obstacles that prevent him from carrying out all the 613 precepts, inwardly and outwardly. This is why the verse says, "The righteous shall *live* by his faith," he shall *live*, it will be just like the resurrection of the dead, so, by analogy, will his soul be revived through this joy he will experience. And it will be a two-fold joy, for in addition to the joy his soul will experience when it discerns that God is near and dwells with him, he will rejoice all the more that God rejoices and the great satisfaction this belief provides to Him, blessed be He.

It is worth noting that the Mitnaggedim, unlike Shneur Zalman, held it to be spiritually dangerous to dwell on this idea that God is all. The reason for their opposition was either that they did not understand the doctrine of God's unity in this way and thought it to be heresy, or they did believe in it but thought that if man reflects too much on it, it will tend to obliterate all distinctions beween good and evil, for it would seem to follow that God is in evil as well as in good. Shneur Zalman, therefore, now goes on to state that evil does not really exist at all. The belief in God's unity in the sense he has described the doctrine reduces evil to nothingness or, in the kabbalistic language Shneur Zalman uses, the "Other Side" (the demonic side of existence), and the kelipot *("shells" or "husks") are vanquished.*

For [the belief in God's unity] will cause the Other Side to be vanquished and darkness will be converted into light, that is to say, the darkness of this material world which obscures and conceals His light, blessed be He. So will it be until the end of days, as it is said, "He setteth an end to darkness" (Job 28:3), referring to the end of days when God will remove the spirit of impurity from the earth and the glory of the Lord will be revealed and all flesh shall see it.

Shneur Zalman refers to the messianic age. In that time all the darkness shall vanish and all men will see the truth that God is all— "the glory of the Lord shall be revealed." The Job passage really seems to mean: "Man sets an end to darkness," but as the text only says "he," Shneur Zalman feels free to say it is God who will do so.

This applies especially in the lands of the idolators, where the very atmosphere is unclean, full of *kelipot* **and the "Other Side," and there is no greater joy to God, blessed be He, than the light and joy which stem from darkness, especially from darkness (i.e., when the joy comes even in a place where there had been deep spiritual darkness). This is the meaning of the verse: "Let Israel rejoice in His deeds" (Psalms 149:2). That is to say, whoever is from the seed of Israel should rejoice that God rejoices and is glad that He resides among those here below, which is called "deeds," which are physical. And that is why it uses the plural** *deeds*. **For this material world full of the** *kelipot* **and the "Other Side" is called the public domain and the mountains of separation. But they are turned into a private domain, to the unity of God through his belief.**

The rabbinic term for "public domain" is reshut ha-rabbim, *literally, "domain of the many," while the term for "private domain" is* reshut ha-yaḥid, *literally, "domain of the one." Hence Shneur Zalman remarks that this world in which there is evil and separation is the domain of the many forces of impurity and the domain of multiplicity and separation, but through belief in God's complete unity all division and multiplicity and evil disappear and the world becomes "the domain of the One." He is again forcing a translation, for the Psalm really says: "Let Israel rejoice in Him that made him," but Shneur Zalman can't resist a broad leap that allows this interpretation.*

II HOW CAN *SCHADENFREUDE* BE AVOIDED?

Tanya, Iggeret Ha-Kodesh, 2, pp. 206–7

This noble letter was sent originally to all his followers by Shneur Zalman after he had returned from his imprisonment in Saint Petersburg. This was a great victory for Ḥasidism, and he sensed that some of the Ḥasidim would take the opportunity to hit back at the Mitnaggedim, so Shneur Zalman here warns his followers to repay hatred with love and not to gloat over the discomfiture of their opponents.

"I am unworthy of all the favors" (Genesis 32:11). The meaning of the verse is that for every mercy shown by the Holy One, blessed be He, to man, he should be all the more humble. For mercy is the "right hand" and "His right hand embraces me" (Song of Songs 2:6). This is the category of the real nearness of God to a far greater state than ever before. Now the nearer a man is to God and the greater his elevation, the more is he required to be exceedingly humble, as it is said: "From afar the Lord appeared unto me" (Jeremiah 31:3). Now it is well known that *everything before Him is as nothing* **so that the more one is** *before Him* **the more he is as** *nothing.*

There are a number of kabbalistic allusions in this passage. First, the saying, "everything before Him is as nothing," is in the Zohar 1:11b. In the context this refers to the insignificance of creatures before God. But in Ḥabad, and to some extent in the Maggid's school in general, this became a favorite text for the view that all creatures are literally "nothing" in relation to God, since all is God in reality. It follows that the nearer one is to God, the nearer to true reality, the less of selfhood will there be. Hence Shneur Zalman's interpretation of the saying,

"Everything that is before Him [i.e., near to Him] is as nothing." When God shows mercy (the term used is Ḥesed, the Sefirah Lovingkindness, *the source of all mercy), He embraces man, as it were, with His right hand (the Sefirot of Mercy are described as belonging to the right, those of Judgment to the left). So when man is shown mercy and God has "embraced" him and thus brought him near, it must follow that he feels all the more unworthy. The verse in Genesis means literally: "I have become small because of the mercies," i.e., I feel all the more inferior because God has shown so much mercy to me. The conclusion is that the Ḥasidim, to whom God has shown special favors, now have to be very humble.*

This is the category of the right hand of holiness and "mercy to Abraham" (Micah 7:20), who said: "I am but dust and ashes" (Genesis 18:27). And this was also the quality of Jacob. That is why he apologized for fearing Esau and not relying on God's promise to him: "And, behold, I am with thee" (Genesis 28:15). For since Jacob had become so very small in his own eyes because of God's great mercies to him, "For with my staff I passed over this Jordan; and now I am become two camps" (Genesis 32:11), and he thus thought that he was unworthy to be saved from Esau. This is what the Rabbis mean when they say (Berakhot 4a) that Jacob feared that sin may have been the cause of the promise being unfulfilled, i.e., Jacob thought he was a sinner.

Abraham, in the Kabbalah, is called the "pillar of Ḥesed," i.e., he represented on earth God's mercies on high. On the basis of Shneur Zalman's analysis we can see why Abraham, in particular, said that he was dust and ashes. Now the Rabbis ask why Jacob was so afraid of Esau. After all, God had promised to be with him and to protect him. The Rabbis say that Jacob feared he might have sinned and so forfeited his right to divine protection. Shneur Zalman gives this a novel turn. God had led Jacob and enriched him so that from a poor wanderer with his staff he had become a rich man with "two camps." God had been very good to him and this caused him to feel even more inferior. Hence, even if he had not really sinned, in his new great humility he thought he was a sinner and had forfeited divine protection.

"God has made one as well as the other (Ecclesiastes 7:14). So it is quite the opposite with regard to Ishmael, who represents the ***Ḥesed***

of the *kelipah*. With him the more mercy he is shown the more he is puffed up with pride and the more ambitious he becomes.

The verse, "God has made one as well as the other" is interpreted in the Kabbalah to mean that whatever there is found in the realm of holiness is also found in the realm of the demonic. That is to say, there are unholy Sefirot, *i.e., profane love, terror, pride, and so forth. Ishmael is the symbol of unholy* Ḥesed. *When* Ḥesed *manifests itself to the unholy man, instead of being humble like Jacob was, he thinks that he deserves even more goodness and becomes proud and demanding.*

Therefore, I come to inform you, in an important proclamation to all the members of our fraternity, of all the kindness which the Lord has wrought for us. It is right, therefore, to seize hold of the quality of our father Jacob, "the remnant of His people" (Isaiah 11:11), "the remnant of Israel" (Jeremiah 6:9), so called because he treats himself like a remnant, like something useless that is left over. Do not, therefore, exalt yourselves over your brethren and do not speak in haughtiness against them and do not hiss at them, God forbid. Let such a thing never be mentioned. I give you a strict warning. You should therefore be very humble in spirit and heart, seizing hold of Jacob's quality in the presence of all men, with a lowly spirit and the kind of gentle answer that turns away wrath. And have a restrained spirit, etc. Perhaps, after all this, God will put it into the hearts of your brethren to behave likewise: "As in water face answereth to face, So is the heart of man to man" (Proverbs 27:19).

When a man gazes into water he sees his own face reflected. So, too, if the Ḥasidim will behave well toward their opponents, there is a possibility that the latter will also respond with love.

III WHAT IS THE EXTENT OF MAN'S GENEROSITY?

Tanya, Iggeret Ha-Kodesh, 9, pp. 226–28

In this letter to his followers, Shneur Zalman urges them to be generous. The background is the extremely difficult time in Russia when many Jewish communities were impoverished. There is an element of extremism in Shneur Zalman's complete negation of family love, but it has to be realized that he was addressing Ḥasidim whom he suspected of placing the family before anything else to the extent that the needy were overlooked. From another version of this letter, however, it seems that his appeal was on behalf of the Ḥasidim in the Holy Land.

Friends, brothers, and companions whom I love as myself! I come now to recall you to your duty, to awaken those who sleep the heavy slumber of vanity of vanities, to open the eyes of the blind that they should see. Let all their desire, longing, and ambition, with all they have, in their innermost being, be for the Source of Life, all the days of their life, whether in things spiritual or material. I mean that they should not engage in worldly things and in earning a living solely with self in mind. They should not be like the idolators who work for, support, and have regard for their wives and children out of their love for them. For it is written (1 Chronicles 17:21): "Who is like Thy people Israel, a nation one *in the earth*." This means that even when attending to earthly matters they should not be separated, God forbid, from the truly One. They should not be guilty of testifying falsely, God forbid, when they recite the *Shema* daily, saying, with their eyes closed, "The Lord is One," and He alone reigns in all four directions, in heaven above and on the earth beneath, and yet, no sooner do they open their eyes, than it has all vanished, God forbid.

It is the practice, when reciting the Shema, *to close the eyes and concentrate on the belief that God alone reigns above and below and in all four directions of north, south, east, and west. Shneur Zalman takes this to mean that the true Ḥasid does everything for God. He only loves his wife and children because this, too, is what God would have him do. But no sooner has he opened his eyes, after affirming it in the* Shema, *that he forgets all about it and thinks only of earning a living for his family*

Through this alone can we be acceptable to God, in that all our efforts in worldly things should be with the motive of reviving souls, portions of God, and to satisfy their needs in pure love. In this way we resemble our Creator, the Lord who is One, whose lovingkindness is all through the day a true lovingkindness, wherewith He revives the world and the fullness thereof at every moment. Only, it so happens that according to the Torah a man's wife and children take precedence over others.

Shneur Zalman means that man is expected to resemble his Maker. Now God's love is entirely untainted by self-interest, for He lacks nothing. It is pure, unadulterated goodness. So, too, man should be entirely disinterested in the good he does. He should not have any self-interest. His aim should be to keep souls alive, i.e., to help others because they have immortal souls (in Ḥabad, as in Levi Yitzḥak's thought, they have an actual portion of God in their souls). Strictly speaking, there ought to be no difference whether a man supports others or his own family. It is only that the Torah demands that he give precedence to his family. Thus his special care for his family should be because the Torah has so commanded.

Therefore, my beloved brethren, consider these things stated here very briefly (please God when we meet face to face, I shall elaborate on them) that the main way of serving God in these times, the times of the "heels of the Messiah," is to give charity. As the Rabbis of blessed memory say (Sanhedrin 98a): "Israel will only be redeemed through charity." The Rabbis only said (Peah 1:1) that the study of the Torah is equal to acts of benevolence in their day when the study of the Torah was their main way of serving God, and that is why they were such great sages, Tannaim, and Amoraim. It is quite different during the time of the "heels of the Messiah," when the Tabernacle of David has fallen to the stage of "heels" and "feet," which represents action. There is no other way of converting darkness into light except through action, namely, the act of giving charity. For those who are wise know that the category of "action" with regard to the divine realm is the category of the influx of divine grace down below to those who have nothing of themselves.

Everything on earth mirrors the divine processes. Consequently, just as in the sefirotic realm there is wisdom and action so, too, in the progress of human history. Now the aspect of "action" in the divine realm is that God acts *in His mercy to sustain the world, giving of His goodness to those who have nothing. Similarly, as mankind progresses toward the messianic age, raising the Tabernacle of David that has fallen, there are stages. In the days of the Rabbis the stage was that of thought, mirroring the stage of thought in the divine realm. But now we have to mirror the stage of action in the divine realm by giving charity. The reference to the "heels of the Messiah" is to this expression found frequently in the rabbinic literature, where it means the time when the "feet" of the Messiah are heard, i.e., just before he comes. But in the Kabbalah the meaning is that man has, as it were, worked his way downward from the head (the thought of the Tannaim and Amoraim) and has now to put right things through the "heels," which denotes action, i.e., the lowest stage of the divine processes, when God's thoughts are being realized. The Tannaim are the rabbis of the Mishnah, the Amoraim of the Gemara.*

Whoever sacrifices his evil inclination in this matter and opens his hand and heart will cause the "Other Side" to be vanquished and will convert darkness into the light of God, blessed be He, who dwells among us in the category of "action" at the time of the "heels of the Messiah." And he will be worthy of seeing God eye to eye when He returns to Zion.

Reading between the lines of this epistle, it would seem that some of the Ḥasidim tried to find an excuse for their lack of generosity in that they served God by studying the Torah, which is just as good as being benevolent. They could quote the passage in Peah in their support, so Shneur Zalman hastens to disabuse them.

CHAPTER 17

Israel Hapstein,
the Maggid of Koznitz 1733-1814
and his son, Moses Eliakim Beriah d. 1828

How can man overcome the evil in his nature?
What is the meaning of "the fear of God"?
Can a man lose himself in God?
Self-annihilation

*Israel Hapstein was a disciple of the Maggid of Meseritch, Levi Yitzḥak of Berditchev, and Elimelech of Lizensk. Israel was a great talmudist and kabbalist—even his Mitnaggedic opponents did not deny this. He was an eloquent preacher, occupying the position of Maggid in the Polish town of Koznitz, and a famed Ḥasidic master. As a zaddik Israel believed not alone in praying on behalf of his Ḥasidim, but also in engaging in miracle working by means of amulets and the like and, it is said, also healing by such natural means as herbs and nostrums. Israel is reported to have been an invalid but, it is said, when he rose to pray in burning enthusiasm (*hitlahavut*) it was as if he had been reborn and had gained new strength. He is known among the Ḥasidim as the "Koznitzer Maggid." Israel was succeeded as a Ḥasidic master and Maggid in Koznitz by his son, Moses Eliakim Beriah (d. 1828).*

Israel's main work is Avodat Yisrael *(Israel's Worship), first published in Yozepof in 1842. (The edition used here is that of Lemberg, 1858.) Moses Eliakim Beriah's work in the same tradition is* Beer Moshe, *published in Yozepof in 1858. (The edition used here is that of New York, 1954.) Both works follow the conventional pattern of comments on the weekly* sidra.

I HOW CAN MAN OVERCOME THE EVIL OF HIS NATURE?

Avodat Yisrael, Mi-ketz, pp. 19b–20a

This is a comment on Pharaoh's dream in Genesis, chapter 41. In verse 4 we read:

"And the ill-favored and lean-fleshed kine did eat up the seven well-favored fat kine. So Pharaoh awoke." Now when Pharaoh related his dream to Joseph he elaborated on this, saying: "And when they had eaten them up, it could not be known that they had eaten them; but they were still ill-favored, as at the beginning." This was not stated previously when it tells of his dream. Now it seems that this has to be understood by way of a hint, for all the narratives of the Torah hint at the way we should learn to love God and serve Him.

*Like the other Ḥasidic masters, Israel understands narratives such as this as affording guidance for the present. The narrative is said to be in the way of a hint—*remez*—the term used for allegorical interpretation of Scripture.*

Now Pharaoh's dream seems to hint at the way of the sinner who behaves so wickedly that his sins bring about, God forbid, the devouring of the seven qualities of the holy by the seven evil qualities of the "Other Side," and they are devoured, God forbid. For in general there are seven ways in which man is obliged to serve his Maker: to love Him; to fear Him; to glorify Him; to be victorious in the struggle against the evil inclination for the sake of His name; to give thanks unto Him; to cleave to the Holy King; and to acknowledge Him as King.

The seven Sefirot*—*Ḥesed, Gevurah, Tiferet, Netzaḥ, Hod, Yesod, Malkhut*—represent the "seven qualities" of holiness and so far as man is concerned they provide seven different approaches to the* *service of God. Ideally man should serve God in all these seven ways. Thus:* Ḥesed = *loving God;* Gevurah = *fearing God;* Tiferet = *glorifying God;* Netzaḥ = *gaining the victory over evil in the service of God;* Hod = *giving thanks to God;* Yesod = *cleaving to God;* Malkhut = *acknowledging God as King. Israel now goes on to say that corresponding to these seven there are seven evil qualities. He quotes the verse used by the kabbalists, "God has made one as well as the other" (Ecclesiastes 7:14) for the idea that everything in the domain of the holy has its "opposite number" in the realm of evil, the* Sitra Aḥera, *the "Other Side." For Israel these are the seven lean cows which devour the seven fat cows.*

"God has made one as well as the other," and the evil inclination and the "Other Side" have been created to entice man to worldly things and stupid nonsense, to lead him along the path that is anything but good. He comes to love strange things, to fear others than God, to take pride in other than God, and so with regard to the other qualities. The fool who walks in darkness and allows himself to be enticed by his evil inclination causes, God forbid, the seven qualities of holiness to be devoured by the seven qualities of the "Other Side."

Now the sinner at the time of his sin, and as he daily continues in folly, and for as long as he fails to repent, becomes completely insensitive to his wickedness, unaware that, as we have said, he weakens the power of the holy, his heart too dull, his eyes too blind to see. On the contrary, he imagines himself to be a righteous man, upright and a man of integrity.

Now all is clear. The first verse speaks of the sinner at the time of his dream. He is then like one who sleeps, for the good in his soul is dormant and he spends his time as in a dream. Of him it cannot be said: "it could not be known that they had eaten them." At that stage he could never say this, since then he does not even know that he does not know. Afterward, however, when the sinner bestirs himself to repent of his sins, he is compared to the sleeper awakening from his sleep. For he, too, awakens from the sleep of folly and returns unto the Lord. His heart troubles him because of his former deeds and he feels his sin to be too great to bear. His eyes are now opened. He can now see the flaw caused by his deeds, for Heaven

helps him to see how by pursuing desolate abomination he has caused the seven qualities of the "Other Side" to devour the seven qualities of holiness. He now sees, too, that he has been guilty of the great sin of not even knowing that these have been devoured. That is why the verse says: "But they were still ill-favored, as at the beginning." Now he is able to see that he had sinned so greatly that he was not even aware at the time that he was a sinner, imagining himself to be a righteous man.

At the time of the "dream," when a man sins, there is no awareness of sin. It is only afterward when he "awakens" in repentance that he becomes aware of his sin and aware of his lack of awareness while he was a sinner that he was a sinner. Now and only now can the repentant sinner say that at the time he did not know that the seven lean cows had devoured the seven fat cows. Israel continues that this is the meaning of "So I awoke" at the end of verse 21. The sleeper is now awake. The sinner has repented.

This is hinted at when the dream is related, for then it says: "So I awoke." This means: The repentant sinner, when he does repent, speaks to himself of the great blindness with which he had been afflicted. He bemoans the fact that he had sinned so heavily that, until he had awakened, he had been unaware that the holy qualities had been devoured. It was only when he woke up that he was able to appreciate it all for himself. When this happens his heart is bitter and he returns unto the Lord. He resolves not to sin again and to walk in the way of uprightness.

Implied in this whole passage is a critique of the pseudorighteous who, not content with sinning, manage to delude themselves into thinking that they are good men. Israel is saying that the first step is for them to be stirred awake sufficiently to realize that they have been guilty of self-delusion. Israel now goes on to quote a similar idea in the name of his teacher the Maggid of Meseritch. This is on the first verse of this chapter in Genesis.

I have heard a similar exposition from the mouth of our Teacher Rabbi Dov Baer of blessed memory, who said that the beginning of this portion hints at a clear rebuke to man. For man's years can be divided into three stages. First, until he reaches the age of twenty,

there are the years of growth, during which times he becomes ever stronger and more mature. Then there are the static years until he reaches the age of forty, during which he remains at the same stage. After forty it is the age of decline, when man's powers begin to wane. Hence Scripture says: "And it came to pass at the end of two full years" (Genesis 41:1), namely, the two periods of growth and stasis, when the evil inclination is in full power because then man has all his strength. But at the "end of these two full years" it should be the time for man to repent, turning aside from his evil way when he considers that he will soon be called upon to render an account of his life. However, since his way of life up to that time has become habit-forming, "Pharaoh dreamed," the evil inclination stiffens his neck and makes him dream. "And behold he stood by the river," namely, on the contrary, he is proud, saying: "Thank God that I am a scholar." That is why it says *ha-yeor* **("the river"), which should be read as:** *hey or* **("five lights"), hinting at the five illuminations of the books of the Torah. He says to himself, "Happy am I." All this is because his evil deeds have become habit-forming. But whoever has been worthy of having his eyes opened, he sees that, on the contrary, he has always been remiss in God's service. His heart is then broken and he returns unto the Lord, who will have mercy upon him.**

The Maggid of Meseritch puns on the word Pharaoh, *connecting it with the word* oref, *"neck." Pharaoh is the symbol of the stubborn evil in man, the stiff-necked refusal to acknowledge the truth. Even when the age of maturity has arrived and man should be ready to repent, the "Pharaoh" in him lets him sleep on so that he stands by the river of learning and, sinner though he really is, imagines himself to be a pious scholar. Again here we have the Ḥasidic critique of the scholars.*

II WHAT IS THE MEANING OF "THE FEAR OF GOD"?

Avodat Yisrael, Avot, 98b

Israel here comments on the passage in Ethics of the Fathers 1:3: "Let the fear of Heaven be upon you." Man's fear of God should be the fear of causing God pain, as it were.

"Let the fear of Heaven be upon you." For there are two kinds of fear: fear of punishment and fear of the Lord. An illustration can be

given of a little child into whose foot a thorn penetrates while he is running in the street, and the foot is in danger of becoming gangrenous. The child's father, realizing that the cure is to cut away a little of the flesh together with the thorn, orders the doctor to do this. The father, though he suffers terribly, hides his pain because he wishes to keep the child quiet and to assure him that all will be well. But later on, when the father sees that the child wishes once again to run about in that place, he rebukes the child by reminding him of the incident of the thorn. The child then becomes afraid and is careful that such a thing does not happen again. But if the child is clever, he is careful because he knows how much his father suffered, and it is the pain of his father that he wishes to prevent. Now when we suffer God suffers with us, as it were, but the suffering is ultimately for our good. Hence it says: "Let the fear of Heaven be upon you." This means that we should so conduct ourselves that we cause no further pain to God, as it were.

In Ḥasidism the stress in all worship is placed on lack of selfhood in the experience. The true Ḥasid knows that God suffers when man suffers, and he also knows that it is through sin that the sufferings come. He avoids sin and thus prevents the sufferings from coming, but his motive is that he knows how much God suffers when His creatures are in pain—and it is this divine suffering that he wishes to prevent.

III CAN A MAN LOSE HIMSELF IN GOD?

Avodat Yisrael, Avot, 117a

Israel comments on the saying in Ethics of the Fathers 4:8: "He who makes use of the crown shall waste away." The plain meaning is, as is clear from the context, that whoever uses the crown of the Torah for his own selfish ends will be punished in that he will "waste away." But Israel interprets the saying in mystical fashion. It is not a punishment at all but a mystical reward. It should be noted that Israel, as a kabbalist, is probably also hinting at the highest of the Sefirot, Keter *(Crown).*

"He who makes use of the crown shall waste away." Whoever occupies himself all the time by using the crown of the Creator, blessed be He, to crown Him therewith and to acknowledge Him as King

with all his might, he shall waste away. This means that his soul will become part of the crown itself, and he will waste away from this world and ascend on high.

Israel does not mean that he will die, but that he will be lost to the world. He becomes "part of the crown itself," losing himself in God. This is a further statement of the Ḥasidic doctrine of bittul ha-yesh, *"self-annihilation," losing the self in God.*

IV SELF-ANNIHILATION

Beer Moshe, Bereshit, 3a

Moses Eliakim Beriah discusses the debate between the School of Hillel and the School of Shammai in tractate Hagigah 12a. Hillel, according to the talmudic tradition, was the most modest of men. The saying of Hillel to which Moses Eliakim Beriah later alludes is in Ethics of the Fathers 1:14. It reads: "If I am not for myself, who is for me?" The first part of this saying, "If I am not for myself," reads in Hebrew: im eyn ani li. *Now* ani, *"I," is the kabbalistic name for* Malkhut, *"Sovereignty," the "I" of the universe; and the word* eyn *means "nothing." Hence the interpretation: "If I am* nothing *then 'I' is with me." Still another example of the doctrine of* bittul ha-yesh.

There is a debate in the Talmud between the School of Shammai and the School of Hillel. The Shammaites say that the heavens were created first, but the Hillelites say that the earth was created first. At first glance there is a difficulty here. The Hillelites were renowned for their meekness; the Talmud records many instances of Hillel's great humility. How, then, could the Hillelites have said that the earth was created first? They were the meek of the earth, those who consider themselves as low as the earth. How, then, could they have been guilty of what seems to be at least a modicum of pride, saying that the earth, which is their quality, was created first?

The "earth" is also the symbol of meekness. Hence the earth is the symbol of that quality the Hillelites had made their own and it does not seem a mark of humility to state that their quality takes precedence. It is rather like someone saying, See how humble I am. Moses Eliakim Beriah's answer is that by "created first" the Hillelites do not mean that their quality is more important, but they are suggesting, as he will say, a way to God's worship. They are, in fact, saying that the way to God is for man to reflect on his own unworthiness, and this is, indeed, what we would expect of humble men.

It seems to me that the difficulty is to be resolved as follows: It is well known and it is recorded in the holy books, especially in the work *Noam Elimelekh*, that it is a great principle of worship and an important rule to hold fast to two ideas. The first is the exaltedness of God, blessed be He, i.e., a man should contemplate on this theme continually. The second is that he should contemplate his own unworthiness. I have been taught this by my teachers, especially by our lord, master, and chief teacher Rabbi Meshullam Susya of blessed memory. He taught me the way of the Lord in these words, "My son! As soon as you arise from sleep in the morning take the holy *tzitzit* ("fringes") in your hand and set your heart and mind to contemplate the exaltedness and majesty of the Creator, blessed be He, and fear Him because of the great dread and awe He inspires. This is true fear, the fear that stems from contemplation of His exaltedness, not the fear that is simply a habit."

The Noam Elimelekh *is the work by Elimelech of Lizensk. Meshullam Susya, of Anipol, is the brother of Elimelech. True fear of God is not fear of God's wrath, but the awe and dread which stem from profound contemplation on God's majesty. As the author goes on to say, this is called "the heavens" because it involves reflection on God as exalted above the heavens, while reflection on one's own unworthiness is called "the earth." Thus the Shammaites are said to give preference to contemplation of God's majesty, while the Hillelites give preference to contemplation of man's unworthiness.*

This was the stage of the School of Shammai. The Shammaites used to contemplate constantly the majesty and exaltedness of the Creator, blessed be He; hence they held that the heavens were created first. They mean, this stage was created first and this is the main principle, that man should always gaze heavenward and above the heavens, thinking always of the exaltedness and majesty of His essential and limitless divinity, blessed be He. But the School of Hillel had a different approach. The Hillelites preferred rather to reflect on their own unworthiness. Hillel himself said: *im eyn ani li*, that

is to say, "If *eyn*," hinting at the quality of *nothingness*, as if to say: "If I am humble and lowly to the uttermost degree so that I am completely nothing and a totally negative quality," then *ani li*, "the Kingdom of Heaven, called *I*, is revealed to me." That is why the Hillelites said that the earth was created first, namely, the quality of humility and such lowliness that it is as the very earth, this was created first. This means, the main thing is for man to reflect as soon as he wakes up on his own unworthiness, that none is as inferior as he.

Once again we have the basic Ḥasidic idea of shiflut, *"lowliness," "humility." This constant emphasis on humility may seem strange to us who see most of the Ḥasidim as abjectly poor and deprived of almost every creature comfort. Of what could they be proud? They did possess treasures of the spirit, a keen appreciation of scholarship, and as in all societies, an order within their own society of the privileged and those who had to look up to them. It is to the privileged that these admonitions were addressed.*

CHAPTER 18

Jacob Isaac, the "Seer" of Lublin

1745-1815

For the sake of Heaven
A critique of spiritual aristocracy
Rules for saints

Jacob Isaac was a disciple of the Maggid of Meseritch, Levi Yitzḥak of Berditchev, and especially Elimelech of Lizensk. There are a number of Ḥasidic tales which tell of his quarrel with Elimelech and his setting himself up as a Ḥasidic master in the lifetime of his teacher, though, as is generally the case in such matters, it is hard to disentangle fact from legend. Jacob Isaac conducted himself first as a Ḥasidic master in Lancut in Poland and later in the town of Lublin. It was believed that he was clairvoyant and was able to tell a man's character merely by looking at his face—hence the name, given to him after his death, of Ḥozeh *("Seer"). The Ḥasidim refer to Jacob Isaac either simply as "the* Chozeh*" or as "the Lubliner* Chozeh*."*

The "Seer's" teachings are found in three works, although there are some considerable doubts as to how these were compiled. These are: Zot Zikkaron *(This is the Rememberance) (Warsaw, 1883);* Zikkaron Zot *(The Rememberance is This) (Warsaw, 1883);* Divrey Emet *(Words of Truth) (Lemberg, 1884). These three works were published in subsequent editions in a single volume with the title* Sheloshah Sefarim Niftaḥim *(Three Books are Opened). The edition used here is that of Germany (no place name), 1947.*

I FOR THE SAKE OF HEAVEN

Zikkaron Zot, Mishpatim, 55–56

"The choicest first fruits of thy land shalt thou bring into the house of the Lord thy God. Thou shalt not seethe a kid in its mother's milk" (Exodus 23:19). So far as I remember, the work *Shevet Musar* **advises a man before carrying out any worldly matters, before eating and drinking, to say, with open mouth, for example: "I am about to eat so that I shall have strength to do the will of God and in order to obey His command to me to look after my health and to eat and be satisfied." And so he should do in connection with all physical things, as it is said in the work** *Ḥovot Ha-Levavot*. **And so, too, when he journeys forth to sell his wares he should say, with open mouth, "I am about to journey forth to sell my wares so that I should have money for the purpose of honoring God, to pay the fees of those who teach my sons so that my sons will grow up to be scholars who busy themselves in the Torah and the** *mitzvot* **for the sake of Heaven, and so that I shall be able to marry off my daughters to scholars, and so that I shall be able to honor the Sabbath and give charity and tithes." In this way a man binds his occupations to God, blessed be He. Even though, afterward, he experiences physical pleasure, the latter is only in his mind, whereas the main intention was both in the mind and in speech, and everything, depends on the way in which it began. The result of it will be that he will be helped inasmuch as his motive is for the sake of Heaven, and his conduct will not prevent his attachment** (*devekut*) **to God, blessed be He.**

The Shevet Musar *is a moralistic work by Elijah ben Solomon of Smyrna (d. 1729). The* Ḥovot Ha-Levavot *(Duties of the Heart) is by Baḥya ibn Pakudah (see Volume 2 in this series). The "Seer" quotes the practice of reciting, before carrying out any worldly task, a formula stating that it is done for the sake of Heaven, not for man's own selfish pleasure. The "Seer" is, however, sufficiently realistic to appreciate that when a man actually engages in worldly things it is very difficult for him to keep his mind only on God and not to enjoy the pleasure. So be it, says the "Seer," but the fact that he had made the declaration at the beginning and made it, moreover, "with full mouth," i.e., uttering it clearly, will help him to maintain his attachment to God. The reasoning is that the initial utterance was a thought and an utterance, i.e., he not only thought so but gave expression to his intention verbally, and this is sufficiently strong to weaken any later intention, in thought alone, to enjoy worldly things for their own sake. The word for "choicest" in the verse,* reshit, *means "the first," and the word translated as "first fruits," is in Hebrew* bikkurey, *which the "Seer" understands as "coming to fruition,"* i.e., *by giving verbal expression to it. Hence, as he goes on to say, the meaning of the verse is: "The beginning in thought and its bringing the thought into fruition by speech will result in your bringing the land—the worldly aspects of your life—to the House of the Lord your God."*

Thus we can explain the verse: "The beginning of the fruition of your land," the "beginning" referring to the thought and the "fruition" to its verbal utterance, will cause you to bring "your land," denoting your worldly interests, to the House of the Lord your God. However, a man should not rely on this principle so far as his studies of the Torah and his prayers are concerned. Here he should have fear and love of God even at the time when he is actually engaged in the task.

The "Seer" has said that it is enough for a man to have the intention of doing it for the sake of Heaven at the beginning. Now the Ḥasidim followed some of the kabbalists in reciting a special formula before carrying out any religious duty. This was: "For the sake of the unification of the Holy One, blessed be He, and His Shekhinah,*" known as* le-shem yiḥud *("For the sake of the unification"). It might have been argued that this suffices as a similar formula does in connection with worldly things. No, says the "Seer"; with regard to religious duties a man must not be content with the formula he has recited, but even during the act itself he should have God in mind.*

Now the thought that a man has to do something in a particular way is called the mother and the root of conduct. If a man relies on the intention he had from the beginning also in connection with the Torah and prayer, relying on the fact that he had this thought and had said *le-shem yiḥud*, this would be held by him to have completed the matter. Now completion is called "seething," as when we say that fruit is ripe [has been cooked, is completed]. Therefore,

the verse continues: "Thou shalt not seethe a kid." The word *gedi* **("kid") is from** *haggadah* **and it means "to tell," referring to the** *telling* **of the thing at the beginning, whether that he wishes to study the Torah or that he wishes to offer his prayers. "Do not complete it through the milk of his mother," i.e., do not be satisfied that you have completed the matter by having it in the milk of the mother, namely, the root idea, in that you thought and expressed it verbally that you do it with this intention. "Milk" means here "the best" and this is an obvious meaning of the word. Do not do this, but even during the act itself also have your thoughts on Heaven and do it in fear and love. The illustration is of infant who has been weaned and who no longer requires his mother's milk but can eat for himself.**

The style of the book is deplorable; mixed with Yiddishisms, it is sometimes difficult to know precisely what the "Seer" means to say. Here he seems to understand the verse, in, of course, a highly artificial manner, as, "Do not imagine that you have seethed the kid by having the milk of its mother," i.e., wean yourself from the original intention and do the act itself for the sake of Heaven.

II A CRITIQUE OF SPIRITUAL ARISTOCRACY

Zot Zikkaron, p. 15

"And Koraḥ took, the son of Izhar" (Numbers 16:1). *Koraḥ* **is from** *koreaḥ*, **"bald." One who is bald, who has no good qualities, thinks of his aristocratic father. Koraḥ took the fact that he was the son of Izhar. (Hence, he should have said also "the son of Jacob," for no doubt he thought of this as well.) And Dathan and Abiram took to their mind that they were the sons of Eliab and On remembered he was the son of Peleth, and they realized that they were the sons of Reuben, who was the first-born. And they arose before Moses and Aaron of whom no descent is mentioned.**

The verse says that Koraḥ son of Izhar took, but does not describe what he took; hence most translators supply the words "men," i.e., he took men. Among the other conspirators were Dathan and Abiram the sons of Eliab and On son of Peleth, all of whom were the sons of Reuben. The "Seer" says that Koraḥ took the fact that he was the "son of Izhar." The Rabbis say that he should have traced back his descent to Jacob but did not do so because Jacob, having foreseen the rebellion of Koraḥ, prayed that he should not be mentioned. Yes, says the "Seer," Koraḥ would naturally have traced his descent to the even more aristocratic Jacob. Reuben, too, was a great aristocrat, because he was the first-born son of Jacob. There is a pun of the name Koraḥ, connecting it with the term for "baldness," i.e., one who is bald, who has none of the hair of the mitzvot, *who is shorn of good deeds. So the man without good deeds prides himself on his noble birth, but the truly righteous, like Moses and Aaron, are content to be themselves and have no need to boast of their genealogy. There can be little doubt that we have here a critique of the Ḥasidic masters who claimed descent from the great zaddikim of the past. An important element in Ḥasidic self-criticism is the scorn generally poured on the* eynikel, *the "grandson," the man who is not much in himself, but claims respect because he is the descendant of a famous Ḥasidic master. The critique is interesting because Ḥasidism does, in fact, normally believe that the sons and grandsons of a zaddik are also likely to be holy men because the zaddik at the moment of conception had holy thoughts and was thus able to bring down an especially lofty soul from Heaven.*

III RULES FOR SAINTS

Divrey Emet, Hanhagaot, nos. 56–63, pp. 7–8

At the beginning of the work Divrey Emet *there is a long list of pious practices which the "Seer" is said to have recorded for his own guidance and which the editor says he has copied from the "Seer's" own autograph copy. The following are numbers 56 to 63.*

I have made up my mind not to think any longer of what people think of me. If the thought happens to enter my mind, I must remember that it makes no difference.

Similarly, I must not be concerned about whether I tell them any new ideas I have in a sweet manner or in an ordinary manner. As long as they are for God, what difference does it make? Whenever these things are said I must always remember that it makes no difference whether it is this way or the other.

I must be careful never to think about money.

I must never want anything from this world, only for the Lord, blessed be He, alone.

I must remember never to forget God.

And never to be wild.

And to prevail over the evil inclination for the sake of the glory of Heaven.

And to be very careful not to reveal that which resembles prophecy and, if it becomes necessary, to do it with great circumspection with the help of God.

I must always recall the meaning of the verse: "Take heed to thyself that thou offer not thy burnt offerings in every place that thou seest" (Deuteronomy 12:13).

We observe here the inner struggles of the "Seer," tempted to take into consideration the attitudes toward him of his followers. He evidently believed, as it seems from the penultimate lines, that he was gifted with some degree of prophecy, but was obliged to keep this to himself. The meaning of the last paragraph is probably that his enthusiasm should be exercised in a circumspect manner, not being "offered in every place."

CHAPTER 19

Meshullam Feibush Heller of Zbarazh d. 1795

How should man worship God?
How can man be humble?

Meshullam Feibush Heller of Zbarazh was a disciple of the Maggid of Meseritch and of the famous Ḥasidic leader Jeḥiel Michel of Zlotchov (d. 1786). The latter knew the Baal Shem Tov in his youth and later became a member of the circle of the Meseritcher Maggid, but generally pursued a Ḥasidic line of his own. There are no works from his pen, but many of his teachings are found in the works of his disciples. Meshullam Feibush is called by the Ḥasidim "Reb Feivish Zbarazher." He was a skilful author, though he wrote very little.

Meshullam Feibush's main work is the little book Derekh Emet *(The Way of Truth), a defense of the Ḥasidic approach. The work was first published in Tchernowitz in 1855. (The edition used here has no place and no date.)*

I HOW SHOULD MAN WORSHIP GOD?

Derekh Emet, pp. 51–52

Meshullam Feibush is writing to his former friend, advising him how to worship God. In this passage he considers the question of fasting.

In the matter of fasting, there is no doubt that for our sins we are obliged to engage in numerous fasts as it is stated in all the moralistic

works and especially in the work *Reshit Ḥokhmah, Beginning of Wisdom*, for who is innocent of youthful sins? But the truth is that people only carry out the *mitzvot* as commands learned by rote. They judge everything by appearance, not as it is in truth when the heart discerns. They do everything like a lifeless lump of clay without any understanding. They imagine that they pray and study the Torah. But in reality the Shulḥan Arukh in section 98 and elsewhere explains how prayer should really be offered properly. And with regard to the study of the Torah there are many rules by which the Torah is acquired. . . . So that, in reality, they do not really pray at all, they only repeat words learned by rote at the commands of their teachers. And so it is with regard to their fasting. They do not scrutinize their deeds at all, and even on the day they fast they "exact all their labors." As Scripture says: "Behold, ye fast for strife and contention" (Isaiah 58:3, 4), for on a fast day they become irritable and then are guilty of many sins such as bad temper, slander, etc. Yet they still imagine that they fast and they take pride in it and believe that all their sins have been forgiven. But the truth is otherwise, for the main thing in fasting is for the heart to be broken, for man's heart becomes puffed up through eating and drinking, and it is humbled through fasting. The word *ani* ("poor") is made up of letters which are found in the word *taanit* (a "fast") as the *Reshit Ḥokhmah* states. And then the heart can experience great remorse for sin and this is the main aim of repentance, as the *Gates of Repentance* by Rabbenu Jonah states. Without it a fast is worth nothing. Even if a man guards himself from sin during the whole day of the fast and studies all day, yet it is nothing without repentance, which involves careful scrutiny of one's deeds and great remorse. How much less it is worth if on the day of the fast, God forbid, he commits a sin, however slight.

The Reshit Ḥokhmah *is the moralistic work by the sixteenth-century teacher of Safed, Elijah de Vidas. Rabbenu Jonah is Jonah Gerondi (d. 1263), author of the treatise on repentance* Shaarey Teshuvah *(Gates of Repentance). The Hebrew word* taanit, *a "fast," contains the letters* ayin, nun, yod, *forming the word* ani, *"a poor man." A poor man is brokenhearted because he has nothing to eat. The purpose of fasting is to make a man humble and aware of his sins. Here we have a typical Ḥasidic critique of soulless religion. The Ḥasidim were ever critical of mere outward behavior which led people to believe that they were excessively pious when, in reality, it was all a kind of behaviorism. The word it reminds us of is* golem, *translated as "lifeless lump of clay," a figure created from clay into which life has been infused by magic, but which carries out everything automatically without any mind in it. If it were not anachronistic, we should translate it as "robot." The criticism is of "robotlike" religious observances.*

But since the Holy One, blessed be He, is so merciful and since there is no limit to His power and since He demands from man only that which man can do, it is possible that the Holy One, blessed be He, does accept the fasting of some of these men who fast in an unsophisticated way, even though they are insufficiently intelligent to carry out the fast as it should be carried out so as to be acceptable to God. As for men like us, however, who do know the truth, if we do not fast in a manner acceptable to God there is no doubt that He will not accept such a fast and it is as if the dogs had devoured it. Such a fast goes to waste, God forbid, to the *kelipot*, **called "waste." And this is a total loss in many ways. The body loses since people in this generation are so weak, and the soul loses, for the faster loses his humility since he imagines that by fasting he has repaid his debt. In reality he has added to his transgression and prides himself to no avail. Now if you are able to fast one day a week and your soul desires it, then do it. But this is only helpful if you do as follows: Leave all your activities on that day and scrutinize your deeds in private. God forbid, do not think that by doing so you have paid your debt, but trust in the Lord who lets off those who sincerely repent, according to Rabbenu Jonah's description of the various types of repentance. If you desire to do more than this, do it, but take care that the defect does not outweigh the advantage. It seems to me, insofar as I have undersood the opinions of the holy men on earth I have mentioned, that in this generation where there is so much weakness, if we fast we cannot pray or study properly. It is therefore undoubtedly better to leave off fasting, but instead to achieve whatever fasting is supposed to achieve without fasting.**

On the whole the Ḥasidic masters were opposed to self-mortification and prolonged fasting. The "holy men" referred to are the Baal Shem Tov, the Maggid of Meseritch, an early Ḥasidic leader called Menaḥem

Mendel of Przemyslani, and Jeḥiel Michel of Zlotchov, to whom Meshullam Feibush refers at the beginning of the book.

As for what fasting should achieve, the following are its desired effects: (1) There must be remorse, as above; (2) breaking the heart and the bodily energy which derives from the "Other Side"; (3) breaking desire; (4) humility; (5) an increase of bodily heat, as it is said, "Everything that may abide the fire, ye shall make go through the fire, and it shall be clean" (Numbers 31:23), as the *Reshit Ḥokhmah* **states, and there are other things, too. But you can achieve all these things if you can compel your heart and the faculties of your body to offer your prayers with pure intention, which, as it is stated in the prayerbook** *Shaarey Shamayyim*, **is called** *service*. **For it involves great** *service* **to compel thought, busily occupied in worldly matters, to concentrate on the meaning of the words of the prayers. For this great strength is required, and this undoubtedly weakens all the limbs of the body. So if God helps you to pray occasionally with proper concentration you will undoubtedly feel remorse for your sins, your body will be broken, your desire humbled, and the burning flame that seizes hold of the heart in prayer purifies instead of the fire of fasting.**

The prayer book Shaarey Shamayyim *was compiled by the seventeenth-century kabbalist Isaiah Horowitz. Meshullam Feibush is saying that all the desirable effects of fasting can be achieved through proper prayer. Note the typical Ḥasidic emphasis on* hitlahavut, *"burning enthusiasm" in prayer. Fasting heats the body and this was said to purify the soul as fire purifies. But Meshullam Feibush argues that as a substitute one can rely on the purifying fire of prayer.*

The truth is found in some new manuscripts I possess from Rabbi Rebbe Baer of blessed memory. There it is stated that a sign of prayer being acceptable in some way to God is whether it produces humility. That is to say, if the heart is still humble after prayer, this is called its effect, that is to say, where there is humility and meekness. But if not, God forbid, it is certainly unacceptable. Perhaps once in our lives we may merit this. It is stated there, too, that the Baal Shem Tov said that he became worthy of all the high degrees to which he attained only because of his regular immersions in the *mikveh*. **In**

truth this is a very great thing, for the *mikveh* purifies both body and soul. But it all has to be done with intention, not, God forbid, as the commands of men learned by rote, for then, God forbid, it is worth nothing. It is necessary first to pull one's self together and to have proper intention.

Immersion in the mikveh, *the specially prepared ritual bath, occupies an important role in all versions of Ḥasidism. But even here Meshullam Feibush is at pains to point out that it must be done with proper intention, not in a mechanical way.*

II HOW CAN MAN BE HUMBLE?

Derekh Emet, p. 54

Meshullam Feibush here advises his friend on the importance of humility. David of Mikulov is mentioned here and elsewhere as a member of the Baal Shem Tov's circle. The reference to ḥutzpah, effrontery, increasing at the times of the "heels of the Messiah," is found at the end of tractate Sotah in the Talmud. As mentioned earlier, the kabbalistic interpretation of the "heels" is that we are now at the lowliest stage of soul, on the analogy of the human body, whereas in former ages the "head" aspect was prominent.

Although one can speak of every kind of lust, envy, and evil character trait, the main thing one has to discuss constantly and always be terrified of, if one wishes to serve God in truth, is pride. The truth is that I heard this from a certain venerable old man, his appearance like that of an angel of God, a chief disciple of the Baal Shem Tov, David of Mikulov by name, with whom I stayed when I lived in my father-in-law's house in Tcharni in Austria. He said that in these generations the *kelipah* of pride is exceedingly powerful, as the Talmud says: In the times of the heels of the Messiah, effrontery is abroad. The reason for it is that now the generations are lowly and are exceedingly remote from the root, just as the heel is far from the head, hence pride exercises its power over them. For this is the sign, the more a man is unworthy the prouder he is, as people say. This pride stems from a lack of understanding and of shame before God who fills all worlds. The more a man is remote from Him through his sins and transgressions, the more brazen-faced and proud he is.

Again, a Ḥasidic teaching about the great importance of humility. Pride is caused by lack of appreciation of the majesty of God. The nearer a man is to God the less pride will he experience. This should be compared with the letter of Shneur Zalman of Liady (Chapter 16).

Whoever wishes to draw near to God has to be most careful in this matter. Even though he does hate pride, yet this is a thing that is in the heart. The heart turns to lust for praise and to hate if it is disparaged. No one in this generation is free from this at all, not even the great zaddikim, with the exception of the chosen few, the men of high stage who were worthy of receiving the teaching from the Baal Shem Tov himself of blessed memory and from his disciples whom they follow. But for our sins all others are caught in this trap, as we observe all the quarrels and envy in this generation. May God have mercy on us. It is essential to entreat God to help us to achieve this, especially when reciting the prayer: "O my God, keep my soul from evil." When we come to the words in that prayer: "and let my soul be as dust to all," then one must entreat God to help one to attain humility, as the *Reshit Ḥokhmah* **says: Consult that work.**

Note the remark about loving praise and hating disparagement. The Baal Shem Tov, following a remark of the author of Duties of the Heart, *is reported to have said that a man cannot really serve God until he becomes totally indifferent to whether men praise him or whether they disparage him. Meshullam Feibush is only too aware of how far his contemporaries had fallen short of this. By his day, evidently, the rivalry among the zaddikim, that eventually became one of the most unfortunate aspects of Ḥasidic life, was already a social evil.*

CHAPTER 20

Ḥayyim Ḥaikel of Amdur d. 1787

How can man love God?
How can man overcome his ego?
How can man provide a home for God?
A critique of Ḥasidic frivolity

Ḥayyim Ḥaikel of Amdur was one of the most prominent members of the circle of the Meseritcher Maggid. After the death of the Maggid, Ḥayyim Ḥaikel became a Ḥasidic master in the Lithuanian town of Amdur near Grodno. Since Lithuania was the great stronghold of the Mitnaggedim, the opponents of the Ḥasidim, Ḥayyim Ḥaikel had to bear the brunt of the conflict. Ḥayyim Ḥaikel's followers engaged in propaganda for the new movement, encouraging young men to leave their families in order to stay, for a time at least, in the zaddik's "court." There are reliable reports about the peculiar behavior of the Ḥasidim of Amdur who, during their prayers, would turn somersaults, the purpose being to symbolize complete self-abandonment. Ḥayyim Ḥaikel is, in fact, an extreme exponent of the Ḥasidic doctrine of bittul ha-yesh, *"annihilation of the self." As will be seen from the following extracts from his book, the idea of man coming near to God through a loss of selfhood is the main thrust of Ḥayyim Ḥaikel's thought.*

Ḥayyim Ḥaikel's book on Ḥasidic doctrine Ḥayyim Va-Ḥesed (Life and Lovingkindness) *was first published by his grandson Bezalel Lewin in*

Warsaw in 1891. (The edition used here is the photocopy of the Warsaw edition; Jerusalem, 1970).

I HOW CAN MAN LOVE GOD?

Ḥayyim Va-Ḥesed, p. 10

God, blessed be He, created day and night. When God is illumined in the world it is called "day." But He also created night, for without the existence of night the value of daylight would not be fully appreciated. That is why the verse says: "Light excelleth from darkness" (Ecclesiastes 2:13). Now in man, too there is day and night. The love of God is called "day" because it comes through clarity of intellect, but the fear of God is called "night," when man serves the Creator simply because he believes in Him and because it has so been ordained. But when man serves God in fear, God gives him the merit of attaining the stage of love. Consequently, when David was in the stage of fear he said: "At midnight I will rise to give thanks unto Thee" (Psalms 119:62), which, say the Rabbis (Berakhot 3b), means that he sang songs and praises until daybreak. And this is also why David said: "O how I love Thy law! It is my meditation all the day" (Psalms 119:97), "all the day" referring to the day together with the night.

Ḥayyim Ḥaikel interprets the verse in Ecclesiastes to mean that we can only really appreciate the light from *the darkness, i.e., from observing the darkness and comparing the light to it. The Hebrew allows this interpretation. For Ḥayyim Ḥaikel the love of God is a mystical experience, when all is as clear as day, when the mind soars aloft. This stage is infrequent. At times of dryness of soul man must simply persevere in his faith, and even though he experiences nothing of the nearness of God he continues to engage in acts of worship because such is demanded of him. This stage is known as "night" because there is no illumination of soul. But this stage also has its uses, since it is only by comparison that the full beauty of the "day" stage is appreciated. When David was in the darkest stage, that of "midnight," he perservered and sang the praises of God until God allowed him to see "daybreak" and worship Him in love. Hence David's meditation was "all the day," which includes the "night." We have noted earlier the mystical "dark night of the soul."*

II HOW CAN MAN OVERCOME HIS EGO?

Ḥayyim Va-Ḥesed, p. 22

Man should long for the Creator, serving Him with more and more self-sacrifice every day and even every hour of the day. He should proceed even to the state of total self-abandon, forgetting his bodily needs entirely and having no ulterior motive, praying to God only to be given a pure heart.

Again, here is the doctrine of complete loss of selfhood. Man does not even pray to God to satisfy his needs, and he has no other motive in praying than to request God to endow him with a pure heart, i.e., a heart untainted by thoughts of self.

III HOW CAN MAN PROVIDE A HOME FOR GOD?

Ḥayyim Va-Ḥesed, p. 139

As long as man is attached to the body, the Holy One, blessed be He, cannot make His *Shekhinah* rest upon him. However, in reality, the body, too, is a home for the Holy One, blessed be He, only since the body is so corporeal the Holy One, blessed be He, cannot rest upon him. This is the meaning of the verse: "Until I find a place for the Lord" (Psalms 132:5). The Holy One, blessed be He, cannot rest there until he "finds a place for the Lord," namely, he should burn out the evil that is in him and then the Holy One, blessed be He, can rest upon him.

This reminds us of a famous Ḥasidic tale of two little boys who later became Ḥasidic masters. Their teachers asked them: "Where does God live?" One replied, "Where does He not live?" The other replied, "He lives wherever He is allowed to enter."

IV A CRITIQUE OF ḤASIDIC FRIVOLITY

Ḥayyim Va-Ḥesed, pp. 154–55

This is a letter Ḥayyim Ḥaikel wrote to his son Samuel, who eventually succeeded him as the zaddik of Amdur. The letter criticizes the Ḥasidim for paying too much attention to the Ḥasidic tradition and insufficient attention to spontaneity in religion, and it also criticizes those who indulge in frivolous pranks in order, as they claim, to promote the spirit of joy upon which Ḥasidism places great stress. In fact, there is reliable evidence that this kind of behavior was not unknown in the "court" of Ḥayyim Ḥaikel himself, and perhaps he is warning his son here to oppose the practice.

My dearly beloved son whom I love as much as myself. How much do I desire to persuade you to allow your intellect to be uppermost in all that you do. Be not like those notorious idiots who have chosen for themselves a new way, making themselves happy by frivolous means and declaring that they are sages and Ḥasidim. Of them Scripture declares: "Seest thou a man wise in his own eyes? There is more hope of a fool than of him" (Proverbs 26:12). Rather see to it that in all your worship your motive should be to draw near to God, blessed be He. His fear will undoubtedly be before you, etc. This is the aim of all the precepts of our holy Torah and it is obviously so. For our Creator only asks us to fear Him. Had He required many other things of us it is obvious that these would have been stated in His Torah, the Torah of truth. It is also well known that the end is always the beginning and it is said, "The end of the matter, all having been heard: fear God" (Ecclesiastes 12:13), and from this end one must proceed to the beginning. Hence Scripture says: "David came to the head of the ascent" (2 Samuel 15:32). And this is sufficient for him who understands.

The "head" of the ascent is rosh, *which can also mean "the beginning." Since the "end" of the Torah is that man should fear God, man should have this intention in mind when he "begins" to carry out a good deed.*

And be not like those idiots who do it all simply because their fathers did so, for this brings many accusers to man for it is a great contraction [*tzimtzum*]. And this is sufficient for him who understands.

To follow simply the way of the fathers is to invite unfavorable comparison with their piety and, in addition, it results in lack of spontaneity, in "contraction" and narrowness of vision.

Rather, it is essential when performing every precept to draw near to Him, in nearness of heart by keeping remote from materialism, and through this all judgment is overcome. This is the meaning of the rabbinic saying (Genesis Rabbah 33:3) that the zaddikim convert the

quality of judgment into the quality of mercy. And this is the meaning of the passage in Ethics of the Fathers (Avot 5:14) that one who goes to the House of Learning but does not do anything has only the reward for going there. This refers to one who only has the intention of going there, but not of drawing near to God. Consequently, he does not "do anything," that is to say, he does not bring about that evil is converted into good, the quality of mercy.

The plain meaning of the passage in Ethics of the Fathers is that one who goes to the House of Learning but does not do anything, *i.e., does not study when he arrives there, has only the reward for going there, not for studying. But Ḥayyim Ḥaikel here understands it to mean that he does study, but only has in mind the actual performance of the religious act, not the means it affords him of drawing near to God. He therefore does not* do anything, *i.e., he fails to achieve the aim of converting evil into good. So far as his personal character is concerned nothing has changed and he is as remote as ever from God. We have here one of the basic issues between the Ḥasidim and the Mitnaggedim. For the latter the deed itself is what God requires. For the Ḥasidim the deed is indeed important, but only because it is the means by which he can come near to God.*

I will give you counsel, my son, and God will be with you. See to it that whenever you carry out a good deed you proceed from deed to speech [i.e., stating verbally that this is the intention] and from speech to thought and there be alone with your Maker as if you had already departed from this world, no one being left but you and the Creator, blessed be He. Then a great fear will fall upon you at first, and resulting from that fear great rapture will come to you so that you will be completely unconscious of whether or not other human beings are with you. Then you will proceed in confidence. No evil, only good, will dwell with you and mercy shall encompass you about. I beg you to reflect on these few words of mine which you will see may be small in quantity, but are great in quality, and your thirst will be slaked. Also see to it that when you do anything pertaining to the world of time you attach this, too, to God, blessed be He. For we have come into this world for no other purpose than to sift the good from evil, the good being the king's daughter and the evil the garment. The Creator, blessed be He, has sent us here to take out

the good from the garment. We, God's people, are called "the good," for it is said, "Say ye of the righteous, that it shall be well with him" (Isaiah 3:10), and it says: "Thy people, all of them, are righteous" (Isaiah 60:21). Good attaches itself to good and our Creator, blessed be He, is All-Good. So good is attached to good and all becomes one in simple unity, and this, too, is called converting the quality of judgment into the quality of mercy. And this is the meaning of the verse: "Kings' daughters are among thy favorites; at thy right hand shall stand the queen" (Psalms 45:10). And this is sufficient for him who understands.

Ḥayyim Ḥaikel's interpretation of the last verse he quotes seems to be that the "kings' daughters" is the good, as above. The good should be man's "favorite." He should not think of the garment but of the princess herself. The "right hand" is the symbol of the quality of mercy.

CHAPTER 21

Ḥayyim Tyrer of Tchernowitz

d. 1816

The holiest hour of the Sabbath
Why is prayer called "the service of the heart"?
Gazing into Heaven
The dedication of a new house

Ḥayyim Tyrer was a disciple of Jeḥiel Michel of Zlotchov and a colleague of Meshullam Feibush of Zbarazh. His magnum opus, Beer Mayyim Ḥayyim, *has long been one of the most popular of Ḥasidic books, and Ḥayyim is generally called by the Ḥasidim after it, "the* Beer Mayyim Ḥayyim.*" Ḥayyim was a distinguished talmudist and kabbalist. He occupied rabbinic positions in Mohilev, Kishinev, and Tchernowitz. In the year 1813 he went to Israel, settling in Safed and dying there, and his grave can still be seen.*

Ḥayyim's main works are Sidduro Shel Shabbat *(The Order of the Sabbath), first published in Mohilev in 1813 (edition used here; Lemberg, 1860);* Shaar Ha-Tefillah *(The Gate of Prayer) first published in Sudlikov in 1820 (edition used here; Jerusalem, 1969); and* Beer Mayyim Ḥayyim *(Well of Living Waters) first published in Sudlikov in 1820 and later, a sure sign of its popularity, together with the pentateuchal text in Tchernowitz in 1849 (edition used here; Warsaw, 1901). The* Sidduro Shel Shabbat *is a lengthy account of the mystical ideas behind the institution of the Sabbath. Ḥayyim always stresses the great importance of the Sabbath. Ḥasidic legend tells how Ḥayyim would grow physically a head taller on this holy day. The* Shaar Ha-Tefillah *is a study of mystical prayer in all its ramifications. The* Beer Mayyim Ḥayyim *is a running commentary to the Torah,* sidra *by* sidra.

I THE HOLIEST HOUR OF THE SABBATH

Sidduro Shel Shabbat, Shoresh 9:1–2, p. 49b

Ḥayyim describes the time of the Afternoon Prayer—Minḥah—*of the Sabbath as the most sacred time of the whole sacred day. It is then that the sanctity of the Sabbath reaches its culmination, when, in the words of Ḥayyim, the crown is placed on the head of the King. So awesome is that hour that man is afraid to speak. Hence, says Ḥayyim, the Afternoon Prayer is shorter than the other prayers of the day. The Ḥasidim attach great importance to this part of the day. It is the time when they come together to hear the discourse of the zaddik.*

The illustration can be given of a king who gave one of his servants the honor of placing the royal crown on the king's head. If that man is wise enough he appreciates the great and awesome act he has been commanded. Before he even touches the crown he washes his hands thoroughly and then wraps them in a clean, spotlessly white, silken cloth. In addition to all this, when he actually comes before the king to place the crown on his head all his limbs tremble and his whole being shudders at the awesome thought of drawing near to the king. When he comes to place the crown on the head of the king, so great is his trembling, dread, and fear that he finds himself unable to place the crown properly on the king's head. But when the good king notices that, because of his great apprehension, the servant has no spirit left in him and is incapable of performing his task, the king himself helps the servant to place the crown on his head. In fact, the king does practically everything himself. I heard a similar idea from the mouth of my master and teacher, the Holy Rabbi, the Candelabrum of Light, the Man of God, the Holy Diadem, Rabbi Jeḥiel Michel of blessed memory, the Maggid of Zlotchov. He commented thus on the verse: "Thou hast dealt well with Thy servant" (Psalms 119:65) and explained it by means of the talmudic saying (Kiddushin 30b) that if God did not help man, he could never overcome his evil inclination. It follows that all the good deeds per-

formed by man are done far more with God's help than by man's own efforts. Therefore, the verse says: "Thou hast dealt well," namely, all the good that is done Thou hast done; only it is "with Thy servant" in that I, Thy servant, am associated with Thee."

The Maggid of Zlotchov gives an unusual turn to the verse (which really means, of course, that God does well to His servant). The new meaning is that man of himself could never do good unless God helped him, so that it all really is God's doing, only He associates man with it. This is like the man who is too terrified to place the crown on the king's head but is helped by the king. As Ḥayyim goes on to say, at the time of the Afternoon Prayer man would be too terrified to speak at all but God helps him.

How much more in every way now at the time of *Minḥah*, when we stand in a most exalted and awesome place, to crown, as it were, the King of the kings of kings, blessed be He, with the great crowns of the prayer and the *Kedushah*, would we be quite incapable of uttering a single word, so great is our dread, were it not that help comes from the Lord and it is marvelous in our eyes?

Ḥayyim goes on to say that the only praise we can utter at this awesome hour is that we cannot praise and we are obliged to remain lost in silent adoration; hence the Afternoon Prayer is so short.

II WHY IS PRAYER CALLED "THE SERVICE OF THE HEART"?

Shaar Ha-Tefillah, Shaar 8, pp. 109c–110a

This is the parable I heard from the holy mouth of the Great and Holy Gaon, Mighty and Exalted Candelabrum of Light, Head of all the Sons of Exile, our Teacher Rabbi Levi Yitzḥak of blessed memory, may his merits be a shield to us, the Head of the Court of Berditchev. He asked why prayer is called "service of the heart." Prayer is surely like other forms of worship such as reciting the Shema, studying the Torah, and so forth. These are never called "service of the heart," so why should prayer be singled out as such? He gave a wondrous explanation by way of a parable. A king set two of his servants to work. To one of them the king gave wonderful precious stones of the highest value, ordering him to cut them and so make them ready to be used in decorating objects belonging to the king. The other servant

was set to work in the royal park and was ordered to clear it of the stones and rubble found there so that it would become clean and tidy as befits a royal park. The king stated that each of these two workers could keep any of the waste products, this one the stones and rubble he removes, the other one the chips from the precious stones he had cut. This wise king is able to discern whether the two men carry out their task lovingly, joyfully, and willingly or whether it is all a burden to them, and his payment of their wages will depend on the quality of their work.

Now from the physical point of view the task of the man who has to clear the rubble is much harder than that of his colleague who has the easy work of cutting the precious stones. But so far as the demands made on the heart are concerned, namely, that each of them is expected to have the sincere motive of doing whatever he does solely because of his love for the king, not for what he will get out of it, the task of the diamond cutter is far more difficult. Since this man knows that the valuable waste products will belong to him, it is very hard, indeed, for him to work solely out of his love for the king. The riches that will be his are very great, his heart covets and desires them. He must set his heart on fire with a most powerful and faithful love, his love for the king burning so strongly in his heart, as with flaming torches, that all the riches he knows he will have are as nothing to him compared with the love he has for the king. His whole purpose is to give delight to the king. He puts all his energy and all his heart, to the very last drop of his blood, working unceasingly day and night, to do his work so that the king might take delight in the result. The man whose task it is to throw away the stones, on the other hand, is not compelled to engage in any inner struggle, since all he has as his reward for the time being are the stones and the rubble that are practically worthless. All he requires is a sufficient degree of love for the king to prevent the task becoming a burden. He undoubtedly does it for the love of the king since in the task he has been set there are no conflicting motives.

The flowery titles applied to Levi Yitzḥak and to Jeḥiel Michel in the previous passage are typical of rabbinic literature at this period and among the Ḥasidim in their veneration of the zaddikim; such encomiums assumed, at times, the most exaggerated forms. Ḥayyim quotes Levi Yitzḥak's parable, but the style is his own. Ḥayyim is undoubtedly one of the greatest Hebrew stylists among the Ḥasidic authors.

The application of the parable is to holy and pure prayer. For the whole idea of prayer is to entreat God in His mercy to allow his flow of grace to come down from on high so that at each benediction the soul is illumined in a particular way by the quality at which that benediction hints.

The meaning is that each benediction has as its aim, according to the Kabbalah, the drawing down of one particular aspect of spiritual light represented by the Sefirot.

This is a form of limitless joy and incomparable delight to those who desire the light of the Lord. Man's heart yearns for it and desires it with every drop of his blood. And yet so great is the furnace of love and fire of yearning in his heart for God's name, to cause Him delight alone, that nothing else matters and his aim in his entreaties is not for the illuminations to shine in his own soul, despite the sweetness of their brightness and the wondrously pleasant nature of the delight they provide. Now since God, blessed be He, has a limitless desire to bestow of His goodness to His creatures, He wishes to illumine the souls of Israel with these illuminations. It is only that first He desires the prayers of Israel, that the impulse from below should come from them, for it was for this purpose that He created the world. As the Rabbis say (Ḥullin 60b), the plants after their creation remained near the surface of the soil and did not begin to grow until Adam prayed for them to grow, when rain came and they began to grow. This is to teach you that the Holy One, blessed be He, yearns for the prayers of the righteous.

The Ḥasidim did not favor selfish prayer. They thought of prayer chiefly as an illumination of the soul, a profound mystical experience. But since God is All-Good, His desire for prayer is because He has so ordained that the spiritual benefits of prayer can only be attained after man has actually prayed. In the language of the Zohar, there has to be "an impulse from below" before there can be "an impulse from above." Thus man prays in order to allow God, as it were, to pour out His graces on the soul. But, says Ḥayyim, the true worshipper, though he longs for these graces, does not want them for himself but because God wants him to have them. This means, however, that there is a powerful conflict in his soul. On the one hand, he wishes to love God without any thought of his own good, not even of his own spiritual good, and yet he does desire profoundly these spiritual illuminations of soul. Consequently, each act of prayer is "service," i.e., hard work, and this is why prayer is called "service of the heart." Note that these spiritual benefits are only said to result from prayer, not from the study of the Torah. It is true that the Ḥasidim elevated prayer over all other religious acts.

Consequently, his main intention in his prayers is to entreat God in His mercy to allow these illuminations to be drawn down into his soul and the souls of all Israel so that this should be a source of delight to God who, as we have said, has the great desire to illumine the world with these illuminations. The result is that his love for God to have this delight is more powerful in his heart than the pleasant delight and the sweet joy of the illuminations themselves. Understand this well.

This is a very subtle idea of prayer. God wants us to enjoy the mystical experience of prayer, and it is indeed a most wondrous delight. But the true worshipper only prays for this to happen because he knows that God so desires. His desire to please God, who wishes him to be pleased by having these delights, is more powerful than the delights themselves.

III GAZING INTO HEAVEN

Beer Mayyim Ḥayyim, Va-yetze, p. 67ff

This is a comment on Jacob's dream of the ladder with its feet upon the earth and its head reaching to the heavens (Genesis 28:10–22).

And he dreamed, and behold a ladder." Now, in reality, there can be no doubt that this ladder as well as the earth upon which it stood with its head reaching to the heavens all hint at wondrous supernal illuminations of the highest degree, only they have been clothed in the category of the corporeal and he saw them in their garments. To be sure, Jacob was worthy of actually seeing the illuminations themselves in all their beauty, not as clothed in the form of an earthly

ladder. The reason for it is on the grounds we have noted earlier. There we said that Jacob did not see what he saw in a prophetic vision, since he was unmarried and could not atone for himself and his household. This is the reason here, too. It follows that if he had seen what he saw in a prophetic vision he would have seen the illuminations themselves, in all their purity without any garments. Hence, our verse states: "And he dreamed." That is to say, because he saw it in a dream and not in a prophetic vision, therefore, "and behold a ladder set up on the earth," he saw it in its corporeal garment. But if he had seen it in a prophetic vision he would have seen the brilliant illuminations in the form they have on high and not in the form of an earthly ladder.

According to the Kabbalah, a man has to be married before he can have a prophetic vision because, as it is said of the High Priest on the Day of Atonement (Leviticus 16:6), he has to atone for himself and for his household. Consequently, Jacob, who was unmarried at the time, only saw what he saw in a dream. In reality, what he saw was not earthly things at all but the highest spiritual forces as they operate in the sefirotic realm. These are called "illuminations." Had he have been a prophet he would have been worthy to see these naked spiritual illuminations by the eye of the spirit. As it was, he could only see them in a dream and through the "garments" of earthly things like a ladder and the ground on which it stands.

IV THE DEDICATION OF A NEW HOUSE

Beer Mayyim Ḥayyim, Ki tetze, p. 208c

"When thou buildest a new house, then thou shalt make a parapet for thy roof, that thou bring not blood upon thy house" (Deuteronomy 22:8).

We have explained this verse at length in our work *Sidduro Shel Shabbat*, **but repeat it here because of some new ideas we now present.**

We explained there that when a man builds the house in which he intends to live, he should not have in mind at all the material pleasure the house will afford him, such as providing him with a place to stay in comfort, the various uses of a house, the ability to

attend to his business affairs from there, and so on. He should rather have in mind when he builds the house to dedicate the very stones to God's service. His motive in building the house should be so as to have a place where he can affix the *mezuzah*, where he can carry out the precept of erecting a parapet, where he can be hospitable, where he can study the Torah and offer his prayers in a proper manner. For this should be the main thing so far as he is concerned, since he knows full well that the main purpose for which he has come into this world is only that he should serve God, blessed be He, pleasing Him and not in order to satisfy his own desires and to enjoy physical pleasures.

Ḥayyim's interpretation of the verse is: When you build a new house do not have in mind your own pleasure but rather build a parapet to prevent someone from coming to harm. Have in mind a good deed like this when you build. For Ḥayyim this is only one illustration of the good purposes to which a house can be put.

If he does this, the very building materials, the stones, the sand, and the mortar, will become elevated in being associated with the precepts of the Lord. The category of evil will then be removed from them and the category of good will rest upon them in a number of ways. It may be that the evil will be converted to good, as Scripture says: "When a man's ways please the Lord, He maketh even his enemies to be at peace with him" (Proverbs 16:7). Or it may be that the evil will vanish completely with only the good remaining there. As the holy Zohar (3:50) says: "Come and see." It is said: "And all the women that were wise-hearted" (Exodus 35:25). At the time when they carried out their tasks they would say, "This is for the Sanctuary." "This if for the curtain," and so on. This was so that sanctity would rest upon the work of their hands and their efforts be sanctified. . . . In the same way whenever a man builds he should mention God's name before he begins to build, saying that his purpose in building is to serve the Holy One, blessed be He. . . . The help of Heaven will then be present and the Holy One, blessed be He, will invite holiness to rest there. . . . But if not, the "Other Side" is invited into his house, . . . so that whoever lives there is in danger from the evil spirit that resides there. . . . For we know that wherever the category of evil is present it is not only

that there can be no blessing, but all kinds of evil are there. These are called "the stripes of the children of men" (2 Samuel 7:14), for all the plagues a man experiences come from them. Hence our verse concludes: "that thou bring not blood upon thy house." This means: If you do this, building your house right from the beginning for the sake of the Lord, to carry out His laws, then "thou bring not blood upon thy house," for there will be none there to do harm.

The Kabbalah believes in the existence of malevolent spirits and so do the Ḥasidim. Ḥayyim here says that if the house is built for God's sake, all evil spirits are exorcised, but if not, the house becomes haunted by them.

CHAPTER 22

Abraham Joshua Heschel of Apt
d. 1825

Reclaiming the "holy sparks"

Abraham Joshua Heschel was a disciple of Elimelech of Lizensk and, for a time, Rabbi of Apt (Opatow)—hence the name by which he is known among the Ḥasidim "the Apter Rov," or, after the title of his work, "the Ohev Yisrael.*" Abraham Joshua eventually settled in Meziboz, the town of the Baal Shem Tov, and he died and was buried there. His great love for the Jewish people is legendary among the Ḥasidim. It is said that he ordered that there be no other inscription on his tombstone than* Ohev Yisrael *("Lover of Israel"), which is also the title of his book. Like all the Ḥasidic masters and kabbalists, Abraham Joshua believed in reincarnation, and Ḥasidic legend tells that he recalled his previous incarnations, in one of which he was a High Priest in the Temple. The legend has it that on Yom Kippur when leading the congregation in prayer, on reaching the section of the Musaf Amidah which relates the service of the High Priest in Temple times, Abraham Joshua instead of saying, "And thus did* he *[i.e., the High Priest] say," declared, "And thus did* I *say."*

Abraham Joshua's book Ohev Yisrael *is in the usual form of comments to the Pentateuch* sidra *by* sidra*. The work was edited and published by his grandson Meshullam Susya in Zhitomer in 1853. (The edition used here is that of Jerusalem, 1962.)*

RECLAIMING THE "HOLY SPARKS"

Ohev Yisrael, Be-haalotekha, p. 177

According to an ancient tradition, still followed, there are inverted nuns *in the scroll before and after the small section: "And it came to pass, when the Ark set forward . . ." (Numbers 10:35–36). These are found in the printed editions of the Pentateuch as well. Rashi, the famous French commentator, explains that the* nuns *are, rather like our use of brackets, intended to point out that "this is not its proper place," i.e., these two verses do not really belong here. Abraham Joshua gives all this a mystical interpretation.*

We have to understand the reason for the two inverted *nuns* before "and it came to pass, when the Ark set forward . . ." and after this section. We need to understand, too, Rashi's comment that these signs are to denote "this is not its proper place." Why, in that case, were *nuns* used (and no other letters)?

If we reflect on it we recall that which is well known and recorded in all the holy books, that the mystery of the children of Israel journeying through the wilderness and other places is the mystery of the elevation of the holy sparks which were immersed in the lowest depths, swallowed up by the fifty gates of impurity and imagining that there they were obliged to stay for ever, God forbid. However, the children of Israel journeyed through the wilderness and the other places in which the sparks resided. There went Moses our Teacher and together with him the six hundred thousand holy souls of Israel and together with them the Holy Ark and the tablets of stone, the work of God. They represented the holy Chariot on high so that they had the power to draw down illuminations from the fifty holy gates of Understanding and even from the fiftieth gate itself. For although even Moses had no comprehension of the fiftieth gate yet, so great was their degree of sancity that they were able to draw down the illumination even of this fiftieth gate.

We have met with the idea of the "holy sparks" more than once in this book. These "holy sparks" have to be rescued and elevated on high, saved for the holy from the attempts of the demonic forces to hold them captive. According to the Kabbalah there are "fifty gates of Understanding" (Binah, *the* Sefirah *of that name). Man can proceed higher and higher in his contemplation of the divine, but even Moses could only attain to a comprehension of the forty-nine gates, not the fiftieth. We have also encountered earlier the idea that everything in the realm of the holy has its counterpart in the realms of the demonic; hence there are also "fifty gates of impurity." The Israelites were obliged to wander through the wilderness and other places in order to rescue the "holy sparks." This was done by means of their extreme sanctity as well as by the Ark they carried with them representing the divine Chariot. This latter reference is to the vision of the Heavenly Chariot seen by the prophet Ezekiel (chapter 1). The Ark surrounded by the holy people was the counterpart on earth of the Chariot on high. The "holy sparks" derive ultimately from* Binah *on high so that, as Abraham Joshua says, they "sprang to meet their source."*

The result was that when the holy sparks residing amid the thick darkness saw their elevated root on high illumined in clear and brilliant light, they sprang forth from their place of shadow and darkness and were thus elevated to their high and lofty source and root. This was in obedience to the idea found in the verse: "He hath swallowed down riches, and he shall vomit them up again" (Job 20:15). They now saw that it was not as they had previously imagined, that there was their place forever.

The sparks are personified. They had imagined that they were doomed to remain in the place of darkness forever, but now they saw their redemption at hand and they were vomited forth out of the mouths of the evil powers to soar aloft to their source on high.

That is why in some places the Israelites did not stay for a long time after they had pitched their camp, while in other places they stayed for a lengthy period after they had pitched their camp. It all depended on the number of holy sparks swallowed up in that particular place. For this reason our holy Torah gives us a hint here before and after the two verses, "And it came to pass, when the Ark set forward . . . ," and, "And when it rested. . . ." This was indictated by two inverted *nuns*, all for the purpose of hinting at that which we have stated. For the top of the *nun*, representing the mystery of gate fifty of the fifty holy gates of Understanding, was revealed in its illumination down below, reaching down to the final

gate of the fifty gates of impurity in order to make these gates spew out that which they had swallowed, namely, the holy sparks. In truth this was not their place, but their true place was in the root of holiness on high. This is what Rashi means when he says: "this is not its proper place," of each holy spark residing there. But they were all elevated on high to their source on high in holiness. There bring a thanksgiving offering. Understand well all this.

The letter nun *has the numerical value of 50. Hence the inverted* nun *denotes that the fifthieth gate of Understanding came right down, as it were, in order to rescue its own from the fifty gates of impurity which, since they are the opposite of the holy, are inverted* nuns. *The upright* nun *allowed itself, as it were, to become an inverted* nun *because it had to descend into the realms of the unholy in order to rescue its own. When Rashi says, "this is not its proper place," he means by "this," of course, "this" section of the Torah. But Abraham Joshua says that he is really "hinting" at "this" particular holy spark, whose "place in not here," i.e., with the unholy. Naturally Rashi could not possibly have intended to refer to kabbalistic ideas still to be expounded and of which he could not have been aware, but, as we have seen more than once, the Ḥasidic teachers were not bothered overmuch by anachronisms. The phenomenon of the inverted* nun *is found in one other place in the Bible, in Psalm 107, which deals with the thanksgiving offering. Here, too, says Abraham Joshua, it is entirely appropriate, since the psalm deals, too, with the idea of rescue for which thanksgiving is offered. Farfetched though all this certainly is, one cannot help admiring its ingenuity.*

CHAPTER 23

Moses Sofer of Przeworsk

d. 1805

What did Moses look like?
What is the true aim of Torah study?

Moses was a scribe—hence his surname Sofer, *meaning "scribe." Ḥasidic legend dwells on the powerful "illuminations" in the letters of the Torah scrolls he used to write. Moses Sofer was a talmudist and kabbalist, serving as rabbi in Przeworsk until his death.*

Moses Sofer was a disciple in Ḥasidic lore of Elimelech of Lizensk, and some suggest that the "Seer" of Lublin was in part a disciple of his as well as of Elimelech. He is known among the Ḥasidim, after the title of his book, as "the Or Peney Moshe.*"*

Moses Sofer's book Or Peney Moshe *(The Light of Moses' Countenance) follows the usual pattern of running commentary to the Pentateuch,* sidra *by* sidra. *The work was first published in Meseritch in 1810. (The edition used here is the photocopy of the poorly printed Lemberg edition of 1840, published in Israel.)*

I WHAT DID MOSES LOOK LIKE?

Or Peney Moshe, Ḥukkat, part 2, 19a,b

In this passage Moses Sofer accepts a medieval tale—severely attacked, incidentally, by many prominent rabbis—about Moses' facial appearance. The article on Moses in the Encyclopedia Judaica *should be consulted for the history of this tale.*

"This is the statute of the Torah" (Numbers 19:2). I have heard the following tale: A certain king, hearing the fame of Moses, how he had performed such miracles and wonders, and being well versed in the art of reading a man's character from his facial appearance, decided to send a skillful portrait painter to the wilderness to paint the portrait of the man of God. Having accomplished his mission, the artist returned to the king, who saw that the portrait depicted the features of a most depraved man, since they were the features of an adulturer, a murderer, one having every evil trait of character. The king therefore ordered the artist to be put to death for having failed to carry out his task. The king then ordered another artist to carry out the same mission. This second artist, when he came to Moses, saw to his horror that Moses' features were, indeed, exactly as the first artist had depicted them. He was terrified that he, too, would suffer the fate of the first artist when he returned to the king. Taking his courage in his hands he approached Moses and asked him: "Why are your features so evil since you are different from every other man on earth?" Moses our Teacher, on whom be peace, replied: "Son of man, formed from dust, you cannot see it and your intellect is incapable of comprehending it. Shall a man be called good simply because his features portray him as good? Such a man is no better than cattle since he is good by nature. Rather, it is only right to call that man good whose features are excessively evil, but who overcomes his physical nature and converts it to good. Such a man truly deserves to be called good for his goodness is due to his own free choice." This is what I heard.

On the face of it, there is room for some uncertainty about the reply Moses is said to have given since it betokens a lack of humility, and yet of Moses our Teacher, on whom be peace, it is said: "Now the man Moses was very meek" (Numbers 12:3). Nevertheless, I believe that he was obliged to give this reply in order to prevent the profanation of the divine name that would have resulted, God forbid, from them saying that Moses the Teacher of all Israel possessed the features that indicated what they appeared to

do. That is why he was forced to tell the truth. Note this for it is a fine point.

Moses Sofer proceeds to read this idea into the scriptural verse he quotes, but in a very farfetched way. It is one of the curiosities of Ḥasidic literature that this strange tale should have been accepted as true by a prominent Ḥasidic master, especially since the majority of the Ḥasidim believe that the holy man has a holy countenance upon which, as the kabbalists put it, the Shekhinah *rests.*

II WHAT IS THE TRUE AIM OF TORAH STUDY?

Or Peney Moshe, Ḥukkat, part 2, p. 19c

The Rema *referred to in this comment is the famous sixteenth-century Rabbi of Cracow,* Rabbi Moses Isserles, *whose commentary to the Pentateuch,* Torat Ha-Olah, *is quoted frequently by Moses Sofer.*

"This is the statute of the Torah" (Numbers 19:2). The Rema of blessed memory asks why the verse says, "This," as if it were the only statute of the Torah. Consult his work. Possibly it can be understood on the basis of an idea I saw in a book that the numerical value of *zot* **("this") is 408 and it has the same numerical value as the total of** *tzom* **("fasting"),** *kol* **("voice"), and** *mammon* **("money"), representing** *teshuvah* **("repentance"),** *tefillah* **("prayer"), and** *tzedakah* **("charity"). The Talmud (Kiddushin 40b) states that study is great because it leads to practice. From this it follows that the main aim of study is for it to lead to practice, so that through his studies a man who has sinned will know the flaws for which he has been responsible and he will know how to put them right. But one who studies with an ulterior motive (***shelo lishmah***), it were better for him if he had never been created. Possibly this is hinted at here. "This," namely,** *fasting, voice,* **and** *mammon,* **the numerical value of which is 408, the same as that of** *zot* **("this"), is "the statute of the Torah," namely, this is man's way that should result from study of the Torah. He should not study for any other purpose than for the sake of Heaven. It should never be in order to show how much better he is than others or for any other of the well-known ulterior motives. And this is easy to understand.**

The word zot *("this") is formed from the letters* zayin = *7,* alef = *1,* tav = *400; total* = *408.* Tzom *("fasting") is* tzade = *90,* vav = *6,* mem = *40; total* = *136.* Kol *("voice") is* kof = *100,* vav = *6,* lamed = *30; total* = *136.* Mammon *("money") is* mem = *40,* mem = *40,* vav = *6,* nun = *50; total* = *136. Thus 3 × 136* = *408* = zot. *The formula* tzom, kol, mammon *traditionally represents the three basic ideas of repentance, prayer, and charity. Hence the interpretation that the purpose of Torah study should be in order for it to result in a life of repentance, prayer, and charity. This is another example of the Ḥasidic emphasis on Torah study only for its own sake* (lishmah).

CHAPTER 24

Moses Teitelbaum of Ujhely 1759-1841 and his great-grandson, Ḥananiah Yom Tov Lipa d. 1904

Which type of pride is legitimate?
Belief in reincarnation
What is woman's role in Judaism?
Why did Isaac Luria die young?
Beyond time

Moses Teitelbaum was a disciple of the "Seer" of Lublin and the great representative of Hungarian Ḥasidism. Ujhely is a town in Hungary of which he was the official town rabbi for many years. Moses was a famous talmudic scholar, author of a well-known collection of rabbinic responsa. But his fame in the Ḥasidic world rests on his Ḥasidic book of homilies published in Lemberg, 1848–1861. This is entitled Yismaḥ Moshe *(Let Moses Rejoice), and, after it, he is called by the Ḥasidim "the* Yismaḥ Moshe."

Moses Teitelbaum's descendants were famous Ḥasidic rabbis. The best known are: his grandson Jekuthiel Judah Teitelbaum of Sighet (1808–1883), author of Yitav Lev*; the latter's son Ḥananiah Yom Tov Lipa of Sighet (d. 1904), author of* Kedushat Yom Tov *(edition used here; New York, 1947); and Ḥananiah's son Joel Teitelbaum (b. 1888), the present renowned Satmarer Rebbe in New York.*

The following selections are from Moses Teitelbaum's Yismaḥ Moshe *and Ḥananiah Yom Tov Lipa Teitelbaum's* Kedushat Yom Tov.

I WHICH TYPE OF PRIDE IS LEGITIMATE?

Yismaḥ Moshe to Genesis 4:7

"If you do well, lift your head up" (Genesis 4:7). At times the evil inclination entices man away from the right path by showing him how inferior he really is. The book *Akedah*, section 67, states that a man is obliged to look at his better qualities, not at his worst. Hence the verse says: "If you want to do well, lift your head up." In order to be a good man one has to lift oneself up and say, "Behold I am a portion of God on high."

The Akedah *is Isaac Arama's* Akedat Yitzḥak *(see Volume 4 in this series). Although Ḥasidism stresses the great virtue of humility, man must never allow himself to forget that he has a divine spark within him. He must not feel proud of his achievements, but he can and should take pride in the fact that he is a creature of God and he should proudly lift his head up whenever he is in danger of surrendering to spiritual despair.*

Again we have an example of a stretching of the meaning of the biblical text, which is usually translated, "If you do well, shall it not be lifted up?"—which is taken to mean, "shall you not be accepted?"

II BELIEF IN REINCARNATION

Yismaḥ Moshe to Genesis 18:8

"And he took curd, and milk, and the calf which he had dressed" (Genesis 18:8). My master the holy zaddik Rabbi Jacob Isaac of Lublin, of blessed memory, once asked me, Why is there no mention of fish in the holy Torah when it relates the story of the angels and their meal, and yet the Rabbis generally speak of meat and fish when referring to a meal? I replied that the main purpose of eating meals is in order to elevate the holy sparks in the food and to put right the souls of those who have been reincarnated. In the writings of the Ari of blessed memory it is said that the majority of zaddikim come back to earth as fish. It is certain that this only applies to zaddikim of lesser rank, but great zaddikim do not need to come back to earth again for further perfection. In the days of

Abraham our father there were only those great zaddikim who are mentioned in the Torah. He greatly praised my reply. And the Rabbi of Lublin said further that for this reason there is no mention of fish in the account of Solomon's feast (1 Kings 8:65) because then the moon was full and "every man under his vine" (1 Kings 5:5). This means that at the time there were only new souls and no souls that had been previously on earth.

All the Ḥasidim follow the Kabbalah in believing in the transmigration of souls. A man's soul can return to earth in order to "put right" any flaws for which he had been responsible in his previous existence and he can, on the second or third time round, even assume the body of a nonhuman creature. According to the Ari, the Safed kabbalist Isaac Luria, the zaddikim, when they have to return to earth to inhabit a nonhuman body, enter the body of a fish. When the zaddik eats the fish in a spirit of sanctity he assists the soul incarnated in the fish to find its perfection. The reference to the moon being full means that, in the Kabbalah, the "moon" is the symbol of the Shekhinah. *In exile the* Shekhinah *is represented by the waning moon, but in the time of Solomon, and in the messianic age, the moon is full. The Lubliner interprets the verse about each man sitting under his own vine as meaning that in that time each man only had been on earth once. No one had a soul that did not belong entirely to his present body so that it was sitting, as it were, under the vine of another.*

III WHAT IS WOMAN'S ROLE IN JUDAISM?

Yismaḥ Moshe to Exodus 10:11

"Go now ye that are men, and serve the Lord; for that is what ye desire" (Exodus 10:11).

An interpretation of this was revealed to me in a dream. For it is the habit of a king to speak cleverly and by hint. Hence he said, "Go now ye that are men," for it is men who have been created to resemble the beings on high, as it is said: "Let us make man in our image" (Genesis 1:26), and this stage they can attain through the service of God. But women were created chiefly for the benefit of men, to be a help to them, and hence women are not obliged to keep (all) the *mitzvot*. That is why Pharaoh said: "Go now ye that are *men*, and serve the Lord," and not women. But Moses, antici-

pating this, said: "for we must hold a feast to the Lord" (Exodus 10:9) this day, and it is therefore proper for us to rejoice together with our womenfolk, for so does reason demand and it is also so from the point of view of the Torah," and thou shalt rejoice, thou and thy household" (Deuteronomy 14:26). And this is the rule as recorded in the Talmud (Hagigah 6a) that even though a woman is exempt from appearing before the Lord on the festivals, yet she is still obliged to go on pilgrimage to Jerusalem on these days in order to rejoice together with her husband.

Moses Teitelbaum's dream interpretation is hardly likely to endear him to the women's liberation movement. Man acquires perfection, resembling the angelic hosts on high, through serving God. But, strictly speaking, this high aim is only for males, not females. That is why Pharaoh objected to women going to serve God. The role of woman is to serve her husband. But Moses replied that women, too, have to participate in the festival, even if it is only because their husbands require their company. This is a peculiar idea, and it is only right to point out that such an attitude toward women is not really typical of Ḥasidism. It has often been remarked that with regard to the poor social conditions of the time, the Ḥasidic woman generally fared better than her non-Ḥasidic counterpart. There have even been instances of women occupying the role of Ḥasidic zaddik.

IV WHY DID ISAAC LURIA DIE YOUNG?

Yismaḥ Moshe to Numbers 24:14

"And now, behold, I go unto my people; come, and I will announce to thee what this people shall do to thy people in the end of days" (Numbers 24:14). On the night after the festival of Shavuot it was told me in a dream that the Ari of blessed memory lived for thirty-four years because he put right all that the wicked Balaam had spoiled during the thirty-four years of his life. Behold this is true. For, as a result of the sin of Baal Peor (Numbers 25:1–3) the wicked Balaam caused much punishment for Israel and he did this by advising Balak to make the Israelites sin. Hence he said: "I will announce to thee what to do." Corresponding to this the Ari of blessed memory put it right so that no decree of apostasy will ever again be issued against Israel.

Moses Teitelbaum is a bit shaky on his facts. Ari (Isaac Luria) did live a short life, but he was thirty-eight, not thirty-four, when he died. There was a tradition that Balaam was thirty-four years of age when he was killed. It is possible that Moses Teitelbaum was aware of the medieval identification of Balaam with Jesus, and it is to this that he hints in this passage. In this and the preceding excerpts Moses Teitelbaum, unlike the majority of the Ḥasidic teachers, claims to have been given the correct interpretation in a dream.

V BEYOND TIME

Kedushat Yom Tov, Mishpatim, p. 62b

It was revealed to me in a dream to explain the words of the prophet: "Seek ye the Lord while He may be found, call ye upon Him while He is near . . . and to our God, for He will abundantly pardon" (Isaiah 55:6–7). The commentators ask why at first it says, "Seek ye *the Lord*," using the Tetragrammaton which denotes the divine mercy, and then it says, "our *God*," denoting the attribute of judgment. A further difficulty is, why it should say, "for He will abundantly pardon" in association with the name "God," denoting the attribute of judgment, and not in association with the Tetragrammaton.

The author, like his great-grandfather, sometimes claims that his interpretations were revealed to him in a dream. According to the rabbinic teaching, wherever the Tetragrammaton appears in Scripture it denotes God's mercy, whereas the name Elohim, *"God," denotes His sternness and judgment. Why, then, the change from one name to the other here? Furthermore, logic seems to demand that when speaking of God pardoning sin the Tetragrammaton should be used, and yet here* Elohim *is used.*

It was revealed to me on the basis of the statement in tractate Rosh Ha-Shanah 18a that "while He may be found" refers to the ten days between Rosh Ha-Shanah and Yom Kippur. Now on the face of it this is hard to understand. We could have understood it if the verse had used the name *Elohim*. For, as it is stated in the holy books, this name has the same numerical value as the word *ha-teva* ("nature"). Although even here all is governed by individual providence, yet this name denotes God's control of the world in a natural way

and so it belongs to the world of time, and here it is appropriate to speak of a particular time. But the Tetragrammaton refers to God in His aspect of the Limitless and Unbounded, higher than nature and time. How then, in association with this name, can the expression "while He may be found," referring to a specific time, between Rosh Ha-Shanah and Yom Kippur, be used? This aspect of God is not governed by time, so that today is also "between Rosh Ha-Shanah and Yom Kippur" and every day is the right time. Consequently, if God, blessed be He, orders us to repent, then every day is the proper time and if man repents, God accepts it at once.

The author is bothered by the rabbinic idea that somehow the Ten Days of Penitence have a special significance because in them God is "to be found." How can God, who is beyond the time process, be limited in any way so that He can only or especially be found during these days? The author states that if the name Elohim *were used, the problem would not be beyond a solution. For this name refers to God as He operates through nature and the time process. But since the Tetragrammaton is used, and this name refers to God as beyond time, what sense does it make to speak of special days? The remark about the numerical value goes back to the middle ages. The letters of* Elohim *are:* alef *= 1,* lamed *= 30,* hey *= 5,* yod *= 10,* mem *= 40; total = 86.* Ha-teva: hey *= 5,* tet *= 9,* bet *= 2,* ayin *= 70; total = 86.*

But it all becomes clear on the basis of the statement in the holy books that the 248 positive precepts have their root in the Tetragrammaton, the side of mercy, while the 365 negative precepts have their root in the name *Elohim*, **the side of judgment.**

According to the rabbinic tradition there are 248 positive precepts, the things we are obliged to do, and 365 negative precepts, the things we must refrain from doing. According to the Kabbalah the positive precepts belong especially to God's mercy. In His love for us He commanded us to do certain things. The negative precepts, on the other hand, are things we must not do and hence we are judged if we do them. These belong to the side of judgment. Since the Tetragrammaton denotes mercy, it is the "root" of the positive precepts, whereas Elohim*, denoting judgment, is the "root" of the negative precepts.*

On the basis of this I gave a fine explanation of why the Talmud says in tractate Yoma 86a that if a man fails to carry out a positive precept and he repents of it he is pardoned on the spot, whereas if he disobeys a negative precept, repentance and Yom Kippur atone for him. The reason is that positive precepts have their root in the Tetragrammaton and with regard to the Tetragrammaton there is no sense in setting aside Yom Kippur for atonement, since today is also Yom Kippur. But with regard to negative precepts whose root is in the name *Elohim*, **denoting God's control of the world in a natural way and governed by time, for these Yom Kippur is required.**

In the next section, omitted here, the author elaborates further on the theme in a kabbalistic way. But we see the point he is making. The special time, the Ten Days of Penitence, is really for the negative precepts. Yet the expression "while He may be found" is made to denote this special period, although in association with the Tetragrammaton, in order that this period be extended, as it were, throughout the year, since this name denotes that which is higher than time; therefore, from this point of view, it is the Ten Days of Penitence all the time.

Hence the prophet says: "Seek ye the Lord while He may be found," using the Tetragrammaton, because by means of this name He will always be found, to have mercy upon us and to pardon us, but only in connection with positive precepts, the side of mercy. But it is necessary to associate the Tetragrammaton with the name *Elohim* **so that we can find pardon even when we have been guilty of transgressing negative precepts, whose root is from the side of judgment. Hence, it says: "And to our God for He will abundantly pardon," also for the negative precepts. Understand this well.**

Although this comment is obviously farfetched, it is a remarkable piece of homiletical ingenuity; it touches, moreover, on the profound philosophical problem of how God, who is beyond time, can be said in some way to be involved in the time process so that there is religious meaning to special days of the years more than to others.

CHAPTER 25

Zevi Elimelech Spira of Dynow

1785-1841

Why do we blow the shofar on Rosh Ha-Shanah?
How far can human reasoning take us?

Zevi Elimelech Spira was a nephew of Elimelech of Lizensk, born after Elimelech's death and named after him. He was a disciple of the "Seer" of Lublin and the Maggid of Koznitz, Elimelech's disciples. He is known by the Ḥasidim, after the title of his main work, as "the Beney Yissakhar *(Sons of Issachar).*

Zevi Elimelech was a very prolific writer with a number of works to his credit, all highly esteemed by the Ḥasidim. But his main and most popular work is the Beney Yissakhar, *first published in Zolkiew in 1850. (The edition used here is that published in Germany in 1947.) The title of the work is based on the verse, "And of the sons of Issachar, men that had understanding of the times" 1 Chronicles 12:33). This refers to the fact that the book is in the nature of a detailed commentary to all the sacred "times," the festivals of the Jewish year.*

I WHY DO WE BLOW THE SHOFAR ON ROSH HA-SHANAH?

Beney Yissakhar, Tishri, Shofar 1, 3, part 2, p. 8a

The Zohar states that on Rosh Ha-Shanah one should not confess one's sins or refer to sin by word of mouth but only *in secret,* **in**

the privacy of one's own thoughts. It is stated in the writings of the Ari of blessed memory that the four sets of shofar sounds (*tekiot*) are to atone for the four main types of sin. The "sitting *tekiot*" are to atone for the sin of idolatry and nullify the inclination toward idol worship. The *tekiot* during the silent prayer are to nullify the inclination toward adultery. The *tekiot* during the repetition of the Amidah are to nullify the inclination toward murder. The *tekiot* before *titkabbal* ("May the prayers be accepted") are to nullify the inclination toward slander. All this we have to carry out by means of a sound (namely, the sound of the shofar) without words, for God forbid that we should refer by word of mouth to sin on this day.

Awareness of sin cannot be avoided on Rosh Ha-Shanah, Judgment Day, but it is psychologically harmful to refer to sin at the beginning of the New Year. Hence the shofar sounds are a compromise. They are a nonverbal expression of the need to atone for sin and nullify it. Ari is Isaac Luria, "the Lion," the famous sixteenth-century Safed mystic. There are varying customs regarding the rite of blowing the shofar on Rosh Ha-Shanah, but according to the Ari the order is as follows: (1) before the Amidah, where the sounds are known as the "sitting tekiot*" because, unlike at the Amidah, when one must stand, it is permitted to sit down at this stage of the service; (2) during the silent Amidah by the congregation; (3) when the reader repeats the Amidah; (4) during the* kaddish *prayer before the word* titkabbal.

It appears to me that this is the reason why the word *ba-seter* ("in secret") occurs four times in the Bible: (1) "Cursed be the man that maketh a graven or molten image . . . and setteth it up *in secret*" (Deuteronomy 27:15). This refers to the nullification of the inclination to worship idols, "in secret," with a wordless sound. (2) "For she shall eat them for want of all things *in secret*" (Deuteronomy 28:57), referring to the inclination to commit murder. (3) Nathan said to David: "For thou didst it *in secret*" (2 Samuel 12:12), referring to the nullification of the inclination to commit adultery. (4) "Cursed be he that smiteth his neighbor *in secret*" (Deuteronomy 27:24), referring to slander. Thus the intention is that all these challenging sins be nullified *in secret*.

Zevi Elimelech finds, very cleverly, a hint in Scripture to the idea he has drawn out of the Zohar and the Ari. It so happens that the word ba-seter, "in secret," only occurs four times in Scripture and in each case the reference is to one of the four main sins mentioned by the Ari. In the next passage, a footnote to this section, Zevi Elimelech similarly displays his ingenuity in reading kabbalistic ideas (anachronistically, of course) into Scripture.

Note: **To my mind this is hinted at in the Torah when the chief butler said: "I make mention of my sins this day" (Genesis 41:9). The whole of this verse seems superfluous, but the words "this day" certainly are superfluous. But you must know that in ancient times, even those who belonged to the "Other Side" were familiar with the mysteries. The chief butler knew, therefore, that it is wrong to make mention of sin on Rosh Ha-Shanah, and the Rabbis say that Joseph was released from prison on Rosh Ha-Shanah, so that day was Rosh Ha-Shanah. Hence the chief butler said: "I make mention of my sins *this day*." He meant to say, "although one should not make mention of sins on *this* day, I am compelled to do so."**

The "Other Side" is the demonic side of existence, to which the chief butler belonged. Even he knew that it was wrong to speak of sin on Rosh Ha-Shanah, but he was compelled to state his faults in order to inform Pharaoh about Joseph. Naturally, all this is very farfetched but extremely ingenious, and it is easy to see why the Ḥasidim found comments of this kind, combining intellectual brilliance with a tinge of mysticism, so appealing.

II HOW FAR CAN HUMAN REASONING TAKE US?

Beney Yissakhar, Tishri, Maamar 7, 5, part 2, p. 23b

I shall tell you of, as it seems to me, the great good that God has wrought for Israel, the people near to Him, in not making known to the human mind how the problem of God's foreknowledge and human freedom can be solved. The human mind is incapable of seeing any solution and yet we are obliged by the Torah to believe it all.

The great problem, discussed at length by the medieval philosophers (see Volume 2 in this series in the section on philosophy) was: Since God knows beforehand all that man will do in the future, how can man be free to choose? Zevi Elimelech later declares that there is, in fact, no solution capable of being grasped by the human mind, yet the Jew still believes both that God has foreknowledge and that man is free. Zevi Elimelech is leading up to the opinion, stressed in all his works, that faith is "higher" than reason. In the next passage he quotes as an illustration the kal va-ḥomer *argument, the argument from the minor to the major, i.e., if A is so, then how much more so is B, which is obviously superior to A. This argument is one of the thirteen principles by means of which, according to the Talmud, the Torah is expounded, i.e., even if a law is not stated explicitly in the Torah it can be derived by the* kal va-ḥomer *argument. Among the other principles are: the* gezerah shavah, *"similar expression," where two laws in the Torah are compared because the same expression is used of both; and* khelal, perat, u-khelal, *"general, particular, and general," where a new law is derived from a Torah statement of laws in the form of general rule, particular instance, and another general rule. Now these latter and the other principles, apart from* kal va-ḥomer, *can only be applied if there is a tradition to that purpose, whereas the* kal va-ḥomer, *based as it is on common sense, can be applied by the unaided human mind. And yet the Talmud occasionally states that the Torah goes out of its way to record explicitly a law that could easily have been derived by means of the* kal va-ḥomer. *According to Zevi Elimelech, this is to demonstrate that even the most convincing type of human reasoning is not immune from failure and that only faith in the Torah is ultimately reliable.*

I say: Note and appreciate that in the great and expansive sea that is our Talmud we find frequently the statement that Scripture goes out of its way to inform us of a law that could in any event have been derived by a *kal va-ḥomer*. **Yet we do not find this of any other of the thirteen principles such as the** *gezerah shavah* **or the** *khelal, perat, u-khelal*, **and there must be some reason for it. Furthermore, if there is a reason for it, why should it only apply to the** *kal va-ḥomer*? **But it seems to me that the answer is to be found in the fact that all the other principles by means of which the Torah is expounded are a tradition going back to Sinai so that human reasoning only has scope here because of the tradition. But the** *kal va-ḥomer* **(even if it were not in the tradition) is a common-sense argument, used, in fact, in worldly affairs. In order for us**

to appreciate that the Torah is the Will and Wisdom of God, blessed be He, and higher than reason, the Torah supplies a verse even for a law that could have been derived in any event by means of a *kal va-ḥomer*, a rational argument. This is in order to demonstrate that the Torah is higher than reason and that human reasoning, consequently, has no business to interfere. Understand this well for it is a delightful idea for those who are wise.

In reality, the very idea of the kal va-ḥomer, *used so frequently by the Rabbis, contradicts Zevi Elimelech's basic contention that human reasoning has no part to play in the Jewish religion. But Zevi Elimelech neatly turns the tables on his opponents by pointing to the talmudic saying he quotes. In fact, he says, the Torah urges us not to rely on the* kal va-ḥomer*—human reasoning—and goes out of its way to provide scriptural authority for the law. Of course, this only happens occasionally, and in numerous other instances the Talmud does use the* kal va-ḥomer *as the basis of the law. But Zevi Elimelech appears to be arguing that since the phenomenon to which he calls attention is to be observed, at least occasionally, it is a blow struck for faith against reason. It is as if the Torah is saying: By all means rely on the* kal va-ḥomer*—human reasoning—but please be aware that it is not infallible and is never to be preferred to the sure knowledge provided by the Torah.*

On the basis of what we have said, God in His mercy and in His desire to justify this people (of Israel), behaves in His relationship with them in His qualty of mercy, higher than reason. For reason is justice; it is just and reasonable that those who disobey the king's commands of their own free choice should be punished. But in connection with this very matter of reward and punishment, God has concealed even from the wise how punishment can be justified, for sins committed due to a bad choice, since God knows it all beforehand. But the children of Israel believe in it by virtue of the Torah, the Torah of mercy, higher than reason. It follows automatically that even from the point of view of justice, it is only right for their sins to be pardoned and for mercy to be shown to them.

All punishment for sin seems reasonable. No one compels a man to do wrong, and if he chooses so to do he cannot escape the consequences. But this only makes sense if man is free. Therefore, the paradox is that man can only be reasonable in his approach to punishment if he believes that man is free, and this he can only believe as a matter of faith, not of reason (since, according to the human reason, man cannot be free because of God's foreknowledge). So Israel only deserves to be punished, ultimately, because of its faith in the Torah. But the Torah is higher than reason and hence higher than punishment, for in the realm of the Torah all is mercy and pardon. Hence by concealing the solution to the problem of God's foreknowledge and human free will, God exercises His mercy, i.e., by making it depend not on reason but on faith.

CHAPTER 26

Israel Friedmann of Ruzhyn

1797-1850

How can a sinner dare to pray?
How do we walk life's tightrope?
Can prayer be confined to special times?
Music versus fasting
Will it be hard to be a good Jew?

The Ruzhyner (with the accent on the first syllable), as he is called by the Ḥasidim, is one of the most fascinating characters in Ḥasidic history. He lived the life of a Polish count with his own horse-drawn carriage, splendid manor, and even, so it is rumored, a silver throne. The Ḥasidim say of him and the dynasty he founded that it is all the reflection upon earth of the divine principle of Malkhut *(Sovereignty). He was venerated as a great saint by many thousands of followers. One of the claims made on his behalf was that his sanctity was so powerful that he never bent his mouth to the food and drink when eating and drinking, but always, in severe self-control, conveyed them to his mouth. The Ruzhyner also acquired a reputation for acute wisdom, though not for deep learning.*

Israel was the son of Shalom Shachna and Eve, daughter of Naḥum of Chernobil. Shalom Shachna was the son of Abraham "the Angel," son of the Maggid of Meseritch. Israel's six sons all became Ḥasidic masters.

Israel wrote no Ḥasidic work, but his teachings appear in various collections. The following selections are from the work Kenesset Yisrael, *containing the teachings of Israel and his six sons, published in Warsaw in 1906.*

I HOW CAN A SINNER DARE TO PRAY?

Kenesset Yisrael, p. 12

"Let everything that hath breath praise the Lord" (Psalms 150:6). Our Rabbis of blessed memory (Genesis Rabbah 14:9) interpret this verse to mean that man should praise his Maker for every breath he draws. For at every moment the soul wishes to leave the body, but the Holy One, blessed be He, restrains it. It follows that man becomes a new creature at every moment of his life. Man can gain encouragement from this when the thought enters his head at the time of prayer and worship, "How dare you, so base a man, full of sin and iniquity, open your mouth to praise God?" But he should then consider that at that very moment he has become a new creature and has not sinned in that moment, so now he is justified in standing in God's presence.

The novel idea is here expressed that, strictly speaking, no man is really worthy to pray to God. Yet at every moment man is, as it were, created anew by God, so that the man who now stands in prayer is not the man who had sinned.

II HOW DO WE WALK LIFE'S TIGHTROPE?

Kenesset Yisrael, pp. 16–17

It once happened that the Ḥasidim were sitting in company when the zaddik, our master of Ruzhyn, came by with his pipe in his hand. The Ḥasidim called out to him, "Master! Please inform us of the way to serve God." The rabbi replied, "How should I know?" But he did tell them the following story: A king sentenced two dear friends to death. The king really wished to pardon them, but could not do so because he was obliged to uphold the laws of his realm and they were guilty. The sentence was, therefore, that a tight and long rope be stretched out across a fierce river and if the men were able to cross the river on the rope their lives would be spared. The first man succeeded in the crossing, whereupon his

friend called out to him, "Dear friend! Please tell me how you managed to achieve such a hazardous crossing on the tightrope so that I, too, shall do likewise." The friend replied, "I really do not know. I know only that as I was crossing on the rope, whenever I felt myself going over to one side I leaned in the opposite direction."

The zaddik does not possess greater wisdom than his "dear friends" the Ḥasidim. He can only offer the counsel that life involves crossing on a tightrope and no one is really secure. For all that, the zaddik has somehow managed to cross sucessfully and is now out of danger. He can give some advice to his followers, but it is only that they must strive always to preserve the correct balance. We have here a realization of the great tensions of the religious life and that great skill is required to balance the different claims it makes.

III CAN PRAYER BE CONFINED TO SPECIAL TIMES?

Kenesset Yisrael, p. 19

When our master of Ruzhyn visited the holy Rabbi of Apt, the rabbi paid him much honor and showed him many tokens of respect. One day our master of Ruzhyn tarried long before reciting the morning prayers. The Rabbi of Apt came into his room to ask when he would say his prayers. Our master of Ruzhyn said that he himself did not know. And he told this tale. Once upon a time there was a great and good king who was kind to all. Whoever had a request to present to the king was allowed to do so at any time and was not required to make an appointment to see the king. But the princes of that realm decided that it was inappropriate for the king thus to be at the complete mercy of his subjects and to be bothered by them all the time. Consequently, they drew up rules whereby only certain hours would be set aside each day when people with requests could present them to the king. At any other time, no one was allowed in. This became unalterable protocol. But one day a begger presented himself at the outer courtyard of the palace and demanded that he be allowed to enter to speak to the king. Since it was outside the time allotted for the purpose the guards would not let him in. They cried out to the begger, "Everyone in the king's realm knows that special times have been set aside when the king's subjects can present

their petitions to him. Why, then, do you come at other times?" The begger replied, "Yes, I, too, know this, but anyone of even the slightest degree of intelligence knows that the rule was only laid down in the first instance for those who come to present requests on their own behalf. It cannot have been intended to apply to me for I come on a matter that concerns the safety of the kingdom. Obviously, no time limit has been here imposed. On the contrary, such a man must be brought speedily to the king as soon as he comes to the palace. And I, too, have a message that concerns the kingdom itself." When they heard this, the guards let him through. "So," said our master of Ruzhyn, "how do I know when I shall offer my prayers?"

Some Ḥasidic masters disregarded the rules laid down in the codes about the proper time for prayer, arguing that the essence of prayer is its spontaneity and it cannot be governed by law. The further rationale given here is that the zaddik does not pray for himself, but for the sake of God. The King will listen to the zaddik at any time of the day or night, since the zaddik's concerns are God's concerns.

IV MUSIC VERSUS FASTING

Kenesset Yisrael, pp. 27–28

It was a time of great trouble for Jacob, God spare us from such, and at that time the holy Rabbi Joshua Heschel of Apt of blessed memory was the doyen of the generation. He ordered that a fast be observed in all Israel's habitations on Monday, Thursday, and the following Monday, and insisted that even folk of weak constitution observe the fast. At that time, our master of Ruzhyn listened to a concert. It is well known that he had his own orchestra, and when he heard of the order of the Apter Rabbi concerning the fast, he called together his musicians and instructed them to play as never before on their fiddles, pipes, and trumpets. The Rabbi of Apt heard of this, and everyone supposed that he would be extremely angry at the zaddik of Ruzhyn for disobeying his order by converting a time of mourning into a celebration. Yet when the report came to the Rabbi of Apt he said, "We are unable to compete with the zaddik of Ruzhyn, for he follows the way recorded in Scripture: 'And when ye go to war in your land against

the adversary that oppresseth you then ye shall sound an alarm with the trumpets; and ye shall be remembered before the Lord your God, and ye shall be saved from your enemies.' (Numbers 10:9)."

A typical tale illustrating the Ruzhyner's emphasis on joy as an antidote to evil.

V WILL IT BE HARD TO BE A GOOD JEW?

Kenesset Yisrael, pp. 33–34

I heard this from a reliable person who heard it from the Ḥasid Rabbi Hitzel of Lutzk of blessed memory. He was sitting at the pure table of our master of Ruzhyn one Sabbath and only a few Ḥasidim, no more than eleven or so, were present at the time. The Rabbi said, "The time will come when it will be well with the coarse person both with regard to material and spiritual matters, but it will be good for the refined person neither in material matters nor even in spiritual; that is to say, he will be incapable of reciting even a single psalm from the Book of Psalms." He concluded his remarks by saying, "The reason I tell you this is so that you do not become discouraged. For so it is and so it must be."

The final words are in Yiddish in the original. Here we have an interesting anticipation on the part of the Ruzhyner of the new challenges to be presented to the Ḥasidic way of life. One of his sons, in fact, though a Ḥasidic master, left the Ḥasidic fold for a time and went over to the camp of the Maskilim, the "enlightened ones," opponents of Ḥasidism, to the scandal of his Ḥasidic contemporaries.

CHAPTER 27

Menaḥem Mendel of Kotzk

1787-1859

Why the outburst of scientific achievement in the 1800's?
The role of righteous indignation
Which type of worship is false?
Should we care what others think?
God helps those who help themselves
Aphorisms

Menaḥem Mendel—"the Kotzker," as he is called by the Ḥasidim—was a highly original Ḥasidic thinker of fiery temperament whose teachings were all based on the need for absolute sincerity in the religious life and who was a severe critic of his contemporaries for their alleged lack of this quality.

Menaḥem Mendel was attracted to Ḥasidism in his youth by the "Seer" of Lublin, whose disciple he became. When another disciple of the "Seer," known as the "Holy Jew" of Przysucha, broke away from his master to found the Przysucha type of Ḥasidism, with the emphasis on intellectual ability, inwardness, and sincerity and with a special appeal to the elite rather than to the masses, Menaḥem Mendel followed him and his successor Simḥah Bunem of Przysucha. When Simḥah Bunem died, the mantle of leadership of the Przysucha group fell on Menaḥem Mendel. It has often been told how, for twenty or so years at the end of his life, Menaḥem Mendel secluded himself from his followers and from the world.

Professor Abraham Joshua Heschel wrote, just before his death, an acute biography of the Kotzker entitled A Passion for Truth *(New York, 1973), in which this master is compared to the famous Danish thinker and existentialist Kierkegaard. (But see the note on Naḥman of Bratslav.) The Kotzker wrote nothing himself, but his ideas, and especially his keen aphorisms, appear in various collections. The following pieces are taken from the collection* Amud Ha-Emet *(Pillar of Truth) (Tel-Aviv, no date).*

I WHY THE OUTBURST OF SCIENTIFIC ACHIEVEMENT IN THE 1800'S?

Amud Ha-Emet, Noah, p. 7

"In the six hundreth year . . . all the fountains of the great deep were broken open" (Genesis 7:11). According to the holy Zohar, this refers to the six hundreth year of the sixth thousand [= 1840]. In this year, the fountains and springs of wisdom will freely flow. Indeed, in that year the fountains of wisdom were opened but, for our sins, we were not worthy of it. The external ones seized hold of that influx of wisdom which came from the fountains of wisdom and used it for their own purposes. That is why we observe the tremendous development in secular science and the new inventions of our day.

The Kotzker was not unaware of the great strides science and technology had taken in his day, in the first half of the nineteenth century. Ideally, he says, the bursting forth of the fountains of wisdom should have produced a tremendous outpouring of the spirit of Torah wisdom, of spiritual truth. As it was, God's word was still fulfilled, but the outburst of wisdom was applied in the secular sphere.

II THE ROLE OF RIGHTEOUS INDIGNATION

Amud Ha-Emet, Shemot, pp. 17–18

A comment on: "And the anger of the Lord was kindled against Moses" (Exodus 4:14). The Kotzker understands be-moshe *to mean not "against Moses" but "in Moses."*

At first Moses refused to go to Pharaoh. But when the anger of the Holy One, blessed be He, at Israel's sufferings in Egypt began

to be kindled in Moses himself, he went to redeem them. And so it should be so far as every zaddik is concerned. Whatever he does on behalf of the community of Israel, he should do because the anger of the Holy One, blessed be He, burns within him.

The righteous indignation of the man who cannot tolerate injustice has a divine quality. But note how the Kotzker typically stresses this aspect of the zaddik's role, unlike the majority of the Ḥasidic masters who would have said that the zaddik should be especially moved by compassion for his people. The Kotzker was generally a little uneasy about the virtue of compassion, considering it to be at times too soft an option.

III WHICH TYPE OF WORSHIP IS FALSE?

Amud Ha-Emet, Yitro, p. 24

"And when the people saw it, they trembled, and stood afar off" (Exodus 20:15).

It is possible for a man to see and to tremble and yet still be far away.

Most of the Ḥasidim made violent gestures in their prayers, swaying the body this way and that. In his passion for complete inward truth, the Kotzker was suspicious of such external demonstrations of piety. A man can have a vision of the divine and can quake and sway in prayer and yet still be remote from God in his heart.

IV SHOULD WE CARE WHAT OTHERS THINK?

Amud Ha-Emet, Shelaḥ, p. 38

"And we were in our own sight as grasshoppers, and so we were in their sight" (Numbers 13:33). This was one of the sins of the spies. We can understand them saying: "And we were in our own eyes as grasshoppers," but why did they say: "and so we were in their sight"? Why should you care how others see you?

A typical Kotzker observation. [Ordinarily the sin of the spies is expressed as, "How did they know what their enemies thought of them?" He goes far beyond that.] The true Ḥasid should think only of doing his duty and pleasing God. Why should he be at all bothered about the opinion others have of him? This attitude led other Ḥasidim to speak of the Kotzker Ḥasidim as ruffians indifferent to all of the social graces. No doubt the Kotzker Ḥasidim admitted to the charge but were delighted by it.

V GOD HELPS THOSE WHO HELP THEMSELVES

Amud Ha-Emet, Ki tetze, p. 48

"Thou shalt not see thy brother's ass or his ox fallen down by the way, and hide thyself from them; thou shalt surely help him to lift them up again" (Deuteronomy 22:4). The Talmud explains "thou shalt surely help him" to mean, only if he, too, plays his part. But there is no obligation at all if the owner of the ox or the ass leaves you to do it all by yourself since it is a religious obligation. The same applies to the help given to man to assist him in his Torah studies and his worship of God. Only if man himself strives hard is this help extended to him.

The obligations we have to help our neighbors does not mean that they can trade on our generosity and leave it all to us. They, too, must play their part and then we must help them. The Kotzker applies this idea to the divine aid given to man. This is only forthcoming if man tries to the best of his ability first. The principle that God helps those who help themselves applies also to spiritual endeavors.

VI APHORISMS

Amud Ha-Emet, pp. 93–95—some aphorisms of the Kotzker

He [i.e., the Kotzker] once saw a man studying a book and he asked him what it was. The man told him that it was [Maimonides'] *Guide for the Perplexed*. **Our teacher said: "For the man full of knowledge of the Talmud and the codes this book is, indeed, a guide. But for others it is only a source of perplexity."**

Someone asked him what he should do in order to acquire a taste for learning. Our teacher replied, "How can anyone possibly fail to have a taste for such a good thing?" But he added, "the way is to study in depth."

He once asked Rabbi Jacob of Radziman, "Jacob! What is the purpose of man's creation?" The Radzimaner replied, "Man was created

in order to perfect his soul." Our teacher shouted, "Jacob! Is this what we were taught in Przysucha? Man was created in order to increase God's glory."

A young man once excused himself that he was a henpecked husband. The rabbi said to him, "And thy desire shall be to thy husband, and he shall rule over thee" (Genesis 3:16). Where the opposite of the first part of the verse obtains, the second half is also reversed.

Our teacher complained about those who go to visit the graves of the zaddikim in the cemetery of Lublin, since the zaddikim are no longer there.

In these typical aphorisms we see the Kotzker emphasis on ruthless self-scrutiny. But his sternness was too much even for some of his most devoted followers. As we shall see, his favorite disciple, Mordecai Joseph of Izbica, eventually parted company with the master to found a rival Ḥasidic community.

CHAPTER 28

Mordecai Joseph Leiner of Izbica
d. 1854

How can man know his specific duty in life?
What should a man do when his faith weakens?
The importance of obstacles
How can we conquer fear?
The spiritual dangers of religion

Mordecai Joseph Leiner was one of the most audacious and extremely original of the Ḥasidic masters, so much so that his thought is more than a little outside the mainstream of the Ḥasidic tradition. Nevertheless, he is held in high esteem by the Ḥasidim and was the founder of the Radzhyner dynasty in Ḥasidism, being succeeded by his son Jacob of Radzhyn (1814–1878) who was in turn succeeded by his son Gershon Henich of Radzhyn (1839–1891).

Mordecai Joseph was a pupil of the fiery Menaḥem Mendel of Kotzk, the Kotzker Rebbe, from whom he eventually parted for reasons that are none too clear, although legend has stepped in where facts are lacking. Mordecai Joseph's teachings are to be found in the work, published by his grandson, Gershon Henich, in Vienna, 1862, entitled Mey Ha-Shiloaḥ, after which work Mordecai Joseph is generally known by the Ḥasidim as "the Mey Ha-Shiloaḥ" (or, sometimes, "the Izbicer"). The title means "of the Waters of Shiloah" and is based on the verse, "The waters of Shiloaḥ that go softly" (Isaiah 8:6). Mordecai did not write the book himself. As has grandson writes in the preface, it was put together by Gershon from the teachings preserved by the master's closest disciples.

Jacob, Mordecai Joseph's son, is known as "the Radzhyner Rebbe" or, after the title of his book, "the Bet Yaakov*" (House of Jacob). This work was published in Lublin in 1904.*

I HOW CAN MAN KNOW HIS SPECIFIC DUTY IN LIFE?

Mey Ha-Shiloaḥ, Likkutim, p. 139

"O God, Thou hast taught me from my youth; and until now I declare Thy wondrous works. And even unto old age and hoary hairs . . ." (Psalm 71:17,18). Behold, man must engage in reflection and increase his understanding while he is still a young man, before his evil inclination has gained too much of a hold on him. At this time of life he should learn how to discern between that for which he has a powerful desire and that from which his heart is remote. From it he will come to appreciate exactly what it is that the Holy One, blessed be He, has prepared as a test for him so that thereby he can refine his character. It is with regard to this particular thing that he is called upon to gain self-control and exercise vigilance. For the Holy One, blessed be He, has given each man some special means of refining his character, and each man is obliged to make himself aware of his own special task. Basically, he can only really succeed in becoming aware of this while he is still young, for once the evil inclination has gained some control over a man it inclines him toward many things and he is unable to recognize his own special task. Hence, our verse says: "O God, Thou hast taught me from my youth." That is to say, man can only discern his own special task while he is still young. The result will be that "even unto old age and hoary hairs," God will not forsake him.

A psychological observation. No two men are exactly alike, each has his own special task in life, since each differs from others in temperament and disposition. One man finds it easy to be kind and generous, but hard to devote time to study. Another finds it easy to study, but very hard to be generous. And so forth. In his youth a man should become aware of that which he finds uncongenial and then train himself to concentrate on overcoming his reluctance, leaving the things he finds easy to do to take care of themselves. This is the way to refinement of character. It is far easier to engage in this kind of introspection in youth because young men tend to see things more in terms of black and white. They are more idealistic and less cynical than older men, who have become too distracted to acknowledge where their particular duty lies.

II WHAT SHOULD A MAN DO WHEN HIS FAITH WEAKENS?

Mey Ha-Shiloaḥ, Likkutim, p. 142

"If I ascend up into Heaven, Thou art there; If I make my bed in Hell, behold, Thou art there" (Psalm 139:8). "If I ascend up into Heaven" means: When you raise and elevate me with an influx of grace and when my intellect is in control, then: "Thou art there"—it is all absolutely clear to me, as it is said: "For all things come of Thee, and of Thine own have we given Thee" (1 Chronicles 29:14). "If I make my bed in Hell, behold, Thou art there." That is to say, even when my intellect does not function adequately, even then my desire is to recognize that "Thou art," that all power is Thine, hence it says: "Thou art there."

Heaven and Hell are interpreted not as places but as psychological states. When man is "in Heaven," when his mind is clear and his religious sense alert, he knows with certainty that God is. But even when he is "in Hell," when all seems dark and obscure, when faith is very weak, he still prays to be worthy of acknowledging his God.

III THE IMPORTANCE OF OBSTACLES

Mey Ha-Shiloaḥ, Bereshit, p. 7

"I will make him a help against him" (Genesis 2:18). The meaning is that it is the will of the Creator, blessed be He, that help and assistance should spring forth for man from that which challenges him. The illustration is from the pupil-teacher relationship. We find that Resh Lakish asked Rabbi Joḥanan twenty-four questions and that Rabbi Joḥanan then gave twenty-four replies to his objection, so that the theory Rabbi Joḥanan advanced became clarified automatically. But it was not so when Rabbi Eleazar simply declared that he could adduce proof from earlier sources that Rabbi Joḥanan

was right. For when a man sees that his position is challenged, he is obliged to defend it with even stronger proofs so that his view appears in far greater clarity.

The story of Resh Lakish and Rabbi Joḥahan is in the Talmud, tractate Baba Meẓia 84a. When Resh Lakish died, Rabbi Eleazar became Rabbi Joḥanan's companion in his studies. Whenever Rabbi Joḥanan would advance a theory, Rabbi Eleazar would immediately quote proofs for its correctness from the earlier authorities, but Rabbi Joḥanan remained dissatisfied. "Resh Lakish," he said, "tried, on the contrary, to refute my views, raising difficulties to which I was compelled to reply, and in the process the whole idea became much clearer." Thus it is true to life that some opposition is required. The verse speaks of Eve as Adam's "helper," ezer, *but says, too, in one reading of our verse, that she was "against him,"* ke-negdo. *Man and woman are, in a sense, bound to be in confliçt with one another, but this very difference in temperament and outlook causes them to be of assistance to one another. Eve is Adam's "help" by being "against him."*

IV HOW CAN WE CONQUER FEAR?

Mey Ha-Shiloaḥ, Shemot, p. 38

"And it came to pass, because the midwives feared God, that He made them houses" (Exodus 1:21). When a man is afraid of other human beings his soul lacks serenity, since fear is a direct contradiction to serenity of mind. But serenity is found where there is the fear of God, blessed be He. This is why it says: "And He made them houses." A house denotes serenity of mind. Since they had this serenity, the fruit of their fear of God, Pharaoh's decree had no terrors for them. Hence our verse says: "He made them houses."

A fine comment. The accusation that religion is based on fear is countered by noting that, in fact, the fear of God is such that it frees man from all other fears. It produces the serenity and peace of mind that enables man to face all obstacles calmly and courageously just as the midwives who feared God were indifferent to Pharaoh's orders that they should kill the Hebrew infants. The commentators find the expression "He made them houses" difficult to understand, and many suggestions have been put forward as to its meaning. Mordecai

Joseph's homiletical but acute interpretation is that their fear of God made them feel with God's help, "as safe as houses."

V THE SPIRITUAL DANGERS OF RELIGION

Bet Yaakov, vol. 2, *Yitro*, no. 113, p. 256

"Thou shalt not make unto thee a graven image . . ." (Exodus 20:4). This means: You must not endow the precepts of the Torah with any existence in their own right, for they are no more than the instruments of God, blessed be He. As the Talmud (Yevamot 6b) says, "It is not of the Sabbath that you must be afraid," and "It is not of the Temple that you must be afraid." Even in connection with such holy and tremendous things as these, you must not worship them, otherwise they are called a graven image. Hence our verse continues, "of any thing that is in Heaven above," referring to the Sabbath, the sanctity of which is fixed in Heaven beforehand and does not depend on Israel to make it holy, "or that which is in the earth beneath," referring to the Temple site. You must only worship Him who resides in them and Him alone must you fear. It goes on to say: "Thou shalt not take the name of the Lord thy God in vain" (Exodus 20:7). This means that for all that, you must not imagine that they are vain things, God forbid, and that He does not reside in them, for if you think this, you will be guilty of taking God's name in vain. For the Sabbath and the Temple are the Name of God and no place is empty of Him.

The commands of God must be obeyed but not worshipped. If a man worships the Sabbath or the Temple he is guilty of idolatry. This is a very courageous statement, pointing to the peculiar temptation to which intensely religious people are prone, of worshipping the institutions of religion instead of treating them as vehicles to God.

CHAPTER 29

Solomon Rabinowich of Radomsk

1803-1866

How important is sincerity?
How can men be holy outside the Holy Land?

Solomon was a disciple of the Ḥasidic master Meir of Apt, one of the chief disciples of Elimelech of Lizensk. He was a talmudic scholar and was, at first, appointed rabbi of the town of Radomsk, only becoming a Ḥasidic zaddik there in the year 1843. One of Solomon's followers was the German thinker Dr. Aaron Marcus, who wrote a book on his Ḥasidic experiences in the modern style in German.

Solomon's Ḥasidic work Tiferet Shelomo *(The Splendor of Solomon) became very popular among the Ḥasidim. The first volume was published in Warsaw in 1867, the second in Pietrikow in 1889. (The edition used here is that of Jerusalem, 1966.) Solomon is known by the Ḥasidim either as "the Radomsker" or as "the* Tiferet Shelomo" *(after his work).*

I HOW IMPORTANT IS SINCERITY?

Tiferet Shelomo, vol. 1, *Bereshit,* p. 10

"Let us make man in our image, after our likeness" (Genesis 1:26).

The capacity to discover various meanings in the commandments is well known. Each zaddik discovers new meanings without number.

However, it is simply not possible during the extremely short period when he is performing the commandment for a man to have in mind all the meanings hinted at in the holy books we have at present and those to be published until the end of time. Take, for example, the verse about Abraham: "And he took the knife to slay his son" (Genesis 22:10). The commentators are innumerable who explain this verse in accordance with the most profound mysteries, each one giving his own interpretation, and all are the words of the living God. But how could it have been physically possible in such a short period for Abraham to have had in mind all these intentions? The same applies to the numerous holy books reading profound mysteries into the Book of Ruth. It has been reported of the holy Rabbi of Meziboz of blessed memory that he once said that it was quite impossible for Ruth at that time to have had in mind such profound mysteries.

The "holy Rabbi of Meziboz" is Baruch of Meziboz, the grandson of the Baal Shem Tov, treated earlier in this book (Chapter 7), where a similar idea of his is quoted. Solomon has a real sense of history. He does not deny the truth of all the meanings recorded in the "holy books," but realizes that it cannot be taken literally to mean that, for example, Abraham or Ruth could possibly have had all these in mind. Solomon's answer is that it all depends on truth in the heart. If a man sincerely intends to do the will of God, all that is implied in that will, even if it is unknown to him, is embraced by his sincere intention.

The basic idea here is that the quality of truth embraces all, from beginning to middle to end. Thus when a man performs a commandment with completely sincerity all the intentions take effect of their own accord. This is the meaning of the verse: "And thou shalt love the Lord thy God with all thy heart" (Deuteronomy 6:5). This means that the main purpose of all the commandments is for the sake of the unification of the Holy One, blessed be He, with His *Shekhinah*, so that the Name should be whole. This is the meaning of: "And thou shalt love. . . ." This means that you should bring love and wholeness to the Name YHVH so that the letters of the Name should become combined without any separation, God forbid.

Solomon is here referring to a kabbalistic idea of great importance to the Ḥasidim. The Tetragrammaton, the four-letter Name of God, represents the unification of all the powers (the Sefirot*) in the Godhead. Man has been given the tremendous task of producing harmony not only on earth but among the divine processes on high as well. Thus the stage on high known as "the Holy One, blessed be He" is to be united with that stage in which God becomes manifest here on earth, known as the* Shekhinah. *When man on earth carries out God's will he makes God, as it were, come down from Heaven, and there is unity in all creation. Thus Solomon's very bold interpretation of the verse in Deuteronomy is to take it to mean: "Thou shalt produce love," i.e., on high, "love" meaning here "harmony."*

II HOW CAN MEN BE HOLY OUTSIDE THE HOLY LAND?

Tiferet Shelomo, vol. 1, *Va-yetze,* p. 54

"And he lighted upon the place, and tarried there all night, because the sun was set" (Genesis 28:11). The early commentators write that all the deeds of the Patriarchs were done for the sake of their descendants, as the Ramban of blessed memory explains. Therefore, when our father Jacob, on whom be peace, left the Holy Land to go outside it, he knew that this would provide an indication for his descendants. That is why he made it his business to pray in that place. For in connection with buildings on the Temple mount, the Rabbis of blessed memory say that the buildings which stand on a secular spot but have their entrance in a sacred spot are holy, but those standing on a sacred spot but which have their entrance in a secular spot have no sanctity.

The Ramban *is Naḥmanides; for his views see Volume 2 in this series. If a building on the Temple mount is erected on the part that has no sanctity, it still has sanctity if its entrance is in a holy spot; but if it is erected on a holy spot but has its entrance on a secular spot, it has no sanctity. Thus all depends on where the entrance is. Solomon is leading up to the opinion that even if prayers are offered outside the Holy Land they are acceptable to God provided that they are at the entrance to the Holy Land, as was Jacob's prayer. By "entrance to the Holy Land" in this connection, as Solomon goes on to say, is meant where man's intention is in holiness. The Ḥasidim, aware of the great sanctity of the Holy Land, were profoundly disturbed that they had to offer their prayers in a secular land. Masters like Solomon sought to reassure them that the devout Jew can offer his prayers in a spirit of sanctity even in Poland.*

The hint here is to provide a model for the children of Israel who dwell outside the Holy Land and hope for the rebuilding of the Temple, as it is said: "And pray unto Thee toward their land" (1 Kings 8:48); and as it is said: "Open to me the gates of righteousness" (Psalm 118:19). Hence it says: "And this is the gate of heaven" (Genesis 28:17). That is to say, it is considered as if they stood in the holy place. God forbid, the contrary is the case, when they dwell in the land of Israel but have their entrance in a secular spot—that is to say, when their thoughts are on the secular—then it is as if they dwelt outside the Holy Land. That is why Jacob set that place aside so that all the prayers of the children of the *diaspora* **should ascend through that place. Hence our verse says: "And tarried there all night, because the sun was set," since exile is darkness. But of the time of redemption it is said: "But unto you that fear My name shall the sun of righteousness arise" (Malachi 3:20). And so it was with regard to all the prayers offered by Jacob, as when he said: "So that I come back to my father's house in peace" (Genesis 28:21). "In peace" means whole and untainted by sin through the long exile, and so shall we return to the house of our Father, speedily and in our days. Amen.**

Solomon ends passages of this kind, in typical Ḥasidic fashion, speaking of the hope of redemption, with a prayer that it may soon happen. It is very probable that, in fact, these passages are the notes of sermons he actually delivered to his followers and that such sermons generally concluded with the prayer for redemption.

CHAPTER 30

Ḥayyim Halberstam of Zanz

1793-1876

Is it possible even today for holy men to be inspired?
What is the way to truth?
Is it true that religious people are bound to be poor?

Ḥayyim Halberstam was the founder of the Zanz dynasty in Ḥasidism. He was a disciple of the "Seer" of Lublin, Israel of Ruzhyn, and Shalom Rokeaḥ of Belz. All eight sons of Ḥayyim became Ḥasidic masters, the most famous of them being Ezekiel Shraga of Sieniawa (1811–1899). Both Ḥayyim and his son were distinguished talmudic scholars and were the official rabbis of their towns.

Ḥayyim wrote a number of works, all entitled Divrey Ḥayyim *(Words of Life). He is called by the Ḥasidim "the* Divrey Ḥayyim,*" after his work. His Ḥasidic discourses were published under this title in Munkacs in 1877 and his responsa, with the same title, in Lemberg in 1875. Ezekiel's work* Divrey Yehezkel *was published in Sieniawa in 1906.*

I IS IT POSSIBLE EVEN TODAY FOR HOLY MEN TO BE INSPIRED?

Divrey Ḥayyim, responsa, *Yoreh Deah,* no. 105

Ḥayyim ibn Attar, referred to in this responsum, was a famous kabbalist whose commentary Or Ha-Ḥayyim, *compiled at the beginning of the eighteenth century, was very popular with the Ḥasidim. For Ḥayyim ibn Attar see Volume IV in this series.*

QUESTION: **A certain teacher of children insulted "the *Or Ha-Ḥayyim*" of blessed memory, saying that his book was not compiled under the influence of the Holy Spirit.**

REPLY: **I have received your letter. I fail to understand why you are in doubt whether even nowadays the Holy Spirit can rest upon one worthy of it even though there are no prophets any longer. It is stated explicitly in the first chapter of Bava Batra (12a) that from the day the Temple was destroyed prophecy has been taken from the prophets and given to the sages. The Talmud asks: But is not the sage also a prophet? The reply is given that the meaning is; Although prophecy has been taken away from the prophets, it was not taken away from the sages. . . . So you see that even after the destruction of the Temple the spirit of prophecy rests upon whomever is worthy of it, that is to say, the Holy Spirit of wisdom, for prophecy is one thing and the Holy Spirit of wisdom is another, as it is stated in Maimonides'** *Guide for the Perplexed*, **part 2.**

Ḥayyim includes here a lengthy discussion on the talmudic passage which we have abbreviated. The gist of what he says is that it is clear from the passage that although there is no longer the prophetic gift, there still obtains that particular kind of inspiration known as the Holy Spirit, and it is given to the sages of Israel.

So you see that it is stated explicitly in the Talmud and in the early teachers that the holy spirit of wisdom has not ceased from the sages. And it is stated explicitly further in tractate Gittin (6b) in connection with Rabbi Abiathar. This is what the Talmud says there: "nay more, Rabbi Abiathar is the authority whose view was confirmed by his Master." Rashi explains this to mean that God revealed to Rabbi Abiathar the secret whereby he could arrive at the correct conclusion regarding hidden matters. So you see that the holy spirit and confirmation by God have not ceased from those sages worthy of it. And it is also proved by the statement of Rabbi Phineḥas ben Jair (Avodah Zarah 20b).

Rabbi Phineḥas ben Jair, in the passage referred to, states that the study of the Torah leads to many high degrees, among them the attainment of the holy spirit.

Even more than this it is stated in the Midrash Rabbah to Naso, in connection with the woman who attended the lectures of Rabbi Meir, that Rabbi Meir "gazed with the holy spirit." So you see that he was possessed of the holy spirit. And Rabbi Judah the Prince, too, uttered words of prophecy on the day of his death, as is stated in tractate Kiddushin 72, even after the time when prophecy had been taken from Israel. The truth is that from this it appears that it is otherwise than Maimonides states in his *Guide*. **For from that passage in the** *Guide* **it would seem that without the type of prophecy produced by man's imaginative powers the sage is only called a great thinker, not that he is capable of uttering things beyond reason which appear as prophecy.**

Note that Ḥayyim naturally takes as literal truth the talmudic accounts of the sages being gifted with the Holy Spirit. He is thoroughly familiar with the work of Maimonides, including his philosophical teachings, and has great respect for Maimonides, but appeals against him to the Talmud. It would seem from the talmudic passage that the true Torah sage is not simply a man of great intellectual ability, but also is gifted with a kind of inspiration, the Holy Spirit.

Be that as it may, all agree that the Holy Spirit has not been taken from the sages. When it is said that after the days of the prophets the Holy Spirit has been taken away, it refers to the spirit of prophecy; but the Holy Spirit of wisdom, and that the sage should have the gift of conforming to the law as given to Moses at Sinai or like Rabbi Abiathar, this has never ceased. Only a heretic will deny this. When you write that the great ones of the generation have stated that the holy spirit has ceased entirely, I do not believe that any such thing was ever said by our teachers, long may they live. Who knows what this scoundrel wrote to mislead them. The truth is that even in our age the true sages who are not committed to material things are possessed of the Holy Spirit. This is stated explicitly in the *Guide* **and by Naḥmanides of blessed memory. Consequently, the author of the** *Or Ha-Ḥayyim*, **his soul is in Eden,**

certainly composed his work under the influence of the Holy Spirit. But not only this author but every author, even in our age, provided he is worthy of it, composed his work under the influence of the Holy Spirit, that is to say, as the Talmud says of Rabbi Abiathar, his wisdom accords with the wisdom of the Torah. "The *Tumim*" even applies this to the actual law. He rules that no one can claim, in cases of doubt, that he follows other authorities than the Shulḥan Arukh, since this work was composed under the influence of the Holy Spirit.

"The Tumin,*" so named after his work, is the famous eighteenth-century talmudist Rabbi Jonathan Eybushütz. The point here is that in a civil dispute, where the law is debated by the authorities, one who has possession can claim that he is prepared to follow the authority according to whom he is in the right, even if other authorities disagree. But "the* Tumim*" states that this cannot apply where the dissenting voice is that of the Shulḥan Arukh, the standard code of Jewish law, since this is an infallible work, having been composed under the influence of the Holy Spirit.*

Consequently, the teacher who denies that "the *Or Ha-Ḥayyim*" was possessed of the Holy Spirit is a heretic, since he does not believe in the great ones of the generation who testified that he was possessed of he Holy Spirit. Furthermore, this teacher denied the main principle about the Holy Spirit, scoffing at the words of the Talmud in Bava Batra, as above. You did well not to allow your children to be pupils of his any longer, and I congratulate you. However, I am unable to render any decision in connection with his salary behind his back without observing how he actually conducts himself, for it may have been in error. In this matter you can rely on the rabbi in your town and all will be well.

Thus Ḥayyim, like many other Ḥasidic masters, believes that the Holy Spirit still works and that the acknowledged works contain infallible truth. The reference to the "great ones of the generation" is to the belief of the Ḥasidic masters—going back, it is alleged, to the Baal Shem Tov—that the work Or Ha-Ḥayyim *was compiled under the influence of the holy spirit. In fact, this work is quoted frequently by the Ḥasidim as if it were a Ḥasidic classic.*

II WHAT IS THE WAY TO TRUTH?

Divrey Yeḥezkel, Bereshit, p. 3a

"In the beginning God created the Heaven and the earth" (Genesis 1:1). The final letters of *bereshit bara Elohim* **("In the beginning God created") form the word** *emet* **("truth"), but the letters are not in the correct order. The final letters of** *bara Elohim et* **("God created the") form the word** *emet,* **and here the letters are in the correct order. This is a hint that man should strive to attain to the truth even though at first he cannot fully attain to it, that is to say, it is not in the correct order. Then God will help him to attain to the quality of truth completely and it will all be in the correct order. A parable can be given from a building. Although when the actual construction takes place it must all be in the correct order, first the foundation, then the walls, and then the roof, for all that, the builder, when putting together the materials for the building, buys whatever he can get hold of at the time and then when he has it all, he builds in the proper order.**

The final letters of the first three words form the word emet, *but in the wrong order, i.e.,* tav, alef, mem. *The final letters of the three words after* bereshit, *"in the beginning," also form the word* emet, *but this time in the correct order, i.e.,* alef, mem, tav *(*et *is the usual sign for the accusative). Ezekiel derives a moral from this. "In the beginning" the truth cannot be in its proper order. But later on the full truth is obtained. He is, in fact, encouraging his followers in their quest for truth and sincerity. They must not be deterred by the fact that truth is hard to come by. Yes, he says, at first mistakes will be made and only a distorted vision of the truth will emerge. But if man presses on regardless, he will eventually be helped to attain to a complete appreciation of the truth.*

III IS IT TRUE THAT RELIGIOUS PEOPLE ARE BOUND TO BE POOR?

Divrey Yeḥezkel, Tehillim, p. 25b

"O fear the Lord, ye His holy ones; for there is no want to them that fear Him. The young lions do lack, and suffer hunger; but they that seek the Lord want not any good thing" (Psalms 34:10, 11). In a playful way in the name of my master and father the holy

Gaon, his memory is for a blessing, and, so far as I recall, in the name of the Alshech, the verse can be said to teach us the incorrectness of the views of the ignorant folk who argue that God-fearing men are always short of money. Therefore, the verse says: "O fear the Lord, ye His holy ones; for there is no want to them that fear Him." The proof is: how many "lions," a synonym for the "wicked," "do lack," and yet how many of "they that seek the Lord" yet "want not any good thing."

The "holy Gaon" is, of course, Rabbi Ḥayyim, Ezekiel's father. For the Alshech see Volume 4 in this series. Ezekiel realizes that this can hardly be the meaning of the verse, but implies that in a "playful" manner this kind of interpretation is not without its value.

CHAPTER 31

Yitzḥak Isaac Judah Jeḥiel Safrin of Komarno 1806-1874

Are unworthy motives ever admissible?
How can one learn from all men?
How can man honor God?
The harm of losing one's temper

Yitzḥak Isaac Judah Jeḥiel Safrin or, as he is generally called, Reb Yitzḥak Eisik of Komarno—or, by the Ḥasidim, the "Komarno Rebbe"—was the son and successor of Alexander Sender, the founder of the Komarno dynasty of Ḥasidism. He had many teachers in Ḥasidic lore, among them his father, his uncle Zevi Hirsch of Zhidachov, the "Seer" of Lublin, and the Maggid of Koznitz. But in many ways Yitzḥak Eisik pursued a line of his own and is very independent in his views, as well as trying to recapture the original insights, as he saw them, of the Baal Shem Tov and his associates. Yitzḥak Eisik kept a secret diary in which he recorded his visions and mystical thoughts. This circulated in manuscript among a few of his chosen followers until it was printed and published by N. Ben Menaḥem in Jerusalem, 1944.

Yitzḥak Eisik was a very prolific writer both on kabbalistic, Ḥasidic, and general talmudic themes. The following selections are from his commentary to the Mishnah, in the section to Ethics of the Fathers. This edition of the text of the Mishnah together with this commentary, known as Notzer Ḥesed, *and three other commentaries to other parts of the Mishnah, were published in Lemberg in 1862, and recently in New York in 1964.*

I ARE UNWORTHY MOTIVES EVER ADMISSIBLE?

Notzer Ḥesed to Avot 1:13: "He who does not study deserves to die; and he who makes a worldly use of the crown of the Torah shall waste away."

"He who does not study." This is a warning against stupid Ḥasidism. True the main thing is to study the Torah for its own sake and in order to be in a state of attachment (*devekut*) to God. But this is on a most elevated plane, and it is impossible for man to arrive at once to the stage of "for its own sake." He is bound to have to study the Torah with ulterior motives (*she-lo lishmah*) until his character has become sufficiently refined to enable him to delight in the Torah. Even when the Torah is studied with ulterior motives, its inner light produces eventually a worthier approach. But the fools try all at once to seize hold of this inner light, and since they are unworthy of it they give up Torah study entirely; for they do not want to study with ulterior motives, since they are Ḥasidim and as for study for its own sake, this is beyond them for the time being. In order to negate this type of folly—folly it is, since the main thing in life is to study the Torah, and there is nothing more precious in the whole world—the Tanna remarks: "He who does not study deserves to die" by the hand of Heaven, for he has no part in eternal life. "And he who makes a worldly use of the crown of the Torah shall find it transformed." He who makes use of the King's sceptre for his own benefit by studying the Torah with ulterior motives, will nevertheless be transformed, as it is said: "But they that wait for the Lord shall renew their strength" (Isaiah 40:31), for out of study from ulterior motives, study out of pure motives will emerge and holy degrees of worship. But one who does not study at all has nothing to be transformed, and he remains on high in a state of great embarrassment.

We have seen more than once in this book the great emphasis that the Ḥasidim, from the days of the Baal Shem Tov, placed on Torah lishmah, *Torah for its own sake, and on* devekut, *attachment to God in the mind. The result was that some Ḥasidim went to the extreme of saying that it is better not to study at all than to study for one's own personal gain and so use religion for one's own ends, rather as if a subject of the king dares to wear the king's crown "to show off." Yitzḥak Eisik calls this attitude stupid. The main thing, at first, is to study the Torah, and this will have its effect on man's character whatever his original motive for studying. He gives a curious turn to the word* ḥalaf, *translated as "shall waste away." He takes this to mean "will be changed," "will be transformed," so that the passage means: "Even one who uses the royal crown should not be too disturbed, for the Torah he studies will transform him and become itself transformed, so that eventually all will be well." The word used in the verse from Isaiah for "shall renew" is* yaḥalifu, *which is from the same root,* ḥalaf. *Yitzḥak Eisik, as a distinguished talmudist and rabbinic scholar, did not wish to allow the impression to be gained that Ḥasidism was to be identified with ignorance of the Torah, as some of the Mitnaggedim maintained and by whom it is possible that he was influenced.*

II HOW CAN ONE LEARN FROM ALL MEN?

Notzer Ḥesed to Avot 4:1: "Who is wise? He who learns from all men"

"Who is wise?" Our Master the divine Rabbi Israel Baal Shem Tov of blessed memory thus explained: "He who learns from all men." He said that a great principle of conduct is here stated. For a man sometimes imagines himself to be completely righteous, but when he sees another committing any kind of sin he should know that he, too, is guilty of something of the kind and he should repent. He related this about himself. Once he saw a very ordinary person profane the Sabbath unintentionally but in a way that he could have avoided had he have taken greater care. The Baal Shem Tov engaged in repentance as if he had profaned the Sabbath until Heaven showed him that he had, in fact, been guilty of profaning the Sabbath in that he had allowed a scholar, who is called "the Sabbath," to minister to his needs. In similar fashion, one who is proud it is as if he had taken a woman forbidden to him, and one who flies into a rage it is as if he had worshipped idols. The wise man takes note of all this and learns from all men how to improve his own character.

Whether or not the Baal Shem Tov actually said this (and Yitzḥak Eisik is somewhat prone to accept as authentic sayings attributed to the Baal Shem Tov without real evidence), it is a typical Ḥasidic idea that all things on earth are sent to man by God for a particular purpose. Why should the Baal Shem Tov have been compelled to witness someone profaning the Sabbath? The answer is that God wanted him to realize that he, too, had been guilty of this sin—not, of course, in its crude sense, but because he had made use of a scholar and had thus "profaned" the Sabbath, the student of the Torah being called "the Sabbath" because even his weekdays are devoted to spiritual pursuits. The wise man, similarly, will never be guilty of the cruder forms of adultery or idolatry, but he may be guilty of pride, which is like adultery in that he claims for himself something to which he has no right, or he may be guilty of bad temper, which is like idolatry since it demonstrates that he has little faith in God.

The wise man can also learn good traits of character from the man in the street. For there is no Jew without some special good quality rare among others, and so, if he has a mind for it, he can learn much from every man. He can even learn something from a Gentile whom he meets in the market place and who tells him some tale or some other matter. He will appreciate that he was not made to hear this for nothing, but in order that he might learn from it some good practice or some good way of conducting himself. Therefore it says: "Who is wise?" This means that he is wise already. And the reason for it is that he has learned from all men.

Again, a typical Ḥasidic idea. Compare the story at the beginning of this book (Chapter 1) of the Baal Shem Tov and his horses. However, Yitzḥak Eisik is not too happy about this idea, for if a man can become wise by learning from all men, what becomes of the Ḥasidic teaching that only by associating with the zaddik and learning from him can a man become wise? Yitzḥak Eisik makes the distinction between the wise man—the zaddik himself—and the Ḥasid. The latter should gain all his wisdom only from the zaddik, not from "all men." The passage about Joseph bar Ḥiyya referred to below is in tractate Ḥullin of the Talmud (18b).

But a disciple should not learn from all men. The Talmud speaks derogatively of Joseph bar Ḥiyya who learns from all. For the main thing so far as the disciple is concerned is for him to attach himself in great and powerful love and with all his heart, soul, and might to his master. Then his way will be correct and the master will bring some of his own spirit upon his disciples, always provided that they cleave to him in great love and withstand all temptations for them to leave their master, and then they will be successful. But all those who have no special master to whom they can cleave with powerful love in heart and soul, they will never be successful. That is why it says here: "Who is wise?" It refers to one who no longer requires a master because he has already attained to wisdom. He can learn from all men good traits of character and many other matters. But this Mishnah does not apply to one who still requires his master. Even though such a man, too, can learn from all men but not the main thing. For the truth is that he can learn everything from his master. If he is sincerely attached to his master, he will hear from his master all he needs to know for the improvement of his character.

Thus Yitzḥak Eisik sees the zaddik chiefly as a guru-type teacher of wisdom, and all the Ḥasid requires is to have such a master. The zaddik himself, however treats all men as his masters in the sense that he learns from all of them, as above.

III HOW CAN MAN HONOR GOD?

Notzer Ḥesed to Avot 5:13

*The text reads: "There are four characters among men: he who says, What is mine is mine and what is thine is thine, his is a neutral character:—some say, this is a character like that of Sodom; he who says, What is mine is thine and what is thine is mine, is a boor; he who says, What is mine is thine and what is thine is thine, is a saint (*Ḥasid*); he who says, What is thine is mine and what is mine is mine, is a wicked man." Yitzḥak Eisik interprets "thine" as referring to God.*

"What is mine," that is to say, the things of this world, "is mine" so that I will enjoy them. "And what is Thine," that is to say, the Torah and the commandments and good deeds, "is Thine," that

is to say, he carries out these for their own sake (*lishmah*). His is a neutral character. But some say that his is a character like that of the men of Sodom who went after worldly desires. For whoever goes after worldly desires is incapable of doing anything really good and there is a spark of atheism in such an attitude since, in reality, no place is empty of Him. "What is mine is Thine," that is to say, he does everything for the sake of Heaven and he overcomes worldly desires, but "What is Thine is mine," that is to say, his worship of God is for the sake of reward. "What is mine is Thine," that is to say, he carries out unifications, "And what is Thine is Thine," that is to say, he only wishes to carry out the will of the Most-High. He is a Ḥasid. But the contrary is when he runs after worldly desires and also carries out the commandments for his own gain and falsely. He is to be sure a wicked man.

The Ḥasidic ideal: Worldly things should be carried out in honor of God, for the sake of "unification," as above, and spiritual things should be engaged in as pure acts of worship, not in order to win fame and the like or even in order to receive reward from God.

IV THE HARM OF LOSING ONE'S TEMPER

Notzer Ḥesed to Avot 5:14: "There are four kinds of tempers"

Know that anger causes an unclean spirit to rest upon man just as joy used to cause the holy spirit to rest on the prophets. That is why the prophets had people play to them on the lyre, the harp, and the flute—so as to draw down to them the holy spirit which comes from the place of joy and expansiveness of soul. In the same way, the opposite is true, that anger is calculated to infuse into man an unclean spirit. In any event, whenever a man allows himself to be annoyed, the holy spirit departs from him. Consequently, it is essential for man always to be patient, great-hearted, and happy, bearing all tribulations with joy in his heart. The indication of this is provided by the fact that the words *lev simḥah* ("a heart that rejoices") have the same numerical value as the word *Shekhinah*, that is to say, God, blessed be He, causes His *Shekhinah* to rest on the happy man.

The letters of lev simḥah *are* lamed = *30,* bet = *2,* sin = *300,* mem = *40,* het = *8,* hey = *5; total* = *385. The letters of* Shekhinah *are* shin =

300, kaf *= 20,* yod *= 10,* nun *= 50,* hey *= 5; total = 385. Here we have the typical Ḥasidic emphasis on* simḥah, *"joy." The man who is happy come what may in his faith in God is in touch with the "world of joy" up above where there is only mercy and grace. Note the references to expansiveness of spirit. The unclean spirit is basically a narrowness of vision, particularly in evidence when a man loses his temper over worldly and petty things, whereas joy is expansiveness and the heart is then ready to be a recipient of the holy spirit.*

CHAPTER 32

Judah Leib Eger of Lublin
1816-1888

The fragrance of a healthy conscience
A good and sweet year
Rejoicing on Sukkot

Judah Leib was the son of Solomon Eger, Rabbi of Posen, and grandson of the famous talmudic scholar Akiba Eger. In his youth Judah Leib came under the influence of Isaac Meir Alter (the founder of the Ger dynasty in Ḥasidism) in Warsaw and, through Isaac Meir, a disciple of the latter's brother-in-law the Kotzker Rebbe, to the utter consternation of Solomon Eger, a determined opponent of Ḥasidism. When Mordecai Joseph of Izbica left the Kotzker to establish his own Ḥasidic "court," Judah Leib became the Kotzker's disciple. In 1854 Judah Leib was persuaded to become himself a Ḥasidic zaddik in Lublin. He is known by the Ḥasidim as Reb Leibele Eger or, after his book, as "the Torat Emet."

Judah Leib's teachings were published by his sons under the title Torat Emet *(Torah of Truth), in Lublin in 1889. (The edition used here is the photocopy of the Lublin edition, Bene Berak, 1970.)*

I THE FRAGRANCE OF A HEALTHY CONSCIENCE

Torat Emet, vol. 1, *Toledot*, p. 29

"And he smelled his clothes and he blessed him, saying: 'Ah, the smell of my son is like the smell of a field that the Lord has blessed' " (Genesis 27:27).

We have to understand why at first it says, "he smelled his clothes," and then it says "the smell of my son." It would seem that when our father Jacob, on whom be peace, went to his father, having changed his clothes so that his identity would not be revealed, his heart was broken for having to do such a thing, to change his clothes so that his holy father would not know him, and it seemed like a betrayal to him. When he came to his father with so broken a heart, the fragrance of that broken heart ascended on high. Therefore, it says "the smell of his clothes." We find a Midrash that interprets "the smell of *begadav*" **("his clothes") as if it were written "the smell of** *bogedav*" **("his betrayal"), that is to say, Jacob, in his own eyes, behaved treacherously. And our father Isaac, on whom be peace, smelled the fragrance of Jacob's broken heart. It is like a piece of wood from a fragrant tree. As the wood is broken the fragrance comes forth in even greater measure. So, too, because of the broken heart of our father Jacob, on whom be peace, who, in his own mind, was guilty of a betrayal, Isaac sensed the fundamental holiness of Jacob. Hence he said: "the smell of my son is like the smell of a field that the Lord has blessed."**

We have here two typical Ḥasidic ideas. First, the significance of the broken heart, essential in the service of God. Second, the idea that holiness can be sensed, almost physically, by the holy man, the zaddik. It is possible that Judah Leib, in his comment, was not unaware of his own personal tragedy, his allegience to Ḥasidism having caused much pain to his father, to whom it must have seemed as a betrayal.

One can say that in this verse there is a hint of the three sacred meals of the holy Sabbath. Thus, "the smell of my son" refers to the holiness of the Lesser Countenance, which, as is well known, is in the category of Jacob. "As the smell of a field" refers to the holy Apple Fields, as it is said in the Zohar. "That the Lord has blessed," refers to the Holy Ancient One, as is well known to the masters of the secret lore. The initial letters of *reaḥ beni* **("smell of my son") and** *reaḥ sadeh* **("smell of a field") have the same numerical value as that of** *shabbat.*

According to the Lurianic Kabbalah the ten Sefirot are grouped in a set of five Partzufim *(Configurations). Three of these in ascending order are: (1)* Hakkal Tappuḥim *(Apple Fields), corresponding to the* Sefirah Malkhut, *the* Shekhinah; *(2)* Zeer Anpin *(Lesser Countenance or Impatience), corresponding to the* Sefirah Tiferet *and symbolized by Jacob; (3)* Attika Kaddisha *(Holy Ancient One), corresponding to the* Sefirah Keter. *The three sacred meals of the Sabbath (very important in Ḥasidic life) correspond to these. Thus the Friday night meal is the meal of* Hakkal Tappuḥim, *Sabbath morning of* Attika Kaddisha, *and Sabbath afternoon of* Zeer Anpin. *The Ḥasidim, like the kabbalists before them, believed that the Torah, even in its narratives, "hints" at the kabbalistic mysteries. The initial letters to which Judah Leib refers are* resh *= 200,* bet *= 2,* resh *= 200,* sin *= 300; total = 702. The letters of the word* shabbat *are* shin *= 300,* bet *= 2,* sav *= 400; total = 702. Judah Leib, incidentally, was all his life a staunch advocate of the great sanctity of the Sabbath.*

II A GOOD AND SWEET YEAR

Torat Emet, vol. 3, *Rosh Ha-Shanah,* p. 32

This passage is dated 1884, i.e., this is the date when Judah Leib delivered this discourse to his followers. The comment was made on Rosh Ha-Shanah eve when it is the custom to dip a piece of apple in honey and recite the prayer: "May we have a good and sweet year."

"May it be Thy will to renew unto us a good and sweet year." We need to understand the form of this prayer, "a good and sweet year." If it will be good what more is required? However, to be sure when good is present nothing can be better, as it is said: "And God saw the light, that it was good" (Genesis 1:4). But the prayer means that even if the time demands that the light and the good be withheld, it should be in the category of sweetness, that is to say, it should be sweetened and become good. Hence the addition of the word "sweet." The time referred to is Rosh Ha-Shanah. It is well known that the holy Zohar says that this day of Rosh Ha-Shanah is called "the second day," hinting at the absence of light, since the words "that it was good" do not occur with reference to this day (Genesis 1:6–8). And yet, for all that, one can sweeten it and draw down into it the category of the good, as it is said: "The Lord is good to all" (Psalms 145:9).

A typical kabbalistic and Ḥasidic idea is that of "sweetening the judgments." The point here is that Rosh Ha-Shanah is, in the tradition, Judgment Day, Yom Ha-Din, *and hence on this day there is divine sternness and an absence of the light of pure mercy. But man by his deeds is capable of converting darkness into light, judgment into mercy. Thus on this occasion in particular it is appropriate to speak not only of a "good" year but also of a "sweet" year. The Rabbis note that on all the other days of creation it is said that God saw that it was good, but these words do not occur in the account of the second day.*

III REJOICING ON SUKKOT

Torat Emet, vol. 3, *Sukkot,* p. 66

"He shall come home with joy, bearing his sheaves" (Psalms 126:6). "Bearing his sheaves" hints at our holy awakening with which we bestir ourselves on these days [between Yom Kippur and Sukkot]. Especially so, tomorrow, the eve of the festival of Sukkot, when each one is busily engaged attending to his *sukkah*, carrying the bundles of covering for the *sukkah* and making himself energetic in carrying out the *mitzvah* of *sukkah*, as the Creator commanded us to do. As a result, we cause an awakening on high so that there is an influx of the sanctity of the holy festival that comes to us in peace and with all goodness. This idea is also hinted at in the song *Haazinu* [recited on the Sabbath before Sukkot]. Because of our efforts on earth there is an awakening on high and there is: "Bearing them on pinions" (Deuteronomy 32:11).

This comment is based on the kabbalistic idea that, as the Zohar puts it, "the impulse from above is caused by the impulse from below," i.e., God's grace flows in direct proportion and corresponds to man's efforts on earth in the service of his Maker. Hence by "carrying the sheaves," the boughs and leaves with which the sukkah is covered, God is, as it were, bestirred on high to "bear them on pinions," i.e., to protect and save them. Because they "carry" on earth, He "carries" them on high.

CHAPTER 33

Zadok Ha-Kohen of Lublin

1823-1900

Never yield to despair
Opposition to secular learning

Zadok Ha-Kohen was born in Courland and received his Jewish education from teachers in the Lithuanian, anti-Ḥasidic tradition. In order to obtain permission to divorce his wife (for which the approval of one hundred rabbis from three different countries was required) he traveled to Poland where he was won over to Ḥasidism. At first a disciple of Mordecai Joseph of Izbica and then of Judah Leib Eger of Lublin, Zadok eventually became himself a Ḥasidic master in Lublin. He is known by the Ḥasidim as "the Lubliner Kohen."

Zadok was a great talmudist, an acute religious thinker, and a prolific author. He is not famous as the author of any one particular book, but all his writings are highly prized—and not alone by the Ḥasidim. The following is from his work Divrey Soferim *(Words of the Scribes), published in Lublin in 1913.*

I NEVER YIELD TO DESPAIR

Divrey Soferim, no. 16, p. 13

Come what may, a Jew must never yield to despair, whether in matters appertaining to the body, as the Rabbis say (Berakhot (10a); even if a sharp sword rests upon a man's neck he should not give

up hoping for mercy, or in matters appertaining to the soul. Even if he has sunk very low and has committed that sin of which the Rabbis of blessed memory say (the holy Zohar 1:219b) that repentance is of no avail, God forbid, or if it is hard for him to repent or if he sees himself becoming ever more immersed in worldly things, he should never despair and imagine that he will never be successful in separating from worldly things. For the Jew must never yield to despair, and he should realize that God, blessed be He, can help, whatever the circumstances.

Ḥasidism stresses joy in the service of God. Despair is the great enemy of joy. Zadok here says that even with regard to spiritual matters, a Jew must never say to himself that he is beyond hope because he is too immersed in the world to have any capacity to rise higher in the world of the spirit.

The very beginnings of the Jewish people only took place after all hope had been abandoned. Abraham and Sarah were old, and "Who would have said unto Abraham, that Sarah should give children suck?" (Genesis 21:7). For no one would have believed such a thing to be possible. And even after the angel had promised her a child and Sarah, being a righteous woman, certainly believed that God's power is limitless, yet she laughed within herself (Genesis 18:12), for it seemed so remote to her that this should happen, since she was fully aware that Abraham was incapable of being a father and that she herself was so old. She thought to herself that if God wanted them to have children they would have had them before now, since the less a miracle is obvious the better, and no miracle is performed where there is no need for it. But the truth is that it was all planned by God that the Jewish people should only come into being after there had been complete despair, so that no one, not even Sarah herself, could believe that it would ever happen. For this is the whole duty of the Israelite, to believe that one must never despair; for God can help in all circumstances, and nothing is too difficult for Him and one should not ask why God did it so.

Zadok is saying that Abraham and Sarah were given a child, Isaac the progenitor of the Jewish people, only when they were quite beyond having children, to teach us that the very beginnings of the Jewish people would have been impossible, judged by normal standards, and yet the Jews did come into existence. Hence, even if it seems to us quite impossible to believe that God still has any plans for us, we must never yield to despair and must continue to trust in Him. Zadok now goes on to say that this also applies to the messianic hope. Even if it seems quite impossible that Israel will ever be redeemed, the Jew must continue to hope.

II OPPOSITION TO SECULAR LEARNING

Sefer Ha-Zikhronot, no. 1, in *Divrey Soferim*, pp. 50–51

In this section Zadok deals with the principles of the Jewish faith. Ḥasidism is generally opposed to secular learning and especially to secular philosophy as harmful to pure faith.

One must refer repeatedly in our generation to belief in God. For there are many Jews nowadays only too ready to entice with their smooth words the young among the children of Israel that they should study Gentile works and languages and read their books. They advance as their reason that by such studies the young folk will arrive at a purer faith, but as all experience shows, the very opposite is true. They try to prove their case by referring to Maimonides and the other sages of old who did strengthen their faith by studying philosophy. The truth is that it is not for us to question whether these sages were right to do as they did. For this at least we see from the great code of Maimonides how strong was his faith in the words of the sages, and it is clear that his studies did him no harm. But we see the opposite of other people is every generation. They, as a result of their studies, become unbelievers, either denying God or rejecting the belief that the Torah is from Heaven, or denying some details of the Oral Law. These latter also deny the Torah, since the verse says: "Thou shalt not turn aside" (Deuteronomy 17:11).

Zadok, in quoting the verse from Deuteronomy, refers to the talmudic interpretation of the verse that one must believe in the Oral Law as recorded by the sages in the talmudic literature.

We see, therefore, that no proof can be brought from people like Maimonides and his colleagues who were so renowned for their knowledge of the Torah and their fear of sin. In addition to man's

duty to become thoroughly familiar with the whole of the Torah and to go far in establishing human wisdom in his mind, it is right that he should know, and this is the main thing that the Rabbis say: "Only one whose fear of sin is greater than his wisdom will have his wisdom endure" (Avot 3:11). If they said this even about the wisdom of the Torah, how much more does it apply to external sciences. At the end of his *Guide for the Perplexed*, **Maimonides explains that the whole purpose of the book and the whole purpose of man's perfection is for man to attain the fear of God in truth and to cleave to Him at every moment. The gist of his words is quoted by Rabbi Moses Isserles in his beginning note to the Shulḥan Arukh, Orah Ḥayyim.**

The "external sciences" are the secular sciences and philosophy. For Rabbi Moses Isserles see the section on the Shulḥan Arukh in Volume 1 in this series.

It was with this in mind that Maimonides studied all those sciences and read all those books, as he writes in his great code, in the section *Yesodey Ha-Torah*, **that the way to attain to the love and fear of God is to reflect on the study of physics and metaphysics. All his industry was solely for the purpose of attaining the stage in which he could cleave to God. In his effort to attain this high rank he discovered that so far as he himself was concerned, and having in mind the particular requirements of his age, there was advantage in reading those books and studying those sciences. As he himself remarks in one of his responsa, these sciences were only like handmaidens and cooks to assist the queen Torah.**

The Ḥasidic teachers were obviously embarrassed by Maimonides' study of secular sciences. Here Zadok argues that Maimonides only studied these because he believed that they would lead him to a greater knowledge of the universe and hence of the Creator.

Consequently, let a man weigh it in his mind, whether his motive in reading such books is that as a result he will attain the stage of cleaving to God and that the fear of God will rest upon him. If he does not fool himself and knows sincerely that his sole purpose is for the fear of God to be upon his face, he must first

of all try to achieve this aim by reading all the works of the sages of Israel on this theme before he enters the dangerous way. I guarantee that in this generation no one will ever dream of reading those books for this purpose. He will find enough and more than enough in the holy books of the true sages of Israel to set his heart on fire to fear the Lord. He will then understand and recognize the truth that reading these books only cause man to turn aside from the way of the Lord, and he will have no inclination to read them if he sincerely desires to arrive at the house of our Father in Heaven. It is only the man who wishes to acquire wisdom for his own purposes who has a longing to digest the pleasant words and the logic of their works, dripping with strange ideas, and whoever studies them with such an aim in mind will not be free from guilt. This is included in the prohibition of reading the external books of which the Rabbis (Sanhedrin 90a and further) have so much to say on the punishment awaiting those guilty of it. The Torah repeats her warning by saying, "Take ye good heed" and "lest ye deal corruptly" (Deuteronomy 4:15, 16), so we can see how extremely careful one has to be.

The question discussed here by Zadok has been a bone of contention throughout the ages. From the days of Maimonides there have been opponents of all secular learning as well as advocates of it as an aid to faith among Jews. Zadok, like all the Ḥasidic masters, comes down heavily against all secular learning; but note his appreciation of the other side of the coin and the reasoned way in which he argues his case.

In this generation, especially, when there are, for our sins, only too many works of this kind in Israel, it is proper for every one to warn his sons and pupils with all the force at his command and to train them from their youth never to look into any book unless it is known that the author sincerely feared the Lord, and that he is not a hypocrite or a fraud, as are some of the hypocrites who pretend to speak of the fear of the Lord and hide their real intention. Many of them were revealed in their true colors eventually or through the works of their disciples or the disciples of their disciples. If a man runs away from the slightest danger to his physical health so that, according to Jewish law, where there is danger to life one must take even a remote possibility into account, unlike with regard to religious matters (Ḥullin 10a), how much more so in this matter where man's eternal bliss is at stake, as the tradition of our true sages has it. Man can therefore appreciate how far he must keep himself from these works.

Zadok's reference to the Talmud is to the rule that if in a certain case it is highly probable that a substance is kosher, it may be eaten and one need not take into account the remote possibility of it being terefa. *But this does not apply where there is danger to life. If, for instance, there are ninety-nine innocent cups of wine and only one contains poison, it is forbidden to drink from any of the cups.*

And even with regard to the works bearing the names of the early sages, the great ones of the world, if the publisher is not known to be a God-fearing man who believes in all the words of the Torah, an investigation is required whether or not he has interpolated foreign matter into the books with the purpose of misleading the children of Israel, since it has become clear to me that they have done precisely this to a number of books. This has been verified by a letter in the handwriting of the head of that group, the one who began to stir up this plague in Germany in a generation before ours and in whose name they all take pride. In a letter to a companion in Poland this man advised his friend explicitly to print works and attribute them to the early sages such as Naḥmanides and his associates, but to publish there whatever he wishes and so make himself popular. And when this counsel was tried unsuccessfully by that companion he left the Jewish fold. So may perish all who wish to cause the public to sin.

Zadok appears to be referring to Moses Mendelssohn, but it is also possible that he means Saul Berlin, who published the notorious forgery Besamim Rosh, *attributing it to the famous fourteenth-century teacher Asher ben Jeḥiel, known as the* Rosh, *which would explain the reference to the "head," in Hebrew the Rosh.*

Every work published by these men requires much investigation and examination lest there be found in it some foreign admixture. How much more so with regard to books they themselves have

written. Here even if nothing is found in the contrary to the teachings of the Rabbis of blessed memory, even by a faint hint, yet generally when one examines the book carefully he will discover what they really mean. Included in this is their habit of scoffing at the sacred customs of Israel and so forth. Maimonides [at the end of the section of his code on the laws of leprosy] has written that this is the way of the wicked scoffers. At first they exaggerate, then they go on to speak ill of the righteous, and this leads them to speak ill of the prophets, and the result is that that they speak ill of God and eventually deny Him completely. This is perfectly true and is attested to daily in the lives of these men. That is why we have here recorded these things in the section dealing with forgetting God. For it is this that brings about that God is forgotten, and eventually it leads to atheism. Enough of this has been said here.

In this passage we have the strongest echoes of the struggle between the Ḥasidim and the Maskilim, the "enlightened ones." The Ḥasidim accused the Maskilim of unbelief, the Maskilim the Ḥasidim of reaction and obscurantism. In fact, as has often been noted, it was the opposition of the Maskilim to the whole traditional pattern that eventually caused the Ḥasidim to make peace with their rabbinic opponents, the Mitnaggedim, in order to make common cause against the Maskilim, the foes of both tendencies.

CHAPTER 34

Judah Aryeh Leib Alter of Ger 1847-1905

The supernatural
How can man learn to follow his conscience?
How can Jewish particularism be reconciled with universalism?

The Little Town of Gora Kalwaria (known to the Ḥasidim as Ger) near Warsaw became the seat of a famous Ḥasidic dynasty. The founder of the dynasty was Isaac Meir Alter (1789–1866), a disciple of the Maggid of Koznitz and brother-in-law of the Kotzker Rebbe. Isaac Meir, a great talmudist, was the author of Ḥiddushey Ha-Rim *(Novellae of the Rim:* Rim *is formed from the initial letters of* Rabbi Isaac Meir*), by which name he is known among the Ḥasidim. He was succeeded as the zaddik of Ger by his grandson Judah Aryeh Leib, who was in turn succeeded by his son Abraham Mordecai (1866–1948). The present Gerer Rebbe, residing in Israel, is a son of Abraham Mordecai.*

Judah Aryeh Leib's main work is in the form of Ḥasidic homilies to the Pentateuch and the festivals. This book is called Sefat Emet *(Lip of Truth) and was first published by the author's family in Pietrikow in 1908. (The edition used here is the revised edition published in New York in 1953.) The title was given by the members of the family because, as they state in their introduction, the last sermon printed in the book concludes with the verse: "The lip of truth [*sefat emet*] shall* *be established for ever" (Proverbs 12:19). Judah Aryeh Leib is known to the Ḥasidim, after his book, as "the* Sefat Emet.*"*

I THE SUPERNATURAL

Sefat Emet, vol. 4, *Maseey,* p. 198

This is a comment on the stages of the Israelites' journey during their forty years in the wilderness (Numbers 33).

This is the significance of the stages recorded in the Torah and why it is written: "by which they went forth out of the land of Egypt" (Numbers 33:1). For these stages through which the children of Israel journeyed were of a supernatural order, and it was recorded so that we should recall God's wonders, as it is said: "And thou shalt remember all the way which the Lord thy God hath led thee these forty years in the wilderness" (Deuteronomy 8:2). It is also to recall the merit of the children of Israel, as it is said: "I remember for thee the affection of thy youth . . . how thou wentest after Me in the wilderness, in a land that was not sown" (Jeremiah 2:2).

Everything in the Torah is there for a purpose. Why, then, is the list of journeys recorded? Of what advantage is it for us to know all this? The answer given here is that the advantage is twofold. The places mentioned were the stages in a long journey that, humanly speaking, was quite impossible. Thus it is both a record of God's supernatural intervention and a record of Israel's faithfulness and loyalty to God.

The truth is that no one could ever have gone to those places except the children of Israel who had come forth out of Egypt and had, as a result, ascended to supernatural heights, as it is said: "That led us through the wilderness . . . through a land that no man passed through . . ." (Jeremiah 2:6). When God created the world, he left certain places in which the natural laws do not operate. And He did the same so far as time is concerned, for there are times during which the natural order is superseded. And He did the same, too, with regard to souls, for there are sublime souls that are beyond the control of nature. All this is evidence of God.

The exceptions to the general rule provide evidence for all that the rule embraces.

Nature has been deprived of its regularity and power in certain places, certain times and certain persons. These exceptions testify to the power of God, they invoke the idea of a supernatural universe and hence testify that nature itself is entirely in God's hands.

This is why the Sabbath is called a "testimony," for on the Sabbath the natural law is suspended. Just as there are forty-eight Sabbaths in the year, [i.e., apart from those which coincide with the festivals] so, too, there are forty-eight stages [mentioned in our portion] in the world, and in these nature does not rule. As for souls, it applies to the generality of the souls of the children of Israel, but in particular to the forty-eight prophets who arose among the children of Israel and whose whole career was of a supernatural order.

The Rabbis speak of forty-eight prophets who arose in Israel. Thus God, the Author of the natural order, leaves room for the supernatural place, the place where miracles abound; the supernatural period, the Sabbath; and the supernatural person, the prophet.

Now these stages were a preparation for Israel to come to the promised land. As a Midrash to Shemot says, "Three gifts [one of them the land of Israel] the Holy One, blessed be He, gave to Israel, and all three were given through suffering." Thus their sufferings in the wilderness were a preparation for their entrance into the land of Israel. For the truth is that the land of Israel is the main spot of earth, for it was from this spot that the whole inhabited part of the earth was formed. Because the children of Israel went after God into a land that was not sown, they had the merit of inhabiting the main spot on earth.

A mystical notion of the land of Israel as the holiest spot on earth through which all the earth becomes blessed. But this is only possible because Israel journeyed into those terrible places and thus were ready to give away all they had. Through giving away—the Ḥasidic ideal of bittul ha-yesh *that we have encountered more than once in this book—all is ascribed to God, and once this happens man can have all back from God.*

II HOW CAN MAN LEARN TO FOLLOW HIS CONSCIENCE?

Sefat Emet, vol. 5, *Shofetim* (dated 1872), p. 69

"Judges and officers shalt thou make thee in all thy gates" (Deuteronomy 16:18).

I have written earlier that every sensation of man, in every single movement he makes, great or small, must be carefully weighed in the judgment of truth. The category of "judges" applies to man's intellect. "Officers" means that man sets at naught all his reasoning and all his wisdom for the sake of God's commands, and he does this by means of his fear of God, the category of an "officer." In reality, the result of the correct judgment in the mind is that man attains to the degree of apprehension in which his intellect, too, is set at naught for the sake of God's will, as above.

The verse refers, of course, to judges and officers (i.e., policemen) appointed when the Israelites entered the promised land. The author however, gives the verse a more individualistic turn. Every man must have a "judge" and an "officer." The "judge" is his intellect by means of which he weighs up things to judge whether or not they conform to God's will. Once he has seen where his duty lies, man must have an "officer," a policeman of his conscience to see that he obeys God's law.

III HOW CAN JEWISH PARTICULARISM BE RECONCILED WITH UNIVERSALISM?

Sefat Emet, *Sukkot*, pp. 237–38

On the festival of Sukkot the children of Israel are separated from the nations by means of the *sukkah*, **the dwelling peculiar to "all that are home-born in Israel" (Leviticus 23:42). That is why, on this festival, especially, seventy bullocks are offered corresponding to the seventy nations of the world. This is to teach us that the more the children of Israel keep to themselves, the more do they benefit the whole of mankind.**

A fine comment on the problem of universalism versus particularism in Judaism. The sukkah *is particularistic, it is the special home of the Israelite. And yet on this festival seventy bullocks (see Numbers 29:12–34) are offered in the Temple, which the Rabbis say are sacrifices on behalf of the "seventy nations" of the world. Thus on the particularistic festival the universalistic note is sounded. In other words, Israel keeps apart not for its own sake but in order to preserve a truth for the benefit of mankind as a whole. Martin Buber said something similar when he remarked that, as a Jew, he stands beside his father's house but witnesses the whole world passing by.*

The Talmud similarly says that if only the nations knew how beneficial the Temple is for them they would cover it with gold. And we find this idea in the career of our father Abraham, who wished to draw the whole of mankind near to the Holy One, blessed be He, who said to him, "*Lekh lekha*" (Genesis 12:1), and when you will be separate, then "in thee shall all the families of the earth be blessed" (Genesis 12:3).

The words lekh lekha *(usually translated as "Get thee out") mean, if taken literally, "Go to thyself," i.e., retreat into your own domain. Abraham wanted to "go out" to the whole world, and yet God told him to retreat into himself. The reason for it is that this was the way to benefit mankind—by preserving the truth that he had seen, unsullied. After he had gone into himself Abraham was told that this was not an aim in itself, but was for the sake of mankind. All men will be blessed through his efforts.*

CHAPTER 35

Aaron Rokeaḥ of Belz
1880-1957

How the Belzer Rebbe rebuked his followers
Finding good in every Jew
Should one's own family come first?
Kindness to animals
The holiness of the Belzer Rebbe

The dynasty of Belz is one of the more famous Ḥasidic dynasties, but it seems that the zaddikim of this house were extremely reluctant to record their teachings in writing. In fact, none of the five zaddikim of Belz published any works at all. Yet it is impossible to omit any reference to the teachings of so important a center as Belz from this anthology. The following selections on Aaron Rokeaḥ are from the full-scale biography of the previous zaddik of Belz, Ha-Rav Ha-Kadosh Mi-Belza *(The Holy Rabbi of Belz) by B. Landau and N. Urtner (Jerusalem, 1967).*

The founder of the Belz dynasty was Shalom Rokeaḥ (1779–1855), a disciple of Solomon of Lutzk, the "Seer" of Lublin, and the Maggid of Koznitz. Shalom was the official rabbi of the town of Belz in Galicia and was succeeded in that office by his descendants. Thus the zaddikim of Belz combined their role with that of town rabbi. Shalom's successor was his son Joshua (1825–1894), who was in turn succeeded by his son Issachar Dov (1854–1927). Issachar Dov's successor was Aaron, who later escaped from the Nazis and resided in Tel Aviv. Aaron's sons were murdered during the Holocaust, and the present Rebbe of Belz, in Eretz Yisrael, is Aaron's nephew Issachar Dov, who was born in 1948.

I HOW THE BELZER REBBE REBUKED HIS FOLLOWERS

Ha-Rav Ha-Kadosh Mi-Belza, p. 37

On the Sabbaths before Rosh Ha-Shanah, from the beginning of the month of Elul, it was the custom of our teacher to add words of rebuke and words of blessing during his discourse at the third meal. This is how he would begin: "My master and father, may his merits shield us and all Israel, had the custom of speaking these words of rebuke at this time of the year. The truth is that it is very hard to deliver words of rebuke to the children of Israel. But when one gives utterance to these words, whoever hears them awakens to his duty of his own accord."

Many of the Ḥasidic masters did not believe in rebuking their followers. The Belzer Rebbe only justified it on the grounds that his words were only the means by which his listeners came themselves to realize the truth, so that he was not really imposing on them.

Our teacher recalled the opinion in the Talmud (Rosh Ha-Shanah 10b, 11a) of Rabbi Eliezer, who says that the Patriarchs were born in the month of Tishri, whereas Rabbi Joshua holds that the Patriarchs were born in the month of Nisan. The Gemara explains that the opinion that the Patriarchs were born in Tishri is based on the verse, "in the month of *Ethanim*" **(1 Kings 8:2), that is, the month in which the mighty ones** (*ethanim*) **of the world were born. But how will the other opinion be understood by "the month of** *Ethanim*"**? The answer is given; It means the month that is "mighty"** (*ethan*) **in** *mitzvot*. **Rashi explains "mighty in mitzvot" because there are in this month so many** *mitzvot*; **the shofar, Yom Kippur, the** *sukkah*, **the** *lulav*, **the willow, and the water libations. Now, the** *Reshit Ḥokhmah* **states that before carrying out a** *mitzvah* **one should repent. How much more so, then, before this month so mighty in** *mitzvot*! **There are so many** *mitzvot* **of biblical origin as well as of rabbinic origin and so many Jewish customs, so that it**

goes without saying that one must repent. However, repentance must be of so powerful a kind that a man puts right thereby all that he has flawed from the day of his birth, and this is extremely difficult. Consequently, God has given us before this month the month of Elul, known as "the days of compassion and acceptance" so that we might be ready for the *mitzvot*.

The Reshit Ḥokhmah *is the popular kabbalistic treatise by the sixteenth-century Safed teacher Elijah de Vidas. We have noted more than once in this book the kabbalistic idea that sin produces a cosmic flaw (*pegam*) which has to be "put right" (*tikkun*).

He continued to explain the meaning of these. *Children*: **This means that God should help all those who have no children to have them, and the children should live and grow up, living to a ripe old age. And those who have children should be able to bring them up without difficulty to lead a life of Torah and the fear of Heaven.** *Life*: **This means that all Israel should merit long life and good years and that all the sick in Israel should be healed with a complete healing, and as for the healthy that God should keep them fit so that no illness befalls them.** *Sustenance*: **Rashi explains that sustenance embraces every kind of sustenance, so that it embraces both that of the body and that of the spirit. The meaning, then, is that God should help Israel find sustenance so that they can serve the Lord without hindrance, whether in material or in spiritual matters. And God should help us that we might be inscribed in the book of life and have a good and blessed year, in body and spirit, and find complete redemption. Amen.**

The Ḥasidic way of Belz was based mainly on simple faith. The zaddik may be, like Aaron himself, an ascetic, enjoying nothing of the things of the world, yet he prays realistically for his followers to enjoy good health and to be able to earn a good living, since thereby they can better serve God.

II FINDING GOOD IN EVERY JEW

Ha-Rav Ha-Kadosh Mi-Belza, pp. 39–40

In his love for Israel he found only good in every Jew. This included real sinners. He would not allow evil to be spoken of them,

and it goes without saying that he himself never insulted any man, not even the lowest of the low.

Speaking to one of the rabbis our teacher explained it as follows: "If in your studies you are confronted with a difficult passage in the works of Maimonides, what do you do? You work hard at it until you find a solution. The same should apply whenever you come across a difficult Jew. You must work hard at understanding him until you find the solution."

A favorite pastime of talmudic scholars was to resolve difficulties in Maimonides' code by showing that Maimonides was right after all. The Belzer Rebbe here suggests that if such effort is displayed in dealing with a text, surely the same kind of effort and ingenuity should be applied in excusing the conduct of others, even when it seems inexcusable. Many of the Ḥasidic masters had this mystical view of the basic goodness of every Jewish soul.

III SHOULD ONE'S OWN FAMILY COME FIRST?

Ha-Rav Ha-Kadosh Mi-Belza, p. 43

In his love for Israel he was ready to bear all their troubles, listening to their complaints and trying with all his might to lighten their burden, whether by giving them good advice or by words of encouragement. The Lord put wisdom and discernment into the heart of our teacher so that he could direct his followers in the way they should go, that it might be well for them in this world and the next.

One day cries were heard in the streets of Belz that a little child had fallen into a well. When the cries were heard in the rabbi's house and the identity of the child was still unknown, our teacher groaned, "Oy! It might be one of my children." But on the spot he exclaimed, "Oy! My evil inclination! What have I said? What have I groaned? Is a child who does not belong to me not a creature of God?" On the spot he began to experience deep remorse for what he had said and he repented of it. For about half an hour he walked around in his room rebuking himself, "Oy! What have I said?" One of his companions who heard this remarked, "If only

we could experience such remorse on *Kol Nidre* to the extent that our teacher experienced remorse for the single moment in which he put the members of his own family before other Jewish children!"

This is an interesting insight both into the concern of a Ḥasidic zaddik for all Jews and the veneration of the zaddik by his followers. In Belz, in particular, the ascetic zaddik is not aloof from the daily concerns of normal human beings.

IV KINDNESS TO ANIMALS

Ha-Rav Ha-Kadosh Mi-Belza, p. 47

He was compassionate and good-hearted by nature and had pity on the living creatures in his possession, as the law demands. Wonderful is the story of his concern for the horses that had been made ready for him to take him out of danger (during the Nazi period). This is how Rabbi Ezekiel relates it in his book *The Saving of the Rabbi of Belz*: "In the evening, when the *gabbai* would enter the zaddik's room with a drink of coffee wherewith the zaddik used to break his day-long fast, the zaddik used to ask the *gabbai*, 'What of the horses? Who has remembered to feed them? The horses have been acquired for me when I shall need them, and according to the Law I am not allowed to taste anything until I make sure that they have been fed.' " It was on this that the zaddik had his mind set during those cruel days during the war—to carry out his duty and to care for God's creatures.

Since we have touched on this subject, it is worth noting that in Belz our teacher bought horses and delivered them to a special coachman to work them during the days of the week, but to allow them to rest on the Sabbath in order to carry out the command to allow one's animals to rest on the Sabbath. It was also to carry out the ruling of the Rabbis (Berakhot 40a) that it is wrong for a man to eat until he feeds the animals under his care. Each morning our teacher would send food for the animals and, as we have noted, he observed this even in the harsh times of war. During his escape [from the Nazis], while the whole household was in great confusion, he would ask if the animals had been fed.

The gabbai *is the special retainer attached to the zaddik. Every Ḥasidic zaddik had one or more such retainers whose duty it was to look after the zaddik and, to some extent, to protect him from being unmercifully bothered by the Ḥasidim.*

According to one report, he always refused to travel in a cart drawn by a single horse out of pity for the horse who was not strong enough to draw the heavy cart on its own.

Compare this with the tales about the Baal Shem Tov's horses at the beginning of this book (Chapter 1).

V THE HOLINESS OF THE BELZER REBBE

Ha-Rav Ha-Kadosh Mi-Belza, p. 50

Belz itself was a poor little town. The majority of its inhabitants were Jews who relied for their living entirely on the Ḥasidim who visited the place. All the houses were of the same height. The streets were without pavements except for the main street. At the center of the town stood the rabbi's house, two stories high, in which the rabbi and his family lived. At the side of this house was another building, the great synagogue, and beside it a third building, the home of the great and famed Yeshiva of Belz. Before you approach these buildings you come to a gigantic open space which serves as the market square. Here you find tens of coaches ready to take the Ḥasidim to the railway station, especially after the festivals and the Sabbath.

In all the three buildings which constituted the "court" of Belz they did not use electricity but candles set in a brass chandelier. It is said that the reason they did not use electricity was because the electric current was used to provide light for the Catholic church.

Belz was in many ways the most conservative of the Ḥasidic groups. In its struggle with the Mitnaggedim, the Belzer dynasty refused to depart in the slightest way from any of the old customs. In fact, the reason the town was called by the Ḥasidim Belza, instead of Belz, was in order to give a "Gentile" town a "Jewish" form.

Chart of the Ḥasidic Masters

Only the names of masters referred to in the book are recorded. Names in capital letters denote founders of schools or dynasties.

1 **ISRAEL BEN ELIEZER, THE BAAL SHEM TOV (1700–1760):** Founder of the Ḥasidic movement

2 **Jacob Joseph Katz of Pulnoyye (d. [c.] 1782):** Disciple of 1

3 **Phineḥas Shapiro of Koretz (1726–1791):** Disciple of 1

4 **Meir Margoliouth of Ostrog (d. 1790):** Disciple of 1

5 **Aryeh Leib, the Mokhiaḥ of Pulnoyye (d. 1770):** Disciple of 1, predecessor of 2

6 **David of Mikulov:** Disciple of 1

7 **Jeḥiel Michel, the Maggid of Zlotchov (d. 1786):** Disciple of 1

8 **Menaḥem Mendel of Prymishlani (d. 1773):** Disciple of 1

9 **Raphael of Bershad (d. [c.] 1816):** Disciple of 3

10 **Zevi (d. 1780):** Son of 1

11 **Jeḥiel Ashkenazi:** Son-in-law of 1

12 **Odel:** Daughter of 1, wife of 11, sister of 10

13 **Moses Ḥayyim Ephraim of Sudlikov (d. 1800):** Son of 11 and 12, grandson of 1, brother of 14, disciple of 1

14 **Baruch of Meziboz (1757–1810):** Son of 11 and 12, grandson of 1, brother of 13, disciple of 3

15 **Gershon of Kitov (d. [c.] 1760):** Brother-in-law and disciple of 1

16 **Feige:** Daughter of 11 and 12; sister of 13 and 14, granddaughter of 1

17 **Naḥman of Horodenka (d. 1780):** Associate of 1

18 **Simḥah:** Son of 17

19 **Naḥman of Bratslav (1772–1811):** Son of 16 and 18, nephew of 12, 13, and 14, grandson of 17, great-grandson of 1

20 **Nathan Sternhartz (d. 1845):** Disciple of 19

21 **DOV BAER, THE MAGGID OF MESERITCH (d. 1772):** Organizer of the Ḥasidic movement, disciple of 1, associate of 7

22 **Solomon of Lutzk (d. 1813):** Disciple of 21 and editor of his work

23 **Abraham ben Dov Baer, the "Angel" (1741–1776):** Son of 21

24 **Shalom Shachna of Probishtch (d. 1803):** Son of 23, grandson of 21

25 **MENAḤEM NAḤUM OF CHERNOBYL (1730–1787):** Disciple of 1 and 21

26 **Mordecai of Chernobyl (1770–1837):** Son and successor of 25

27 **David of Talnoye (1808–1882):** Son and successor of 26, grandson of 25

28 **Menaḥem Mendel of Vitebsk (1730–1788):** Disciple of 21

29 **Abraham of Kalisk (1741–1810):** Disciple of 21, associate of 28

30 **ELIMELECH OF LIZENSK (1717–1787):** Disciple of 21

31 **Susya of Anipol (d. 1800):** Disciple of 21, brother of 30

32 **Zeev Wolf of Zhitomer (d. 1800):** Disciple of 21

33 **Levi Yitzḥak of Berditchev (d. 1810):** Disciple of 21

34 **SHNEUR ZALMAN OF LIADY (1745–1813):** Disciple of 21 and 23, associate of 28, founder of the Ḥabad movement in Ḥasidism

35 **Dov Baer of Lubavitch (1773–1827):** Son and successor of 34

36 **Menaḥem Mendel of Lubavitch (1789–1866):** Grandson of 34,

son-in-law, nephew and successor of 35

37 ISRAEL HAPSTEIN, THE MAGGID OF KOZNITZ (1733–1814): Disciple of 21, 30, and 33

38 Moses Eliakim Beriah of Koznitz (d. 1828): Son and successor of 37, disciple of 31

39 JACOB ISAAC, THE "SEER" OF LUBLIN (1745–1815): Disciple of 21, 30, and 33

40 Meshullam Feibush Heller of Zbarazh (d. 1785): Disciple of 21 and 7

41 Ḥayyim Tyrer of Tchernowitz (d. 1816): Disciple of 7, associate of 40

42 ḤAYYIM ḤAIKEL OF AMDUR (d. 1787): Disciple of 21

43 Samuel of Amdur (d. [c.] 1800): Son and successor of 42

44 Zevi Hirsch of Zhidachov (d. 1831): Disciple of 14 and 39

45 Meir of Apt (d. 1831): Disciple of 30 and 39

46 Abraham Joshua Heschel of Apt (d. 1825): Disciple of 30

47 Moses Sofer of Przeworsk (d. 1805): Disciple of 30

48 MOSES TEITELBAUM OF UJHELY (1759–1841): Disciple of 39

49 Jekuthiel Judah Teitelbaum of Sighet (1808–1883): Grandson and successor of 48

50 Ḥananiah Yom Tov Lipa Teitelbaum (d. 1904): Son and successor of 49, great-grandson of 48

51 Joel Teitelbaum (b. 1888): Son of 50, Satmarer Rebbe in New York

52 ZEVI ELIMELECH SPIRA OF DYNOW (1785–1841): Nephew of 30, disciple of 37 and 39

53 ISRAEL FRIEDMANN OF RUZHYN (1797–1850): Son of 24, grandson of 23 and 25, great-grandson of 21

54 JACOB ISAAC, THE "HOLY JEW" OF PRZYSUCHA (d. 1814): Disciple of 39

55 Simḥah Bunem of Przysucha (d. 1827): Disciple of 39, disciple and successor of 54

56 Menaḥem Mendel of Kotzk (1787–1859): Disciple of 39, 54, and 55

57 MORDECAI JOSEPH LEINER OF IZBICA (d. 1854): Disciple of 56

58 Jacob Leiner of Radzhyn (1814–1878): Son and successor of 57

59 Gershon Henich of Radzhyn (1814–1891): Son and successor of 58, grandson of 57

60 Solomon Rabinowich of Radomsk (1803–1866): Disciple of 45

61 SHALOM ROKEAḤ OF BELZ (1825–1894): Disciple of 22, 37, and 39

62 Joshua Rokeaḥ of Belz (1825–1894): Son and successor of 61

63 Issachar Dov of Belz (1854–1927): Son and successor of 62, grandson of 61

64 Aaron Rokeaḥ of Belz (1880–1957): Son and successor of 63, grandson of 62, great-grandson of 61

65 ḤAYYIM HALBERSTAM OF ZANZ (1793–1876): Disciple of 39, 53, and 61

66 Ezekiel Shraga Halberstam of Sieniawa (1811–1899): Son of 58, disciple of 61

67 YITZḤAK ISAAC JUDAH JEḤIEL SAFRIN OF KOMÅRNO (1806–1874): Disciple of 37 and 39, nephew and disciple of 44

68 Judah Leib Eger of Lublin (1816–1888): Disciple of 56 and 57

69 YITZḤAK MEIR ALTER OF GER 1789–1866): Brother-in-law and disciple of 56

70 Zadok Ha-Kohen of Lublin (1823–1900): Disciple of 57 and 68

71 Judah Aryeh Leib Alter of Ger (1847–1905): Grandson and successor of 69

72 Abraham Mordecai Alter of Ger (1866–1948): Son and successor of 70